Dedicated to the Master

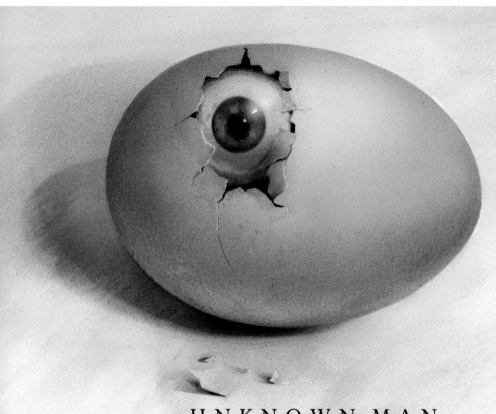

U N K N O W N   M A N

Yatri

Original Illustrations and photography by Yatri

A Fireside Book
Published by Simon & Schuster Inc.
New York London Toronto Sydney Tokyo

Simon and Schuster/Fireside Books,

Published by Simon & Schuster Inc.

Simon & Schuster Building

Rockefeller Center

1230 Avenue of the Americas

New York, New York 10020

SIMON AND SCHUSTER, FIRESIDE and colophons are
registered trademarks of Simon & Schuster Inc.

Designed by Yatri

Unknown Man was produced by
Labyrinth Publishing S.A., Switzerland
Printed in Hong Kong by Leefung Asco Printers Limited
Color Separation by Fotolito Toscana, Florence, Italy
Typesetting by Leadercomp S.R.L., Florence, Italy

10 9 8 7 6 5 4 3 2 1
10 9 8 7 6 5 4 3 2 1 Pbk.

Library of Congress Cataloging in Publication Data

Yatri, 1936-
Unknown man.

"A Fireside book."
Bibliography: p.
1. Man. I: Title.
BD450. Y36 1988 128   88-4472
ISBN 0-671-66069-1ISBN 0-671-66070-5 (pbk.)

C O N T E N T S

INTRODUCTION

Unknown Man is neither a scientific hypothesis nor a mystical truth. It might best be described as an English eccentric needing an introduction.

Its genesis was one of those awakening visions which happen once in a lifetime when the miraculous landscape of reality is lit up by a sudden flash of lightning only to disappear again into the normal twilight world. But once the *real* universe has been tasted the old familiar one can never be quite the same.

It miraculously happened for me one spring morning in the bleak surroundings of a slum in the East end of London. Why it should have chosen such an incongruous setting is one of the mysterious jokes of existence. For the last fifteen years since that moment I have often found only helplessness in my attempts to explain how this real world appeared to me in that brief glimpse.

All that really can be said is that It just *was*. Time stopped, all and everything was intensified a thousand-fold and existence shone in full ecstatic wonder.

As I watched Londoners in the street going about their lives there appeared a dark luminosity within each being. Yet at the same moment there was a strange feeling that they were no more than sleepwalking robots utterly oblivious to that shining nature within themselves. The life force of each person was somehow entrapped within a dull dreaming shell which seemed to prevent any contact with the real and what could have been aflame with consciousness was gray and lifeless.

Only seconds before I had been exactly like that and the awful recognition came that while only a hair's breadth divided the two states, I would also fall back into forgetfulness. What had gone wrong? What had happened to everyone?

In the six months following this event there were a few sporadic encounters with reality, but one in particular was significant for the germination of this book. The image which appeared was of a new being, a tremendous magnification of our own potential yet at the same time an entirely new line, discontinuous with all that had happened before.

Perhaps with a different cultural or religious background the vision might have been of Krishna, the archetype progenitor of mankind, Adamel, the Logos or Sophia. But the brick had fallen by chance upon a very skeptical and agnostic sculptor. And with such a background what he saw was a luminous, androgynous figure ablaze with intelligence, humor and beauty.

I rushed off to India to clinch the deal on what I fondly imagined was instant enlightenment. In that I was to be disappointed, but those seven years in the East did convince me that beings such as those in the vision do exist "in the flesh." I have met and listened to men and women in their natural enlightened state each of whom have that same elusive quality. Yet even though these rare individuals seem miraculous, there is the feeling that they may still be isolated fragments of what humankind could become if the whole species followed their path.

For the last two years I have attempted to give some substance to that original insight, to award it some plausible shape and form by which it can be shared. Originally there was no idea where to look for such evidence and what is offered here is only the first cursory glance. The non-scientist and unwary 'sunday' mystic is confronted by many pitfalls when examining the whole New Age lexicon of pseudo- science and pseudo-mysticism. When surrounded by so much information often third or fourth-hand in content, it is hard to avoid even the most obvious traps.

The ancient Upanishads always start with "Thus we have heard..." and it would be well to remember that virtually all our knowledge and most of our thoughts are at best second-hand. I have had to take on trust much of the evidence assembled in this volume.

In compiling the text one cautionary tale is worth the telling in order to illustrate the problems encountered when trying to substantiate a personal vision with *the knowledge of others*.

Crucial to one of the proposals to be met in this book is that when a new form occurs, be it a new pattern of behavior or a new man, a certain number of such mutants must appear before the new 'habit' sticks, before a field comes into being of sufficient strength to ensure that everyone is doing it or being it.

In the original manuscript of *Unknown Man there had been* an attempt to demonstrate this by using the well-known 'hundredth monkey' story. This had originally been told very entertainingly by Lyall Watson in "Lifetide." A female monkey on an island of Japan had learnt to wash potatoes before eating them. She had passed on this valuable piece of information to her peers but it had proved a relatively slow process. Then quite suddenly, so the story unfolds, something extraordinary happened. It was as if when the hundredth monkey learned the trick in the morning the number somehow nudged the critical mass across a threshold so that by evening almost every monkey was doing it.

Now it is easy to overlook the fact that Lyall Watson was not using the example as a hard piece of scientific fact. From a recent communication with him, it is clear that he uses the situation as a metaphor for the way in which he believes such things may work. This in no way invalidates the overall concept of critical mass and it probably does actually happen much as described, but as Watson points out, it is one thing to see the concept as a potentially useful research tool and quite another to elevate it, through New Age enthusiasm, to an established truth.

Rupert Sheldrake, a scientist who has proposed one of the most rewarding theories of our century, was marvelously direct in his criticism of my first draft manuscript. He drew my attention to this particular case and to a number of other even more embarrassing misconceptions. So in the revision I have attempted to set the facts straight, eliminating at the same time many of the more tempting scientific and mystical fables of our epoch. This tale is important, however, for it clearly demonstrates that this book is essentially one of symbols, or if you like, a parable of our time rather than factual research. Approach its pages as if viewing an artwork or a menu pointing at the food — it was never intended as the food.

The book is as much about you and me as the new visitors. We are as much the new men and women as caterpillars are to butterflies. My major question is why have we chosen to remain in the cocoon so long? Hopefully this volume will suggest some of the reasons why.

Yatri
Tuscany, Spring 1988

PRELUDE

A survey of the technological and psychological thresholds which we, as a species, have stepped across in the last 40 years and the subsequent effect upon the evolutionary development of mankind.

THRESHOLD — TURNING POINT — INNER CRISIS — PHOENIX — DANGEROUS OPPORTUNITY — POPULATION BOMB — MORE = LESS — POISON IN THE SOUP — UNTHINKABLE WARGAMES — SICKBED — MEDIA MAN — ATOMIC EVOLUTION — COMMUNICATIONS EVOLUTION — SPACE EVOLUTION — ARTIFICIAL INTELLIGENCE — GENETIC EVOLUTION — SOLAR REVOLUTION — MINDSETS

Golden Visions

"A new world is born. It is not the old world that is changing. It is a new world which is born. And we are right in the middle of the transition period, when the two overlap, when the old is still all-powerful and entirely controlling the ordinary consciousness. But the new slips in, still very modest and unnoticed — so unnoticed that externally it disturbs hardly anything... for the moment, and is even absolutely imperceptible in the consciousness of most people. But it is working, it is growing."
(The Mother)[1]

THE ENDING OF OUR CENTURY has more than its fair share of predictions and omens. No other century has had such a wealth of apocalyptic prophecies surrounding its closing years. And yet interwoven throughout the visions of a cataclysmic end to our dark warring age is one very particular thread of light — the supposed appearance of a totally new being who heralds a new age of consciousness.

Our collective consciousness is abundantly saturated with such archetypes and the fascination with a popular superman image is all the more likely to occur at the end of a century. The final years of any century are notorious for wacky ideas which sweep across the planet and coming "golden ages" are the perfect stuff for the end of our seventh millennium. One of the prime requirements of our dreams of golden ages is that they never happen now. Such glorious epochs are invariably reserved for the distant past or the far future. The Hindu golden age is safely ten thousand years old while John's Christian vision of Revelation sets the coming age of Light and Peace two thousand years into *his* future.

But, like that apocalyptic vision, other prophecies are also coming home to roost. And most of them firmly place the golden egg on our present doorstep.

Gurus, psychics, mediums and channelers, all add their voice to the gathering mystery of the forthcoming age, each with his favorite hero of higher consciousness. The golden boy has become a commodity to be sold in the New Age market place even before he has left the womb.

Dreams of Superman

EVERY AGE HAS HAD ITS FUTURE AND ITS DREAM. The dreams of the thirties now seem sinister and totalitarian — fascists dreaming neo-romans and Soviets dreaming over-life-sized comrades in superstates. Even as early as the 1920s, Karl Gustav Jung prophesied that a blond monster would arise in Germany. He had been shocked to find this archetype in so many of his patients' dreams. It took another fifteen years for the Nazi Aryan ideal to come into being. But all these supermen proved to be inhuman monsters, horrendous parodies of the collective mirage.

With such tragic failures so fresh in the memory just how realistic is the new dream? Is this unconscious collective vision of a new magical hero destined to end up in the same dark grave as his monstrous brothers of the thirties?

Supposing we were to assume that a new changeling is a possible reality. At this stage it really doesn't matter whether he or she has arisen in the collective mind, awaiting actualization, or that some-where deep within us is a global *precognition* of an event which will send our species into oblivion. The simple question is, how might we go about looking for him or her?

Clearly, as investigators, we are at a considerable disadvantage right from the start. These new entities are, by definition, unknown. There is no description of what or who they might be like. There are no photo albums, passports and forwarding addresses.

Testimony of their existence is, to say the least, questionable, being totally confined to such vague announcements as the "dawning of the new man" or the coming "herald of the new age". And it certainly does not help that most of the prime "witnesses" have been dead for centuries. So we must now look further afield than either the prophets or their prophesies if we are to satisfy our curiosity concerned with such predictions.

We might start the inquiry by asking whether there are any pre-requisite conditions in the environment for such a profound evolutionary change. There are many conflicting evolutionary theories, but there is one fact that does emerge, which seems to be shared by most biologists. Available evidence points to the fact that any major evolutionary jump is preceded by some kind of crisis within the environment of the organism. This usually happens when there is an imbalance or extreme in the natural habitat which triggers powerful adaptive, evolutionary responses.

Never before has humankind faced so many crises all together at one time. We stumble over critical threshold after critical threshold in a long chain of events running parallel to one another which are destined to clash simultaneously any moment. Any one of these thresholds of pollution, population explosion, destruction of the ozone shield or the dramatic climatic changes brought about by the greenhouse effect is, even by itself, sufficient to detonate an evolutionary bomb which could totally change the direction of our species.

However, if we then add the new technological thresholds which we overstep daily in atomic physics, communications, artificial intelligence, space technology, genetic engineering, solar energy and the revolutionary new conceptual models of science, we have the most volatile mixture ever concocted in our little solar system. From the sheer number and magnitude of these accelerating lines of change all converging at the one crossroads in the last years of this century, something quite shattering is about to happen. On close examination the choice does not seem to be whether it *will* happen, but whether we manage to destroy ourselves before it happens.

If, for the moment, we assume that by some miracle we do survive the chaos of the next decade what would then be the most likely coming scenario?

Before we can even begin to envision such a happening, some plausible context, some background must be created. So as a prelude to the event let us take a good look at the crossroads upon which we stand at the present moment. Only by carefully surveying the landscape can we hope to discover whether the claim, that we are about to walk across an evolutionary minefield, is reasonably justified.

Most of the issues are so well-known and popularized that it is unnecessary to enumerate them in detail. However, the main point to be made is that, despite the sheer weight of evidence, we still overlook the magnitude and range of changes we are living through.

Turning Point

IN THE FIRST TEST OF THE HYDROGEN BOMB in 1952, an entire island in the Pacific was vaporized by a fireball five kilometers in diameter.

Today we reap the scientific harvest that was set in action in the hurricanes following the explosion. We now face a planet-wide scourge, grown since this explosion which has in turn sponsored so much pollution, famine and the destruction of so much of our natural environment. And always in the background there is the ever-present threat of a nuclear holocaust. Strangely, in that spectacular monument to the progress of scientific materialism exploded above the Marshall Islands, there was the very "virus" which would eventually lead to the collapse of the whole system and vision it was planned to create. For the central theme of those confident ideas of the 1950s was the concept of man as a separate observer of nature. This was man, able to dominate and bend existence to his bidding, wresting nature's innermost secrets from her on the altar of science. Our own generation has felt the awful cost of such an arrogant vision and is urgently seeking new ways of looking at both existence and ourselves, to find harmony and an understanding of how we, as a species, fit into the greater whole of the universe.

As we approach the last decade of the present millennium we might look back on that atomic event as the phoenix of our past; it is out of those ashes which rained down from the star blast over the Pacific, almost forty years ago, that a new spirit was born.

The event can be seen as the turning point: the first division of an evolutionary cell which has continued to divide and multiply ever since.

"This was how I saw the horses and their riders in my vision: they wore breastplates, fiery red, blue and sulfur-yellow; the horses had heads like lion's heads, and out of their mouths came fire, smoke and sulfur. By these three plagues that is, by the fire, the smoke and the sulfur that came from their mouths, a third of mankind was killed."
(Revelation)[3]

"The unleashed power of the atom has changed everything save our modes of thinking and thus we drift toward unparalleled catastrophes."
(Albert Einstein)[4]

Inner Crisis

"Each time a new element is introduced among existing combinations, it creates a tearing of the limits, we could say... The perceptions of modern science undoubtedly come much closer to expressing the next reality than, say, those of the Stone Age. But even they will be suddenly completely outdated, surpassed, and probably made obsolete by the introduction of something that did not exist in the universe we have studied. It is that change, that sudden alteration of the universal element which will most certainly bring a sort of chaos into our perceptions, from which a new knowledge will emerge."
(The Mother)[7]

PERHAPS NOWHERE IS THE HUMAN MYSTERY more paradoxical than in the difference that exists between man's history and man himself. We belong to a uniquely gifted species whose latent powers, as we shall discover, are those of a God, yet whose actions appear to be those of a maniac.

Few of us suspect that there is anything inherently wrong with our way of life. Violence, war, disaster, terrorism and insanity have all become so habitual that we meet them, equally, with bland indifference, as though we had lost the capacity to be touched by life. We accept that it is a natural part of being human to be lonely, anxious, insecure, alienated and in perpetual fear of death. There is growing suspicion that somewhere along the road humankind took a wrong turning, becoming an insane species and, like all those in such condition, we are the last to know it.

So it is all the more poignant, in this present period of crisis, that we are increasingly being afforded brief glimpses of our condition and evidence that the way we live now may not in fact be the natural state of man. Simply, we have at last begun to examine just who we might be and what we might be doing on this planet.

"A new world is being born, a new kind of man is springing up today. The great mass of mankind, destined in our time to suffer more cruelly than ever before, ends by being paralyzed with fear, becoming introspective, shaken to the very core, and does not hear, see or feel anything more than everyday physical needs. It is thus that worlds die. First and foremost, the flesh dies. But although few clearly recognize it, the flesh would not have died if the spirit had not been killed already."
(Henry Miller)[5]

"Countries like ours are full of people who have all of the material comforts they desire, yet lead lives of quiet (and at times noisy) desperation, understanding nothing but the fact there is a hole inside them and that however much food and drink they pour into it, however many motorcars and television sets they stuff it with, however many well-balanced children and loyal friends they parade around the edges of it......it aches!" (Bernard Levin)[6]

Phoenix

"There is a certain bird which is called a Phoenix. This is the only one of its kind and lives five hundred years. And when the time of its dissolution draws near that it must die, it builds itself a nest of frankincense and myrrh and other spices into which, when the time is fulfilled, it enters and dies."

This description, given two thousand years ago by Clement, goes on to tell of the bird's renewal and flight into Egypt where the young phoenix places the remains of the old one on the altar of the sun. The Egyptian myth depicts the body of a man and the wings of the bird and the nest of incense and flames probably originates from the flames of the sun worshipers. To the mystics of Persia the phoenix was the symbol of the immortality of the human soul reborn from its own dead body. To medieval Hermeticists the bird was a symbol of the alchemical transformation and phoenix was the name given to initiates as those who had been born again.

The crisis of the phoenix was the burning, and out of the ashes came the re-birth. Crisis can be seen, therefore, as a positive aspect of change.

THERE SEEMS TO BE A GENERAL AGREEMENT amongst modern evolutionists that before any evolutionary initiative is provoked there is likely to be a crisis in the environment. It can be a dramatic change in the climate, a food crisis, a poisoning of the atmosphere with waste products or some other drastic upheaval in the planet's ecosystem.

We face just such a crisis now. Humankind consumes vast amounts of energy in the form of food and fossil fuels, chemicals and nuclear material, in such a way that widespread pollution and the wholesale destruction of our environment seem inevitable.

It appears that not only have our technological overspills created havoc within the environment, but our present cultural and technological transformation has exploded so dramatically in the last four decades that it seems to far outstrip any previous evolutionary event of our species.

In biological terms such massive, simultaneous and, in our case, global fluctuations appear as a crisis in which organisms are forced to adapt to the changed conditions by jumping to higher levels of organization or to head off down some evolutionary cul-de-sac and ultimate destruction.

If an environmental crisis is the trigger needed to detonate an evolutionary time-bomb, then our generation certainly qualifies for a transformation of the species. It is said that trouble likes company. The company of crises far exceeds the three categories of seven listed below but at least set the scene of our present situation and serve as indications of how many could collide at any moment.

Technological and Social Overspills

1) Population explosion and exploitation of the natural habitat
2) Pollution, the "Greenhouse Effect," acid rain and toxic, chemical soups
3) Severe damage to the ozone shield and dangerous levels of UV radiation
4) The dumping of poisonous wastes
5) Radiation leaks and hazards
6) Unthinkable wargames and nuclear terrorism
7) Stress and illness

Fritjof Capra once pointed out that the Chinese ideogram for crisis, *Wei Ji*, is composed of two interlocked characters. One is danger and the other is opportunity. Thus the beauty of a crisis is that it holds within its image inherent change. The Chinese Book of Changes demonstrates that existence is a cyclic movement where the process of breakdown is also the moment of breakthrough. Disintegration becomes renewal. We live in a time of immense danger, yet also mankind has never been offered such an opportunity.

"Greater dooms win greater destinies."
(Heraclitus)

Technological Innovations

1) Atomic Engineering
2) Instant Global Communications
3) Space Travel
4) Artificial Intelligence
5) Genetic Engineering
6) Solar Energy
7) Evolutionary Mindsets and New Paradigms

Crises in Natural and Mystic Cycles

1) Possible planetary shift of axis
2) Planetary line-up and volcanic cycles
3) Psychic cycle of consciousness (532 years)
4) Astrological cycle
5) End of the century
6) End of the millennium
7) Turning of the "Great Wheel of Dhamma"

THERE ARE SEVEN MAJOR CYCLES which converge in the next decade. Some are natural and explicable and some are subtle and mystical. There is for instance the obvious cycle of the ending of a century which may elicit a strong collective emotional response. On this occasion it is the end of the seventh millennium. The end of the last thousand year cycle in the 10th Century saw Western Europe in turmoil. Hysteria gripped the Christians during that period, as it was believed that the year 1000 would bring the end of the world and that a new spiritual universe peopled by the heavenly host would take its place.

These are cycles within the gigantic seasons of the Earth itself. Five planets will be aligned with Earth during spring of the year 2000. In fact the whole Solar system is lopsided at that moment and there is no knowing what effect this might have on the delicate balance of either the sun or our globe. It is believed that this occurs about every six thousand years. Already there are predictions which bear serious consideration of a major and possibly cataclysmic shift in the Earth's axis. Many observers feel that the ecosystem is anyway in a highly

Full Circle

Possible shift in the Earth's axis during spring of the year 2000. Variously thought to be a cycle of 6 to 7 millennia. The Egyptians recorded it on one secret magical papyrus as *The South becomes North and the Earth turns over.*

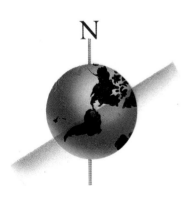

"There are seven ages, each of which is separated from the previous one by a world catastrophe"
(Visud-dhi-Magga)[7a]

volatile and dangerously unstable state. The vast ice sheets of Antartica lie precariously off the south polar center and are creating a wobble to the planet. Billions of tons of ice pressure are effecting the cracks and faults in the delicate plates which make up the Earth's crust. It is predicted that a cycle of volcanic eruptions could add to the natural disasters and droughts which plague us at present.

There are esoteric cycles upon which psychics and channelers are focusing, for one of the periods of five hundred and thirty-two years, which supposedly provides the stepping stone towards higher consciousness, is about to begin.

The better-known astrological Age of Pisces gives way to the Age of Aquarius. Yet such esoteric revolutions seem tame beside a cycle which is known in the East as the "Great Wheel of the Dhamma."

Gautama the Buddha, among others, told his disciples in the Diamond Sutra that every twenty-five centuries there is a period of intense chaos and strife as the Dhamma (the truth or the Tao) starts a new revolution. At that time the "Wheel" is once more set in motion and with it an entirely new phase in the consciousness of the planet. Two thousand five hundred years ago exceptional men of genius, who had entered the "natural state" of self-realization or enlightenment, emerged simultaneously all over the planet.

In India there was *Buddha* and *Mahavira*, who were contemporaries. In Greece *Heraclitus* "the obscure," *Socrates* and *Pythagoras* all appeared while *Zarathustra* was supposedly born laughing in the Middle East.

In China came the extraordinary gathering of *Lao Tzu, Chuang Tzu* and *Sosan*. The four major religious orders of Buddhism, Taoism, Zoroastrianism and the spiritual rebirth of Jainism all appeared together. Two of the greatest philosophical schools of Greece and the West's first great, enlightened mathematician all appeared in the space of one single century.

Buddha predicted that the next turn of the Wheel would see an unprecedented change in man of a magnitude never before reached in the history of the species. We exist at exactly the time of that "turn of the Wheel."

Population Bomb

"My African friends don't understand the link between the population explosion and the natural destruction of their environment. The entire African environment is in the process of being destroyed. But they believe that national riches are measured in the number of inhabitants. In the last twenty years the standard of living in the (sub-Saharan) Sahel has declined: population is increasing by three percent per year, which multiplies the population by twenty times a century. Production is increasing by one percent a year."
(René Dumont & Charlotte Paquet)[8]

In Rumania birth squads are sent out to women at home, demanding why they are not having children. The Rumanian president recently stated: "The fetus is the socialist property of the entire society. Giving birth is a patriotic duty which is decisive for the fate of the country."

Growth of world population since the beginning of the century:
1900 - 1,500 million
1950 - 2,500 million
1960 - 3,000 million
1970 - 3,700 million
1980 - 4,500 million
1988 - 5,000 million

"In 1955 the population of South Korea was 21.5 million, 18 percent of whom lived in or near Seoul. During the next 25 years more than half the population growth in the country took place in the region of the capital. By 1980 the total had reached 37.4 million and 36 percent of all South Koreans lived in or near Seoul. Furthermore in 1980 more than half of all the economic production in South Korea took place within 25 kilometers of the center of the capital."
(Daniel R. Vining Jr.)[9]

More Equals Less

DEMOGRAPHY, THE STATISTICAL STUDY OF HUMAN POPULATION, is at best an inexact science. Many of the doomsday predictions of the 1970s preparing us for an overpopulated, famine ridden world by the late 1980s have largely proved unfounded. However, a number of anomalies have surfaced.

Why is it, for instance, that there is such a disparity between the explosive population growth rates in Africa, the Middle East, South America and India and the declining rates of Europe and North America?

European governments complain that their birthrates are dwindling, while in the poor, but vast baby factories of the Third World countries the story is the opposite. Even the Draconian measures in China, attempting to restrict families to one child, tend to prove ineffective in a land where big families have always been a tradition. And the tragic consequences of Africa's famines, India's incredible over-population and the overwhelming social problems of other Third World countries are seen daily in the news media.

Religious orders such as the Hindus, Catholics and Jainas of India actively resist birth control which many critics point out is a strategy to keep the number of their own sect higher than their rivals.

As the story becomes more and still more complex, we tend to lose touch with a very simple equation — more people means more food, more space, more energy is needed therefore more waste, more pollution and a drastic reduction of natural resources is created.

The world in fact does produce enough food to feed everyone, but the poor simply do not have enough money to pay for it.

In an ideal world, with no national prestige at stake or borders to protect, the population could rise above our present levels with no real hardship. But in our present state man becomes a pawn, a mere number and a national number at that. It is numbers which are most lethal in a divided world and it is by numbers, as we will find, that the evolutionary initiative is triggered.

Poison in the Soup

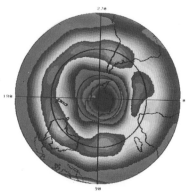

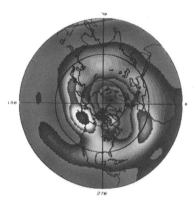

THE POPULATION EXPLOSION is intimately connected to another crucial issue — the excessive use of polluting sources of energy. The two most widely publicized effects of pollution are the warming of the Earth's surface through what is called the "greenhouse effect" and the depletion of the delicate ozone shield which filters out the harmful ultra-violet radiations of the sun. Carbon dioxide is produced whenever fossil fuels are burned. Such industrial expulsions are so essential to modern economics that environmentalists despair of ever being able to do anything to limit them. The industries and agencies which produce such pollution have just too much political muscle and any effort to curb emissions from their factories and generating plants are hardly likely to be either feasible or effective. It looks as though humankind will have to live with this fact and adapt to the new climatic conditions.

Above: **The ozone layer as computed at the North and South poles, by backscatter UV instrumentation aboard the Nimbus 7 satellite. The blue areas show the extent of a serious ozone depletion.**

"The population increase from two and a half billion in 1952 to five billion now, the four-fold increase in the global economy since 1952 and the five-fold increase in the use of fossil fuels are beginning to push us beyond many key thresholds. Many of these — the sustainable yield of forests, the extent to which agricultural development accelerates soil erosion — are local thresholds. We are seeing thresholds being crossed almost willy-nilly in all countries. What is new is not that thresholds are being crossed, but that so many thresholds are being crossed in so many parts of the world."

(Lester Brown)[11]

The activity of five billion human beings has become the major dynamo of environmental and evolutionary change, and we are fast overrunning nature's ability to counterbalance our activities. Effectively we have already begun to suffocate in our own waste.

POLLUTION: The burning of such fossil fuels as coal and oil has both poisoned the atmosphere and caused a vast chemical thermal blanket, trapping heat from the sun. This can wreak unimaginable havoc, turning much of the temperate zone into desert and totally changing the coastlines of America and Europe. The destruction of the ozone shield has already caused anxiety to scientists who are concerned by the effects of increased ultra-violet radiations.

ACID RAINS: The exotic photo-chemical cocktails issuing from industrial complexes, power stations, car fumes and chemical plants have created acid hazes and ozone smog which contaminate and corrode whole countrysides. Over half the forests of Central Europe are dead or dying, victim of the twin effects of ozone and acid combination. Virtually all the waterways, rivers and lakes are affected and many are already sterile. Decades of acid fallout have turned soils into vast acid bogs unable to support life. Deaths from overtaxed and weary respiratory organs are tragically increasing in both Europe and the United States.

WASTES: Heedless and criminal disposal of toxic chemical wastes has poisoned many of our rivers, streams, lakes and coastal waters. Leaks from natural gas drilling and oil spills endanger both fish and marine

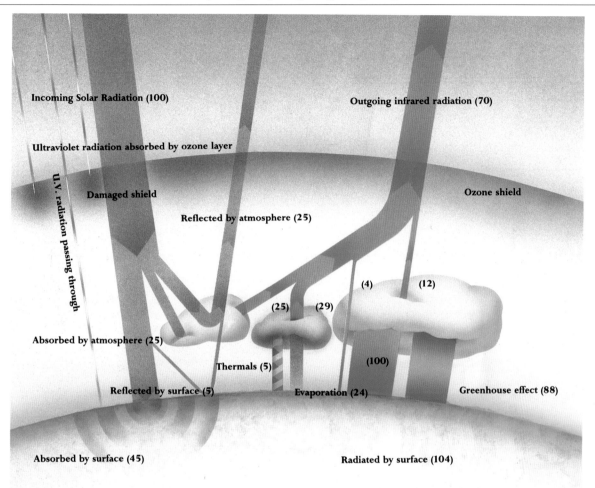

Incoming Solar Radiation (100)

Outgoing infrared radiation (70)

Ultraviolet radiation absorbed by ozone layer

U.V. radiation passing through

Damaged shield

Ozone shield

Reflected by atmosphere (25)

(4)   (12)

(25)   (29)

Absorbed by atmosphere (25)

Thermals (5)

(100)

Reflected by surface (5)

Evaporation (24)

Greenhouse effect (88)

Absorbed by surface (45)

Radiated by surface (104)

organisms in the oceans. Many chemicals enter the food and water chain to emerge in lethal and unsuspected amounts many years after.

RADIATION: In nearly every step of the nuclear-power industry some radioactivity leaks into the atmosphere. Accidents occur with frightening regularity. The recent disaster in Russia at Chernobyl showed the extent of the threat. It was also a sobering demonstration of how governments, with vested interests, withheld or falsified information as to how dangerous the situation was. That particular radioactive cloud at some time covered most of Europe. Radioactive crops had to be destroyed, animals slaughtered as countless long-life isotopes entered the soils and water systems. These will continue to be active for hundreds of years. Human fetuses were profoundly affected by the radiation and a distressingly high number of children have been born, in Germany and Poland, with gross deformities and brain damage as a consequence.

The "greenhouse effect" is caused by a number of interlocking man-made chemicals: carbon dioxide, chloroflorocarbons (CFCs) and an exotic soup of photo-chemicals. The CFC molecule has ten thousand times the effect of one carbon dioxide molecule and some varieties have life spans of over a century. All these chemicals absorb infra-red radiation from the sun which normally escapes into space. This raises the temperature near the Earth's surface. The climate is already changing drastically with heat wave even seven in the Arctic; polar icecaps are beginning to melt, raising the level of the sea. In the next decade ports and coastal cities will be seriously threatened by catastrophic flooding. Once fertile regions could be turned into deserts and the concentration of world power in the hard hit temperate zones could be seriously challenged for the first time in known history.

Unthinkable Wargames

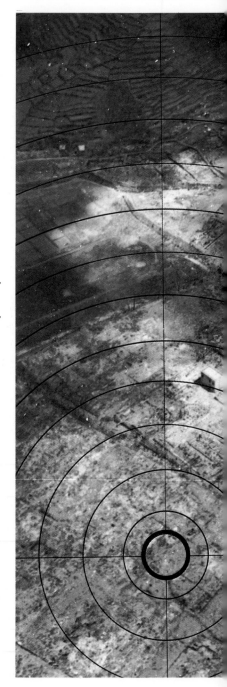

Mother and child, Nagasaki, 1945. The realities of war are seldom considered by the strategists of the wargames, as they play with their targets on computer screens.

OUTSIDE THE DANGERS of environmental and "natural" destruction we have also our own efforts at self-destruction, and if anyone needs proof that our species is utterly insane then we only have to invoke the doctrine of the *nuclear deterrent*.

The central proposition of the deterrent is that each sovereign nuclear power is capable of destroying its potential aggressor. There are two possible outcomes to the nuclear scenario. If the deterrent strategy succeeds, then both sides find themselves paralyzed by inaction. If it fails, of course both sides annihilate one another, destroying all life on Earth. *Mutual-Assured-Destruction*, MAD for short, is the logical child of such a policy.

Simply stated, the deterrent theory states that in order to avoid extinction from nuclear weapons we need *more* nuclear weapons. The strategists, who so enthusiastically stockpile these lethal arsenals, lead a strange double life, as if in two separate and closed-off worlds. In one they act with compassion in relation to their own families and friends and have feelings of real horror at even having their pet dog put to sleep, while in the other they suspend all human concern and play unthinkable scenarios in the wargames amusement parks of the military bunkers. The ultimate decision to walk down the terminal nuclear path, taking along five billion other humans, rests with a handful of politicians. Three out of every four of the planet's citizens know nothing of these men nor do they even understand the language they speak.

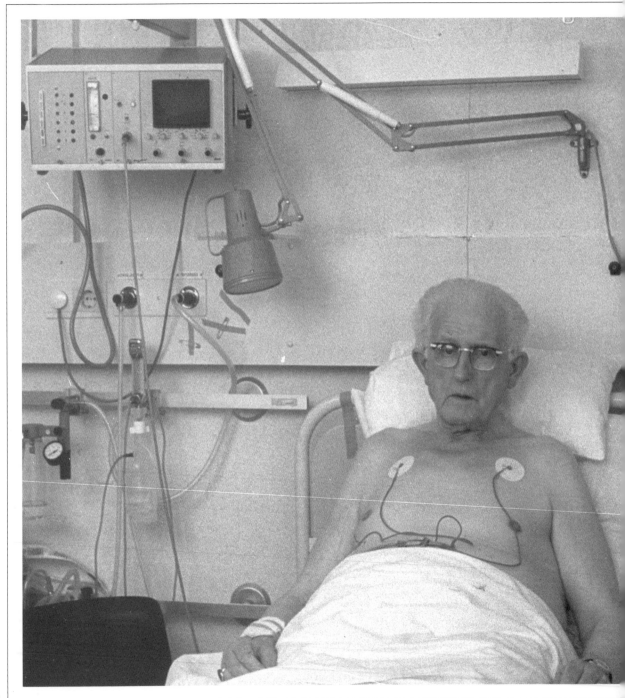

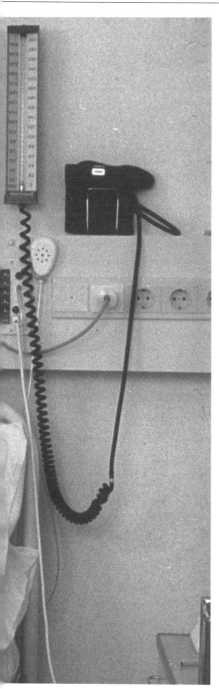

Sickbed

IT WOULD SEEM THAT WE ARE SPELLBOUND by the mystique surrounding medicine. So often we surrender the entire responsibility for our illnesses to the "doctor-priest" who is supposed to know what is wrong with us. The body is still seen as a machine whose parts wear out and need replacing, while disease is viewed as an outside invader which can be repulsed only by the heavy artillery of drug weapons.

But, as is now clear, stress is one of the greatest causes of illness. Temporary stress is a natural aspect of life and any healthy organism thrives on short-term stimulations. However, once that temporary state of excitement extends into a permanent or chronic condition, our natural mechanisms are overwhelmed. Prolonged stress suppresses the body's immune system and with it all the normal defenses against infections and disease. In cancer patients that critical stress can occur some six to eighteen months before actual diagnosis. Feelings of despair, helplessness or depression may create a situation in which serious illness or even death is welcomed.

This attitude towards the body and its health is nowhere more apparent than in AIDS research, which assumes that any cure can come only through drugs and hard technology. Perhaps the thought of exploring the factors of stress and the role played by the mind in altering the defense strategies of the immune system are too daunting to researchers. The epoch of change in which we currently live has so profoundly challenged all the old established values and norms that too many vulnerable human beings feel cast adrift and consciously or unconsciously find their lives pointless. Collectively we may simply be in the process of losing the will and wonder to live. If this is so, then AIDS may be one of the epidemics of that loss.

"AIDS is without question a psycho-neuro-immunological disease. A typical patient who is told he has been exposed to the virus often goes into severe depression and since depression can adversely affect the immune system he ends up with a double dose of immune suppression."
(Nick Hall)[14]

Children die in orphanages from seemingly trivial illnesses, even when the premises are clean, well organized and the children well-fed. When love and physical tenderness are missing the children just give up the will to live and shrink within themselves. Victims of AIDS, cancer and other stress related diseases may be viewed as this generation's existential orphans.

Media Man

HAVING SUMMARIZED some of the dangers of the present crisis which we face, let us turn to the other aspect of *Wei Ji*, the Chinese ideogram for crisis — the opportunities.

A century ago, the writer of Utopias, Samuel Butler, observed that the evolutionary process had been fantastically speeded up by machines. He had recognized one of the most unique factors which characterizes the human animal: human beings actually extend their whole central nervous system by means of machines. "Man-machines" or "media-man" is a perfect symbiosis, an intimate union of two totally dissimilar systems ending up with a mutually beneficial organism. A stick is an extension of an arm, language is an extension of memory and perception, the wheel an extension of the legs.

Yet symbiosis is a two-way process, for just as man creates his media, so media shapes the man. Whenever we examine the phenomenon of mankind it is evident that man cannot be separated from his media, machines, symbols or languages howsoever unsophisticated these might be. Of course we have no examples of man without his programs and his acquired knowledge. Man seems indivisible from mankind. In the natural wild, a solitary primate is invariably a dead primate.

Group life is essential for maintaining the complex social interactions which stimulate media learning. In man the whole biological evolution is inseparable from cultural evolution. This is in the amazingly rapid growth of our hominid brains — three-fold in three million years — much of it caused apparently by the novelty of communicating by language. Man shapes the language and language shapes the man.

Now media man has invented some extraordinary new playthings. But this time these technologies and innovative ideas are of such a magnitude that they threaten to disturb the balance between man and machine and are already shaping their creators in unforeseen ways.

Any one of these new innovations could have signaled an evolutionary jump of great significance. The arrival of so many together, simultaneously acting as catalysts on each other and spawning new technologies almost daily, is having a profound effect upon

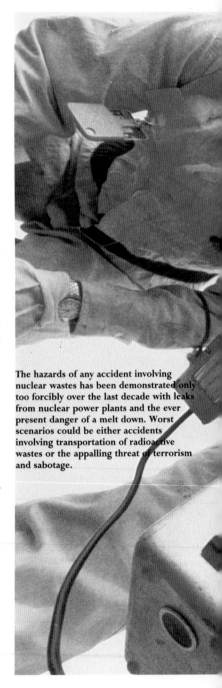

The hazards of any accident involving nuclear wastes has been demonstrated only too forcibly over the last decade with leaks from nuclear power plants and the ever present danger of a melt down. Worst scenarios could be either accidents involving transportation of radioactive wastes or the appalling threat of terrorism and sabotage.

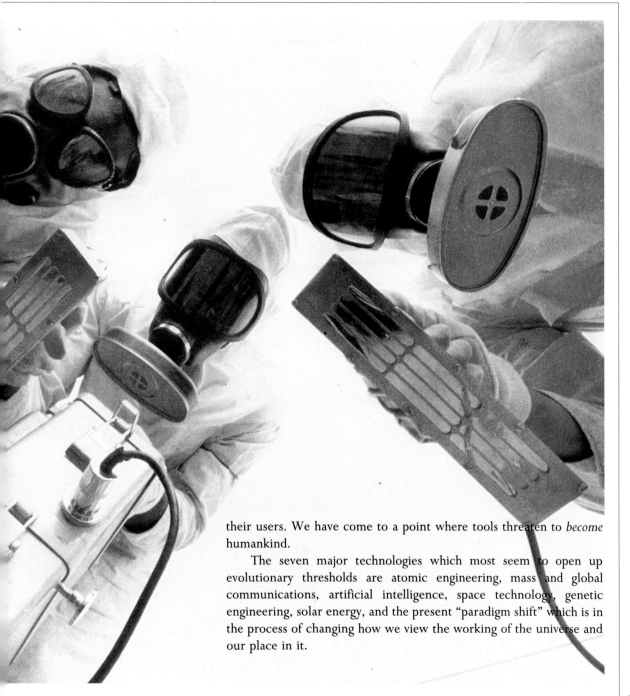

their users. We have come to a point where tools threaten to *become* humankind.

The seven major technologies which most seem to open up evolutionary thresholds are atomic engineering, mass and global communications, artificial intelligence, space technology, genetic engineering, solar energy, and the present "paradigm shift" which is in the process of changing how we view the working of the universe and our place in it.

Atomic Evolution

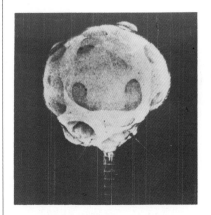

Above: **The first millionth of a second into an atomic explosion. The wires and the tower supporting the bomb are captured milliseconds before vaporization.**

Opposite: **The dancing arabesques of the "vapor trails" of particles in transit.**

DURING THE LAST THREE DECADES the most fundamental questions about the nature of existence have been asked within the framework of the physical sciences.

The twin models of Einstein's Theory of Relativity and Quantum mechanics have governed the ways in which we look at the universe and the way in which we think it works.

Few physicists would openly admit there are any flaws within these models or that there is any theoretical crisis. The discipline of physics has demonstrated such spectacular successes in this century that to many it seems inconceivable there might be a crack within the foundations.

Yet, of course, no one has ever seen an atom, let alone a positron, an electron, an elementary particle or a particle of a particle — a quark. These exotic events live only inside the minds of scientists. The reality of the subatomic world of physics lies in a set of mathematical abstractions. The sophisticated machines which watch out for evidence of these hypothetical particles are designed in such a way that the technician will find only what he *expects* to find.

"*... scientists simplify, they abstract, they eliminate all that, for their purposes, is irrelevant and ignore whatever they choose to regard as inessential; they impose a style, they compel the facts to verify a favorite hypothesis, they consign to the waste-paper basket all that, to their mind, falls short of perfection.*" (Aldous Huxley)

In short a scientist often makes a square machine to catch square holes in infinite emptiness. Yet the very methodology of science highlights the dangers of trying to fit facts to theories. It underlines the fact that scientists haven't really a clue how the universe works, while we laymen always thought they did. This only becomes disquieting when the scientist acts as if he *does* know and we, who only have a superficial understanding of the limits of his discipline, blindly accept it.

So far technician scientists apply certain formulae or recipes which seem to work, ultimately resulting in a product. The technician guesses and so far his guesses have proved right, at least most of the time. For example, no new elements have been created in this corner

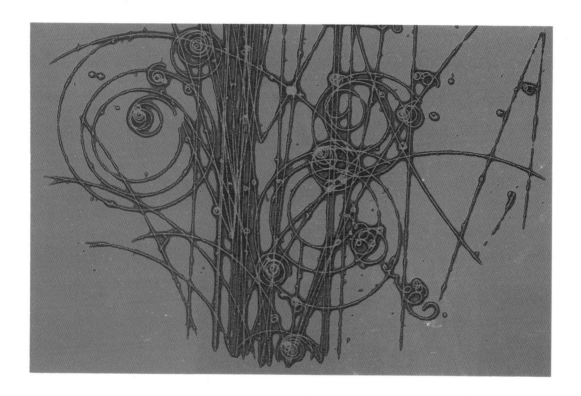

of the galaxy for billions of years. The supernova which spawned the matter of our solar system was part of a vast inter-connecting process of unimaginable complexity. Every part interacted within the whole. Now entirely new elements have been created which have no known purpose within the scheme of our holistic periodic table. We rush forward in our belief in "scientific progress" while our machines quietly out-strip us. But we *are* the machines we create, as part of the whole symbiotic process called humankind, and we can expect that the birth of these magnificent yet dangerous monsters will have inevitable and profound biological and evolutionary repercussions.

Communications' Revolution

ONE HUNDRED YEARS AGO, Earth, if observed from space, would have appeared as a completely silent planet, apart perhaps from the occasional static caused by thunderstorms. Today it is a noisy beacon in space, broadcasting its thoughts non-stop, far into the galaxy. That leap in the complexity of our global communication systems has occurred since World War Two.

It has been pointed out by many observers that the communications network of the world is beginning to resemble the neuronic pathways of the human brain. Instant communication of information holds together the disparate human activities of the planet as links are made from mind to machine, mind to mind and machine to machine.

The developed world relies upon a network which includes radio and television, information retrieval, video conference and cellular telephone, facsimiles, videotex, teletex, telecontrol along with all the computer and satellite linkups.

Already, by the late 1980s integrated digital service networks were being installed which allow an incredible spectrum of information. They allow home access to huge scale mainframe computers with outlets for videophones, multi-media terminals and devices which can transmit and receive simultaneously voices, images and data. Linkups with simulated artificial realities could engage whole populations in single shared experiences which are beyond our present imaginings. It is not inconceivable that this could be our reality by the mid-1990s.

With the addition of new artificial intelligences to the network and the developing richness and quality of the flowing information Marshall McLuhan's "Global Village" has changed into the "Global Brain" — an entirely new kind of consciousness and a new kind of planetary species.

The overall data processing capacity is doubling every three years and if this rate is maintained, the complexity of the world network could approach the order of magnitude of a human brain in the number of its interactive processes or connections. In biological terms it is not unreasonable to conclude that human beings might well be the Earth's way of gaining global consciousness.

Evolution in Space

WE ARE WELL ON THE WAY to colonizing space. In evolutionary terms this could be viewed as significant an event as when the first hominids began to walk upright in the savannahs.

Astronauts and cosmonauts who have experienced the Earth from space seem to share a mystical connection with the planet. It is also easy to forget that man has taken a look at his home from the outside only in the last twenty years and the profound and almost mystical effect upon the astronauts has been embraced by the species as a whole. We can see our planet as an exquisite, luminous, living globe hanging undivided in the silence of space. The testimonies from space bring home with a fresh impact just what a rare and precious opportunity of life we share with the planet as one whole ecosystem and us as a part of it.

Orbiting Earth, the astronaut Rusty Schweichart had this to say: "*As you pass from sunlight into darkness and back again every hour and a half, you become startlingly aware how artificial are the thousands of boundaries we've created to separate and define. And for the first time in your life you feel in your gut the precious unity of the Earth and all the living things it supports. The dissonance between this unity you see and the separateness of human groupings that you know exists is starkly apparent.*"[16]

"*Once a photograph of the Earth, taken from the outside is available, a new idea as powerful as any in history will be let loose.*"
(Fred Hoyle)[15]

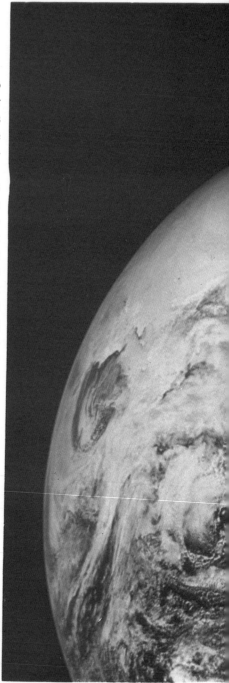

Evolution of an Artificial Intelligence

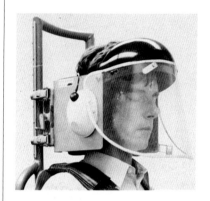

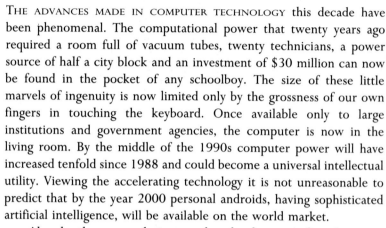

THE ADVANCES MADE IN COMPUTER TECHNOLOGY this decade have been phenomenal. The computational power that twenty years ago required a room full of vacuum tubes, twenty technicians, a power source of half a city block and an investment of $30 million can now be found in the pocket of any schoolboy. The size of these little marvels of ingenuity is now limited only by the grossness of our own fingers in touching the keyboard. Once available only to large institutions and government agencies, the computer is now in the living room. By the middle of the 1990s computer power will have increased tenfold since 1988 and could become a universal intellectual utility. Viewing the accelerating technology it is not unreasonable to predict that by the year 2000 personal androids, having sophisticated artificial intelligence, will be available on the world market.

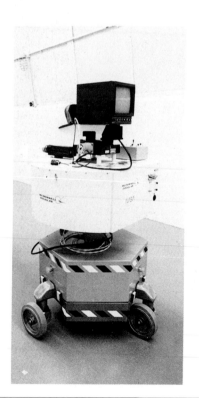

Already there are designs under development for electronic cognitive and prosthetic devices which can act as vast storehouses of ready packaged information, when transplanted in the brain. If such devices are found to be feasible they could give us access to the Encyclopedia Britannica and leave enough room for the entire Chinese vocabulary. When these developments are coupled with the chemical packages, such as the hormones ACTH, alkaloids or drugs that improve memory or alter the spectrum of emotions and feelings, then the range of consciousness available to the human race could be enhanced beyond imagination.

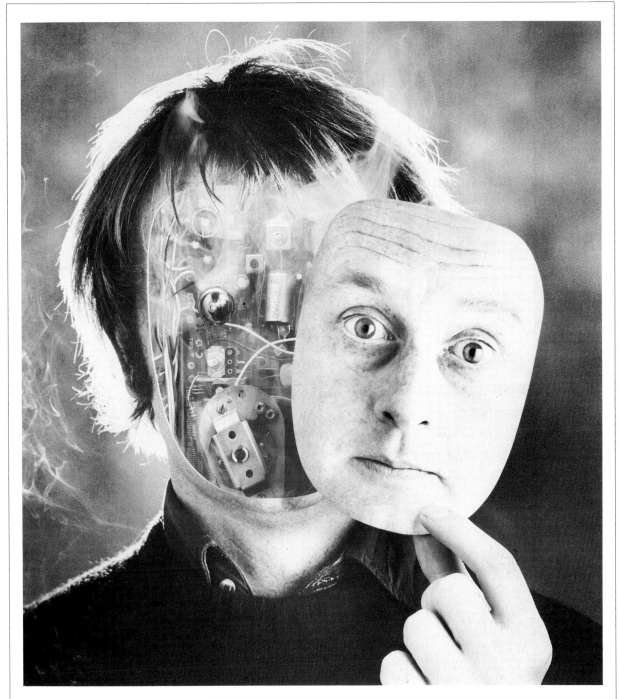

Genetic Evolution

"The feeling grows that scientists are finding it increasingly difficult to predict the consequences of their work; that technology has become the sorcerer's apprentice of our age. The concept of dangerous knowledge appears in a variety of images — the mushroom cloud, the usurping robot, the armless child of thalidomide."
(Van Rensselaer-Potter)[19]

"Recombinant DNA technology promises to give man power over nature of a more fundamental kind than that afforded by any other technology. Hitherto evolution has always seemed as inexorable and irrevocable a process as time or entropy. Now at last man has a handle on the force that shaped him."
(Nicolas Wade)[17]

"Somehow it is presumed that we know a priori that none of these recombinant clones will be harmful to man or to our animals, or to our crops, or to other microbes. I don't know that, and worse, I don't know how anybody else does either."
(Robert Sinsheimer)[18]

TWO BILLION YEARS AGO SEX WAS INVENTED, making it possible for two cells to unite, producing offspring containing combinations of that original genetic material. This was an extraordinary expansion of life and an incredible opportunity, through an abundance of success and failures, to create new adaptations or mutations of the original stock. Suddenly evolution moved as if on greased wheels.

In the last decade, biologists have made as significant a jump by learning how to modify genes in a cell in a way which can lead to entirely novel life forms and even a new species of mankind. We are already compressing life processes, which have taken millions of years to evolve, into the frame of a few months. As extravagant claims for genetic engineering become a reality, we are faced with some unpalatable truths.

Two decades ago we had the technological and operational ability to design new strains of viruses. Even at this moment completely novel, man- made hybrid plasmids and viruses are being created by recombinant DNA technology. Work now proceeds to produce food crops with altered genetic structures which can extract nitrogen from the air rather than from the exhausted and overburdened soils.

As we rush headlong into such unknown realities we haven't the slightest idea of how nature is likely to respond. Yet there are both scientists and governments, while still being ignorant of the foundational laws which govern life, who are prepared to step across barriers of no return to create potentially lethal strains which could totally overwhelm the delicate balance of the planet.

The biologist's ultimate dream of creating his own unique species or even a new advanced model of *Homo sapiens* may sadly prove too much of a temptation to resist. Perhaps one major question of our time is not whether we can devise methods of controlling genes in a cell, but whether we can devise methods of controlling scientists and governments from *abusing* such power.

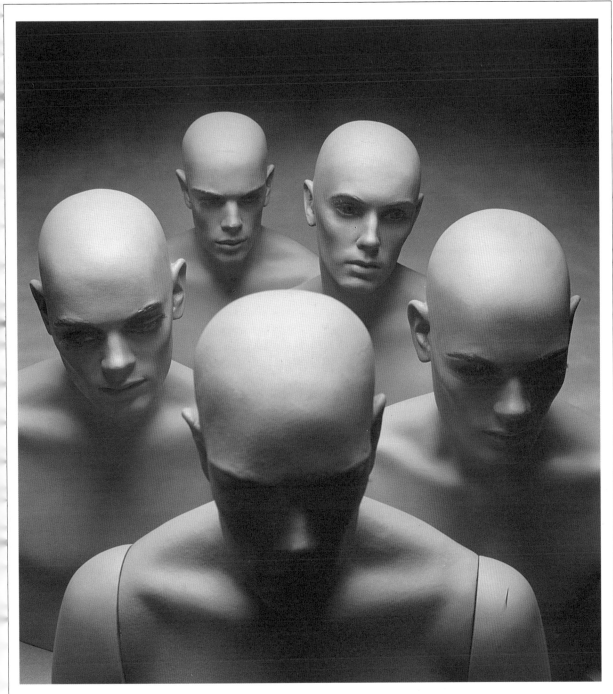

Solar Revolution

WHEN THE FIRST SIMPLE CELLS emerged on the planet they used the revolutionary life process of converting sunlight into energy: the process of photosynthesis. These bacteria gained an evolutionary foothold which eventually led to the plants we know today. A billion years later oxygen-eating bacteria appeared and set off in the opposite evolutionary track towards animals and eventually man.

Now we use vast amounts of fossil fuels created by that first line in order to pollute our atmosphere and destroy the ecological balance on Earth. Most of that precious energy has just gone up in smoke. Today, however, a whole new age of soft technology has sprung into being. The recent sophistication of photo-voltaic solar panels, wind generators, organic recycling bio-mass technologies, fuel cells and the creation of plant fuels and gases all share the sun as the central energy giver. Many of these conservation techniques are simple, non-polluting, non central and cost effective. The political muscle of the present utilities companies, reluctant to lose their age-old monopolies on electricity, coal and oil, remain the major obstacle to the rapid development of solar technology. Given the explosive development in computers within a decade, it is easy to foresee a similar sudden advance in the use of photo-voltaics. Indeed the Japanese who have been pioneering research into solar energy have already come up with a new amorphous silicone solar panel in the form of a roofing tile which could drastically reduce costs, bringing such technology straight into the back yard. This could mean a total revolution in the use of decentralized power with the possible decentralization of populations throughout the world. Such a revolution would be welcomed in the sun-rich Third World countries, for they would benefit the most. The huge polluting and inefficient industrial complexes could be dismantled and there would suddenly be a novel and unpredictable redistribution of wealth throughout the world.

The solar cell brings to an end the epoch of centralized control and heralds a revolutionary future with immensely exciting possibilities.

Opposite page: artist's impression of the proposed permanently manned space station. Solar panels can be seen with a 50 kilowatt solar dynamic system, mounted on the ends of the transverse boom (NASA.)

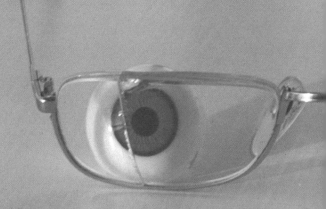

Evolutionary Mindsets

WHILE THE PREVIOUS SIX DOORWAYS to evolutionary re-organization have been firmly rooted in the technologies of the physical world, the seventh threshold is perhaps more subtle. It is directly concerned with the mindsets which actually created those technologies and which form our ways of thinking and perceiving. These mind programs are the ones which are being seriously challenged today.

In this century we have been dominated by very particular kinds of scientific and cultural ideas.

Although for the most part we may not notice them, our everyday perceptions are determined by these models of reality.

Isaac Newton proposed, over three hundred years ago, in his *Principia*, that the universe is somewhat like a vast clockwork mechanism composed of matter and forces and that we somehow stand outside of it as wondering observers. This particular model has long ago been exposed as a fiction, but because that "mindset" has become so collectively habitual most of us still perceive life much in this way. We still see ourselves as essentially separate observers of creation; we still believe that existence can be reduced to its atomic parts, which will eventually tell us how everything works; and we still believe that science equals progress and knowledge.

The revolutionary perspective of the 15th Century Renaissance

One day perhaps mankind will invent new words for "sunset" and "sunrise" which fit the facts of a revolving planet. Until we do, the tyranny of those words force us to see the sun moving about us and not us moving about the sun. This is one paradigm shift that never happened.

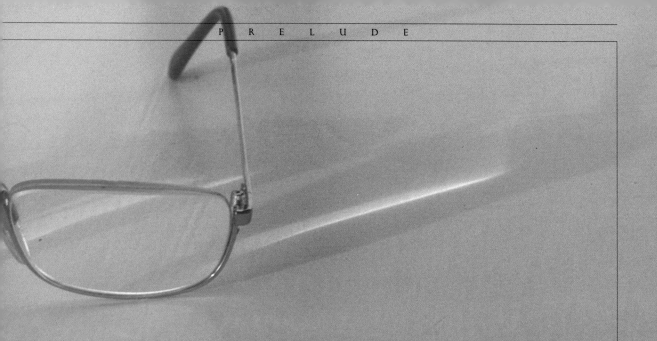

world is a beautiful example of just how persuasive and all-consuming a powerful new model can be.

Artists of that time created a novel way of picturing reality. For the first time they assumed an observer standing, as it were, before a window frame looking out at a fixed situation where all the imaginary lines drawn from the object would meet at a single point of a fixed horizon. Two hundred years later the new science endorsed this mechanical point of view of a standard uniform space by reducing phenomena into uniform standard units. Even later, the camera seemed to confirm once again all our ideas about the nature of life by using precisely the same principle of a fixed hole with light falling onto a flat plate behind it.

Now it is still tempting to see reality like this especially as our simple movie screens and televisions and our magazines all confirm that the real world is like a photograph and we are separate onlookers.

New pictures are gradually emerging, however, of a reality which might be synchronous, or a constantly shifting holographic mosaic. The phenomenal world could be more like a vast thought field, which changes depending on how we look at it. Reality has been elevated from that of a fixed and static noun to a fluid, living verb.

The new scientific visions have also completely changed the actual position of the classic observer. Not only does man no longer stand on the outside of the rest of creation, looking on, but he is an integral part of that whole creation. Even more shattering to the older image is the implication *that man is also the whole.*

It is perhaps this understanding which has prompted a sudden surge of interest in the nature of consciousness, of self-reflective awareness and the whole mystical renaissance of the 1970s and 1980s. It is predicted that within the next decade the Human Growth movement, with its focus on altered states of consciousness, could overtake our present "Age of Information" as the major industry of the Western world. Far-fetched as it might seem, if the current trends are sustained we will enter the Age of Consciousness by the year 2000 or even earlier.

This whole paradigm or pattern shift in our collective mindsets is the single most powerful doorway to evolutionary change. As we shall discover later, the way we view the world largely determines what we find in it. Change the way of looking and the world is changed. Alter the model we have of ourselves and mysteriously man is altered too.

In a classic experiment by Mark Rosenzweig at Berkeley, two colonies of laboratory rats were kept in totally different environments. One environment was impoverished, dull and repetitive, whilst the other was lively, varied and rich in all the things which rats find exciting. The group in the latter environment displayed a striking increase in the mass and complexity of the cerebral cortex as well as unexpected changes in the brain chemistry. This suggests that distinct physiological alterations accompany intellectual and perceptual experience. Changes of conceptual and perceptual models can precipitate release of hormones, changes in the glands and profound alterations within the brain and nervous system.

We have now examined just some of the critical thresholds of our present epoch. Given the fact that evolutionary changes generally appear at just such points of crisis within an environment we have also seen we are preeminently qualified for a change within the organism. The next part of the case is whether the original blueprint of Homo sapiens carries with it any functions or secret codes which might act as a foundation for such a transformation.

Part I

T H E   S O N G   O F   M A N

CHAPTER ONE

The Original Blueprint

What is man, where did he come from and where is he going? The
following is a reconstruction of the original blueprint of Man and the
evolutionary environment of the species.

A Map for All Seasons — Philosophia Perennis — Sleepers — A Matter
of Life and Death — Patterns for the Time Being — Vortex —
Creation Zero — All Things Great and Small — Holo-ground —
Being and Becoming — Mirror — Brainwave — In Two Minds —
Dialectics — Glands and the Heart of the Matter — Body Electric —
The True Environment of Evolution — Flight of the Swan —
Symbiosis — Rainbow on the Seashore of Time — Mixed Metaphors

CHAPTER TWO

Paradise Lost

Has mankind taken a wrong turning and if so what have we lost on the way?
Man Made Man — the creation of a humanoid.

Brief Encounter with a Disposable Man — I, Robopath — Humanoid —
Divided Within — The Other Half — Devil's Gate — Divided Without
— Slaughterhouse Planet — Misanthropy — Economics of Starvation
— Immune to Life — Insane Species

CHAPTER THREE

Stranger in a Stranger Land

The underlying reasons behind the loss of our extraordinary inheritance and
an examination of the world in which the new men and women are to be born.

Let There Be Two — False Identity — Blind Belief — Priest, God and
the Hereafter — Four Horsemen of the Apocalypse — Prisoner of
Knowledge — Parent and the Family — Politician and the State —
Blind Alley — New Priesthood — Tapes of Beliefs and Tapes of Doubt

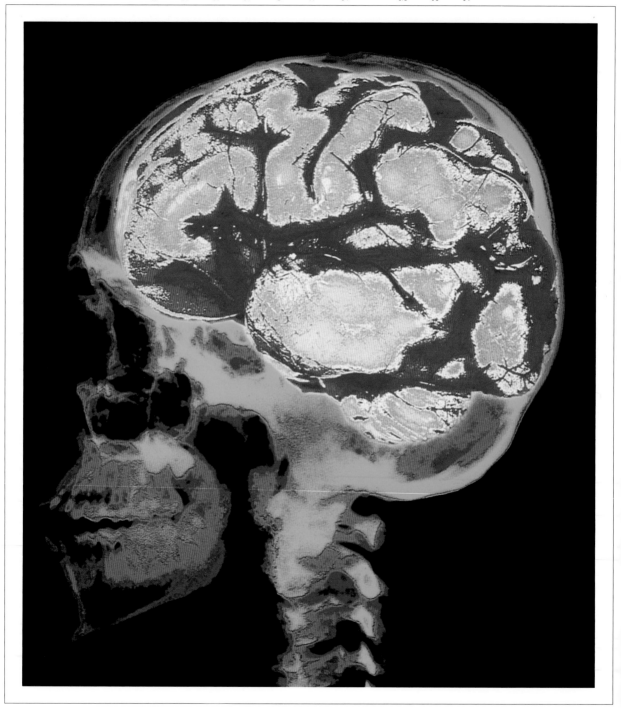

CHAPTER ONE   The Original Blueprint

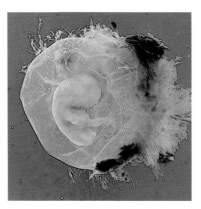

AN ATTEMPT HAS BEEN MADE in the prelude to show that we live in a time of unprecedented change and shifting perils; that never before has mankind had to face so many critical thresholds at one time. We suspect from past evidence that any evolutionary transformation of a species maybe is preceded by a crisis in the environment. It has also been shown that many of our present critical thresholds are destined to collide at any moment and that each hour brings us closer to that apocalyptic event. Each single critical pathway is, of itself, sufficient to trigger an evolutionary time-bomb which could detonate a transformation of our species. The magnitude and number of these thresholds compels us to conclude that something of a revolutionary nature is imminent.

We turn now to the second part of the investigation. From where does the new species arise?

It is hardly likely, from what we know of evolutionary strategy that a new species will appear from nowhere, fully cognizant and ready to take over the planet. If a new species appears at all, it will be born of normal men and women like us and will inherit most of our genetic make up. Modern man was a huge leap forward from his predecessor, but the earlier *Homo sapiens* provided a clear form from which to develop.

So the next question that naturally arises is: "What do we really know about *ourselves*?"

Perhaps after all, there is something within that old fellow Homo sapiens which we have somehow overlooked. Perhaps we are not at all what we first appear to be and have been carrying around a treasure which we have never used. There are countless testimonies that man has a treasure of miraculous powers which have remained dormant.

A Map for All Seasons

BEFORE EMBARKING ON ANY QUEST for the original blueprint of man we need an overview which gives some indication of where to look and what to look for.

In the present confusion and turmoil of the sciences no unified map seems readily available. All that we can find are tiny fragments from the different disciplines of physics, Quantum Mechanics, molecular biology or evolutionary biology, each with their opposing camps and factions. Few of their theories seem to fit together and in many cases even those that do seem often hopelessly out of date.

Where else then can we look for our map of the species?

In the world of the mystics there are some profound and beautiful maps which appear not to suffer from the ravages of time. Here we find a host of ancient and modern disciplines as widely different as Taoists, Gnostics, the Sufis and the monks of Zen.

This diverse spectrum of human experience has been handed down through living teachings and scriptures with an admirable thoroughness. They all, of course, differ in details, yet the major landmarks and the terrain are uncannily similar. Aldous Huxley, who was fascinated by the fundamental teachings of the various mystical traditions, used Leibnitz's original coin and called that thread of experience "Philosophia Perennis" or the Perennial Philosophy. He defined it as the "*ethic that places man's final end in the knowledge of the immanent and transcendental Ground of all Being.*" It is that abiding philosophy which seems to survive all seasons and changes of age.

Anyone who is skeptical about using such mystical and non-scientific "theories" as maps, might do well to reflect that the originators who compiled such charts did not *theorize* — they *knew*. The sages and seers who created these cosmologies had supposedly experienced them at first hand. Such "philosophy" is not really what we might normally term philosophy in the West but neither is it a science in our usual understanding of the term. For just as the "Western" world chose to explore the *exoteric* boundaries, the external phenomena of life, the Eastern explorers chose the internal, *esoteric* territory. They used rigorous and detailed procedures to determine the topology of inner space, much as a Quantum physicist might do in mapping the structure of an atom.

But while the scientist uses theories which have to be changed and updated in the light of new evidence, his mystic counterpart uses no such device. A blind man has a "*theory*" of how the sun rises; a man with his eyes open needs none for he has *seen* it.

The real problem for the mystic is translating his overwhelming experience into words which have meaning to the blind man. The problem for the blind man, however, is that he must trust the mystic blindly. And here we see the necessity of having an overview which is balanced by the sciences.

Philosophia Perennis

The very first principle of the Perennial Philosophy is that of *hierarchy*. The map is, at first glance, a tiered structure, a series of planes, dimensions and levels. The levels, however, are not seen as separate dimensions but rather as a child's set of nestling dolls which unscrew to reveal a smaller and smaller doll within each of their bodies. Each *ascending* level includes all the levels below it, so an atom on Level One would be included in the living organism of Level Two. But it does not work the other way around. The atom does not contain the living organism. Put in another way, the more highly evolved organism includes the less evolved, but not vice versa. These levels are a stairway which ascends or descends.

And here we are introduced to the essential theme of all the scriptures. On the one hand we have the fall of "Involution" and on the other the ascension of "Evolution." In asserting this we already fall into the trap of generalization for the mystic Meher Baba upends this model by using a conceptual schema with a very different terminology (see page 147.) However, as an introduction to these mystic models we will use a simplified, perhaps personal interpretation of these exquisite insights and teachings.

In the beginningless beginning there is timeless, spaceless, dimension-less, all-pervading eternal and infinite "Oneness." This is the original source from which everything arises. It may be called "Primal Consciousness." It is not really a level at all as it embraces all planes and levels, including itself. For our present purposes and in order to build a bridge between the Eastern map and the Western mind, we will adopt the numbered level system to exemplify the hierarchy: we will assign Primal Consciousness to Level Seven — the level of unity.

For some ultimately unfathomable reason, what Meher Baba has called "God's whim," a wave forms in this limitless void. A moment arises when the wave feels separation, although any sense of division from the "One Ocean" is very subtle indeed. This is the "Causal Level Six," the realm of the "Formless Radiance of Transcendental Being." And even at this exalted mystical level we find the first symptoms of a divine *dis-ease*. A deep restlessness and disquiet appears within the wave.

On the one hand there is the thirst to return to the "Source," out of which the wave originally arose, but on the other this could inevitably mean "death" to the newly discovered sense of self.

In returning to the Ocean, the separate and unique individual wave would have to disappear. This moment is the first recoil from the awful possibility of that death of "it-self." In the withdrawal, the contraction from that state, a substitute universe is born over which the wave at least feels it has control. This is the "Primary Illusion," for of course the wave cannot actually ever be separated from the Ocean; but somehow it forgets this and creates a kind of false replica of the original Ocean.

This now corresponds to Level Five, or the "Subtle Plane" of the "transpersonal world of archetypes." With each recoil from that fear of death and extinction comes a further and even stronger contraction of consciousness. Each attempt to identify with a particular level results in the formation of lower levels which are further and further away from the "Original Primal Consciousness." The subtle consciousness of Level Five gives way to the mental Level Four, the Psychic Heart and the thresholds of the realms of power and energy. This is the no-man's-land bordering mental Level Three which in its turn spawns

Level One: Physical Matter

Level Two: Living Organisms

Level Three: Consumers

Level Four: Psychic Heart

Level Five: Subtle

Level Six: Causal

Level Seven: Original Unity

the biological Level Two — the plane of life. At the final level the wave passes into unconsciousness. This is the Fall.

This brief summary is much like drawing two rough circles and claiming them to be a map of the world. However, such a map does establish a number of fundamental processes which are overlooked in our everyday life or in any of our scientific models. It clearly shows that the coin of life has two separate aspects: Involution, going down the levels, and Evolution, going up.

Evolution strives towards higher and higher levels of consciousness, while the contractions of involution condemn it to insentient equilibrium — a kind of unconscious entropy. The Hindu sages inform us that existence is all "Leela" — or God's infinite play. The essence of this divine comedy lies in the self-forgetting. By becoming a separate wave, God is playing hide-and-seek with himself. The play revolves around the exquisite piquancy of the "remembrance" — that moment when God comes rushing around the corner and catches sight of Itself in the mirror. The final aim of evolution is for existence to re-awaken as Primal Consciousness, having tasted the novelty of creation, the restrictions and the sufferings from the contraction and the ultimate beauty of that image in the mirror. Evolution is simply the way back home.

Evolution, as expressed in man, has now reached Level Three, which is the plane of thought. Some rare "evolutionary pioneers" have managed, throughout history, to transcend this level and move to Level Four, and beyond.

The next evolutionary step, therefore, is for the species as a whole to do the same. Whether we do this by self-transformation or through an evolutionary quantum leap is the subject of the second part of this book.

However, before we explore these possibilities we must acquaint ourselves with Levels One to Three, by examining a few theories of creation, of life and the consciousness of man within our new map.

And it must be remembered that these theories only cover the first three levels of life: the realms of physics and chemistry (Level One), those of biology and the life sciences (Level Two) and those of philosophy and psychology (Level Three). They are all only indications, very, very rough approximations of the real, and while we all remain at level Three it cannot be otherwise.

Sleepers

HOWEVER POWERFUL THE EVOLUTIONARY DRIVE MIGHT BE to ascend to higher and higher levels of existence, its direction "upwards" does seem to have a curiously disjointed pattern. From the evidence of fossils nothing seems to happen for long periods and then suddenly a crisis appears in the habitat of an organism and almost overnight a brave new world is born.

While it is true that no one has ever witnessed a full-blooded evolutionary jump there is enough convincing evidence to support the "sudden jump" theory notwithstanding the conventional neo-darwinist's view that evolutionary change is a gradual affair. The term "overnight" is, of course, used in an evolutionary context to mean hundreds or thousands of years, an abrupt change only when compared to the normal evolutionary spans of billions of years.

The greatest mystery to biologists is just how the changes arise. From where does the new species obtain the information to change? Is it purely a random, accidental affair where the fortunate individual passes his winning sequence on to the genetic pool which quickly capitalizes on the advantage? Recent discoveries in microbiology might give us some first clues.

DNA is conventionally regarded as the master plan of life. It was always assumed to be a complete set of blueprints of how to build an organism and replicas of that organism. But biologists in the early 1980s found that instead of the complete "blueprint" being engaged, astoundingly only 3 percent of the DNA information was actually being used in the cells of many organisms and only 1 percent in man. Even that was in an almost fortuitous and accidental manner. John Rogers, writing of "Genes in Pieces" in The New Scientist back in 1977, reflected on the severe shake up to the biologists' world when he admitted: *"There is an air of bewilderment bordering on incredulity in molecular labs at the moment."* Although much has been learned since then, the question still remains that if we only use 1 percent of our genotype, or the genetic constitution of our organism, what about the other 99 percent? The research around this new discovery is still conflicting but we can surely conclude at least that our genetic pool is vast beyond our original imaginings.

Within the interacting matrix of our individual ecosystems, that precious library of DNA could give instructions for the organism to be many different things. There is evidence to show that, on occasion viruses and bacteria can, and do, transfer genetic information between species which are only distantly related.

The fact that every now and again the virus gives information that the cells cannot handle, resulting in a breakdown of the immune system and an outbreak of a viral infection, is just a small penalty for such a vital system.

It is calculated that there are over a million genes in our nuclei alone which we are not actually using. Nature is always super-abundant, she is never miserly. Many of these programs could be ancient scriptures, the records of our whole genetic history from the very first stirrings in the early oceans or the life crystals in some primordial clay. The first tentative proposal within our present investigation is that the higher level fields, the evolutionary initiative, have left a series of evolutionary time bombs quietly ticking away on Level Two.

It is as if these are doorways left ajar to the upper levels or clues left behind by the Primal Consciousness of how to get back up there, so that the game of hide-and-seek with Itself can reach a crescendo of fulfillment.

In accord with evolution's upward drive towards higher and higher levels, it is possible that nature has planted perfectly developed seeds, potential functions, which lie dormant until triggered by some other biological or physiological event. As will be seen, thousands or even millions of years could elapse while a species carries around the treasure of its future. Sometimes through an accident or a freak set of biological or cultural circumstances the seed is activated in a single individual.

But nature seems to need numbers for the "seed" to take properly. It not only needs the right conditions but a minimum number of similar individuals to trigger a full evolutionary transition to a new level or a new species. So, in any investigation of the original blueprint of man, we must be alert for any function which might qualify as a "sleeper."

"If you want to experience the body, you must live in the body! That's why the ancient sages and saints didn't know what to do with their body: they left it and they meditated, so the body didn't participate at all."

(The Mother)[1]

A Matter of Life and Death

The "*Belousov-Zhabolinsky*" chemical reaction is the best known far-from-equilibrium or dissipative structure, which uncannily resembles life forms. Four chemicals, malonic acid, bromate, cerium ions and sulfuric acid are left in a shallow dish. Within a few moments spirals and concentric patterns spread across the dish and continue to fluctuate and change for many hours. The appearance of these ordered patterns represents a decrease in the entropy within the dish by dissipating even greater amounts into the environment.

The two images illustrate the effect of far-from-equilibrium systems, acting on an ordered beach scene. Living organisms require a constant flow of energy and materials from the environment to maintain their forms. Extreme fluctuations and instability which build up within any dissipative structure lead to the emergence of novel levels of organization. Looking at the crisis of mankind today we see the increased flow of energy and matter characteristic of a typical dissipative system combined with high entropy in the form of both ecological and psychological disorders.

IT IS OUR NEXT INTENTION, in examining what man *is*, to review three of the classic questions which have puzzled the species during its entire history: "Who am I?," "From where did I arise?" and "Where am I going?"

These questions naturally fall into the framework of our concept of time. "Who am I?" can only be answered in the present and is the fundamental question of the mystic-sage. It is the door to all existential levels. But, as we are not mystics, we shall be obliged to investigate this somewhat obliquely by rephrasing it to "What are we?"

The second question, "Where do we come from?" is more in the realm of the scientist, the so-called objective observer. Here we will summarize some of the most relevant theories of creation.

The third question, "Where are we going?" is of course the whole subject of this present quest. This will be a survey of the subtle, internal landscape of the species and the various evolutionary crossroads and road signs which indicate our general direction.

We begin, appropriately enough, with a matter of life and death or, more precisely, the life and death of *matter*. We start with the physical roots. There are two fundamentally different scientific viewpoints which might best be described as the "Science of Dying" (Level One) and the "Science of Living" (Level Two), and it is their conflicting overviews which have a profound effect on how we see ourselves. One of the unique properties of Newtonian physics is that there is no arrow of time built into the theory. We know, existentially, that neither can our cosmic movie be run backwards nor can *cause* follow *effect*. But such non-sense all makes perfect sense to the equations of modern mechanistic physics. Neither of the two foundation stones of modern physics, Einstein's Theory of Relativity or Quantum Mechanics have any built-in arrow of time.

Patterns for the Time Being

However, a new wave of scientific theories holds that time is *irreversible*, it is a one-way street, and at the same time the fundamental stuff of the universe. In the present re-conceptualizing of modern physics a pioneer like Ilya Prigogine can boldly assert: "*I would even dare to say that time precedes existence, just as irreversibility precedes the creation of the universe.*"

The Reaction (illustration)
The autocatalysis is in the circle around A. C1 and C2 are the chemicals starting off the system. A reacts to form B which in turn produces C which in turn produces more A. D and E are the products of these reactions. The autocatalytic cycle A'B'C' renews itself continuously and also acts as a catalyst transforming C1 and C2 into more of D and E. This process occurs spontaneously in both far-from-equilibrium states including those reactions which take place within living cells.

THE CLASSICAL "PHYSICS OF DYING" has always insisted that, while the energy of the universe remains constant, the whole cosmos is running down as a result of less and less of that energy being in an available form. Burn a log of wood or petrol in a car and energy is released in heat. No energy is actually lost; it has just taken a different form in the air, in ashes, exhaust fumes or in a new arrangement of atoms, but, and this is a big but, it no longer exists in any available form for further use. "Entropy" is a measure of that unavailability. Entropy is constantly endeavoring to increase chaos and disorder. According to the "Physics of Dying," at the final death of our universe a theoretically perfect equilibrium will be achieved with disorganized atoms ending up in a vast thin particle soup stretching in all directions.

Directly opposed to this view is the "Physics of Life." Central to this theory is the concept of a *far-from-equilibrium* state. While entropy strives for a perfect equilibrium this "Life" state is in a constant flux, adapting, adjusting and *evolving* into more and more complex arrangements and organized forms. These far-from-equilibrium forms have to get rid of, or dissipate, entropy so that it does not overwhelm the organism with equilibrium. In order to dissipate this entropy, a constant input of energy and matter has to be drawn from the surrounding environment. These so-called dissipative structures can only survive by allowing matter and energy to flow through them and from them, like a vortex in a stream of water.

A vortex in any liquid is a perfect example of a dissipative structure, as is the body-mind of an individual human being or the species as a whole.

Vortex

I<small>N A DISSIPATIVE STRUCTURE</small> (a far-from-equilibrium state), whether it is chemical, physical, or organic, some reagent sets off gigantic oscillations in the reactive systems. As the fluctuations become increasingly turbulent a crossroads or what is known as a "bifurcation point" appears, at which point the system could go in any direction. It is impossible to predict in which direction it will go until suddenly the whole system jumps across the threshold and a new order takes shape. In essence this is the evolutionary process. The whole nature of *being* is really *becoming*; a moving flow which continually reproduces itself, a perpetual recreation and transformation.

Modern theoreticians are increasingly drawn to such concepts for they go a long way to explain some very tricky paradoxes.

The cosmos can be seen as an *infinite dissipative structure which somehow feeds off the far-from-equilibrium state itself.* In such a model life is no longer seen as an isolated phenomenon, briefly flaring up in what otherwise is a dying, entropy-filled universe, but as part of a whole living organism. Dissipative structures live or occur by allowing matter and energy to flow through them like the vortex in a stream of water. In this new vision the Infinite Endless Livingness is viewed as a flowing through everything, which is also "Itself." Man is both the flow and the flow-er, observer and observed, a wave within an infinite ocean. The cosmos begins to look more like an elaborate artwork as we live and flow as an ever transmuting order of creativity.

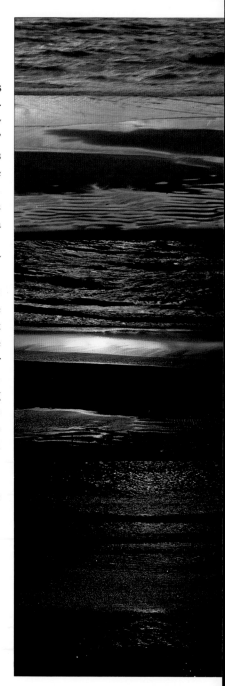

Eddies and ripples and vortices in water are examples of far-from-equilibrium structures. The slightest change in the flow or any external condition creates a crisis in the fluctuations and suddenly a vortex appears. It is an ordered, autonomous form, yet inseparable from the water itself. The vortex remains stable and resistant to change although that stability depends on the constancy of the continuing flow. Its stability is in fact an instability because of its dependence on the environment. If there is any perturbation in the flow then it will spontaneously abort, disintegrate or evolve into a new form. In this tidal stream the feedback loop is such that the flow acts upon the environment (sand) creating ripples which slowly build up until the vortex form of the water has its mirror image in the sand. This in turn creates a new turbulence and then another vortex takes its place. Here the form acts upon the field and the field on the form. Evolution can be thought of in this way.

"*You can never step in the same river twice.*"
(Heraclitus)[2]

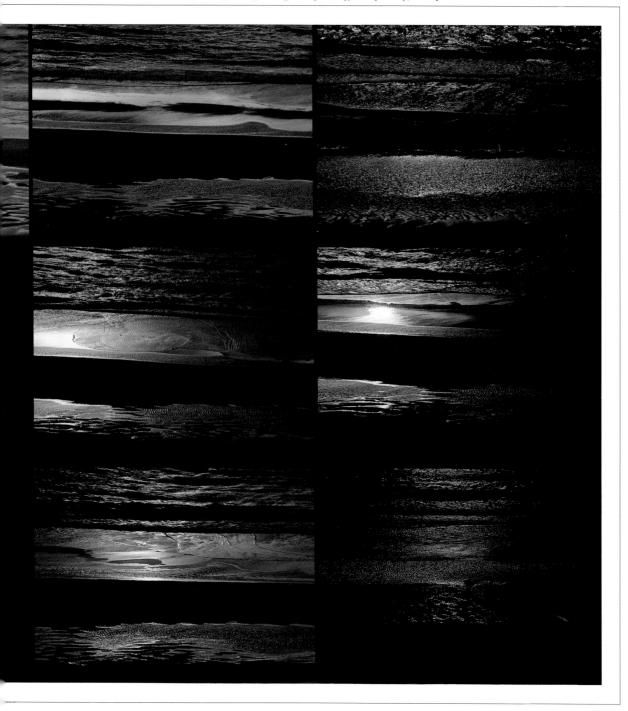

Creation Zero

WE DON'T ACTUALLY KNOW HOW THE UNIVERSE BEGAN. The only thing we can be reasonably sure of is that our present environment evolved from an intensely hot, dense state. It may have been a bifurcation point, a gigantic thermodynamic instability which suddenly made a quantum leap into the order and form of our universe.

The most currently acceptable theoretical model of Western physics starts with a brief period of unimaginable expansion before turning into a cosmic fireball ten to fifteen billion years ago.

It proposes that existence appeared in nothingness, as a sudden, vast expanding sphere of radiation at an unimaginable temperature of one million million degrees centigrade. There is no physical state known today which even shadows such a source of pure energy.

Existence cooled as it expanded as a cloud of "gas" from Creation Zero. As it continued to cool atomic nuclei formed and simple atoms began to appear. Atoms which managed to survive the cataclysmic forces of radiation now clustered together under the spell of a new force — gravity. Over eons of time these gathered into the primordial galaxies. Clouds of helium and hydrogen condensed into the gigantic masses which became the first stars. As the cooled gases collapsed under colossal gravitational forces, many early stars generated so much heat that they exploded into supernovae, brighter than an entire galactic center. The explosions hurled heavier and increasingly complex elements even further out into space and time. This rich debris would condense into new stars, only to implode and explode again and again like some vast stellar breathing. As atoms stabilized they combined in ever more complex configurations of matter, creating the planets and their satellites.

Some recent theories dramatically depart from the conventional scenario at this point, for they propose that living and non-living microstructures flowed together as if in a cooperative venture, rather than in a competitive environment of survival of the fittest. Primordial Earth was at that time a far-from-equilibrium chemical reaction regulated by "autocatalytic" events. The intense fluctuations in the primitive atmosphere and oceans caused a multitude of critical threshold points, and structures similar to the Belousov-Zhabolinsky reaction might have appeared. These could have reproduced and

"And spontaneously there occurred a sort of eruption, disrupting the individual poise and the unconscious tranquillity of the Infinite Soul with a recoil or tremendous shock which impregnated the unconsciousness of its apparent separateness from the indivisible state."
(Meher Baba)[3]

"When thought contemplated itself in your beginning, what it expanded itself into was the principle of thought called light. Light was created first, because whenever thought is contemplated and expanded, it is always lowered into a vibratory frequency that emits light. Light is thus the first lowered form of contemplated, expanded thought.
"Whenever you contemplate thought and emotionally embrace it, the thought expands into the vibratory frequency of light. If you slow the movement of the particles of light and condense it, you create electrum — an electromagnetic field that has positive and negative poles which you call electricity. If you slow and condense the thought still further beyond the electromagnetic fields, the electrum coagulates into gross matter. Gross matter then coagulates into the molecular structures called form. And the form is held together by the thought that the soul envisioned as an ideal of creation.
"All things are created by taking that which has no speed — thought — and expanding it into that which does — light — and then slowing the light down until you create this and that and all that is around you."
(Ramtha)[4]

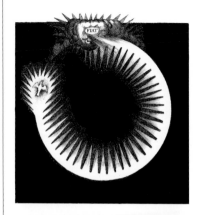

gradually evolved into what became life.

This breakthrough into life could have happened in the oceans, in the tidal pools or even in the primitive crystals of clay. In fact this last theory, that man has descended from mud, is an evocative theme which appears in religious myths all over the world. As larger molecules, amino acids, enzymes and proteins began to link together in increasing complexity, simple cells formed which changed the chemistry of the whole biosphere. This in turn created new fluctuations, creating new dissipative structures. This is a holistic unfolding. It involves the smallest and the largest in a *whole* pattern in which nothing is greater or lesser. Life and Non-life are seen as one evolutionary process.

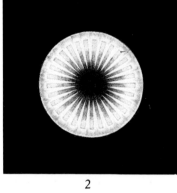

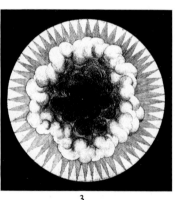

1

2

3

The creation according to the 18th Century alchemist Robert Fludd. In many ways we remain as mystified as he was and hardly offer better models of how it all began.

1. The Great Darkness, Mysterium magnum, the Great Mystery
2. The Appearance of Light
3. Division of the Waters (Duality)
4. Chaos of the Elements
5. Solar Creation

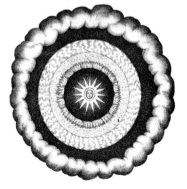

4

5

All Things Great and Small

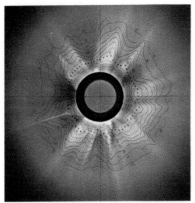

ONE VIEW IS THAT THE WHOLE OF PRIMORDIAL EARTH is a vast dissipative structure, an immense chemical vat of far-from-equilibrium reactions. In this conceptual scheme the whole biosphere was like some choreographic latticework. Microscopic bacterial events could then have acted with profound effect upon macroscopic happenings, the size of the planet and vice versa.

In the Age of the Bacteria, which lasted two hundred thousand times as long as the recorded history of mankind, bacteria entirely transformed the Earth's atmosphere, stabilizing the oxygen content, as far as is known, at 21 percent, which is its present level. Why bacteria should ever have started this action is one of the unsolved mysteries of biology. For although, as we have seen, there were simply too many bacteria and eventually too little food, up to this point the bacteria had proved, in a Darwinian sense, to be perfectly adapted to their oxygenless environment. It is true, that *in retrospect*, it can be seen that oxygen allows the bacteria to be far more efficient in metabolizing glucose, yet how were they to know that in advance? And when the new breed had reached maximum efficiency with 10 percent oxygen why go on producing more to double that figure, poisoning themselves into the bargain? It almost seems they purposefully sacrificed a bacteria paradise in order to act as *catalysts*, enriching the planet for far more complex and exotic forms to supplant them. It would, however, make perfect sense if life on the planet was in some way seen as a cooperative venture.

We are the evolutionary product of fifteen billion years of ceaseless dissipative action. The dissipative structure of the planet as a whole is supported by the constant flow of matter, energy and other life forms through its vast system. Humankind is supported by the same process.

Simple cells began to combine with others, giving birth to ever more complex cells with the beginnings of a well-defined nucleus which held the cell's genetic material. Two cells could come together and from their merger could produce offspring carrying both of the original genetic codes. Sexual reproduction opened up spectacular opportunities for mutations to spread throughout the populations. The invention of sex created great variety and the novelty of both "individuals" and "death."

About one billion years ago a quantum leap in evolution happened. Cells had grown so large they could no longer feed themselves fast enough through their walls. Thus they started clustering together in communities, creating the first blob-like multi-cellular beings such as jellyfish or sponges. Slowly, different cell clusters carried out different tasks which allowed the colonies to adapt more easily to the environment. Six hundred million years ago complex organisms appeared which led to the incredibly intricate and interdependent life chain upon the planet.

Above: Solar eclipse.

Opposite page: Division of cells. The action of the microcosmic world upon the macrocosmic world and its reverse, in an everchanging flux, is central to the theme of co-evolutionary universe.

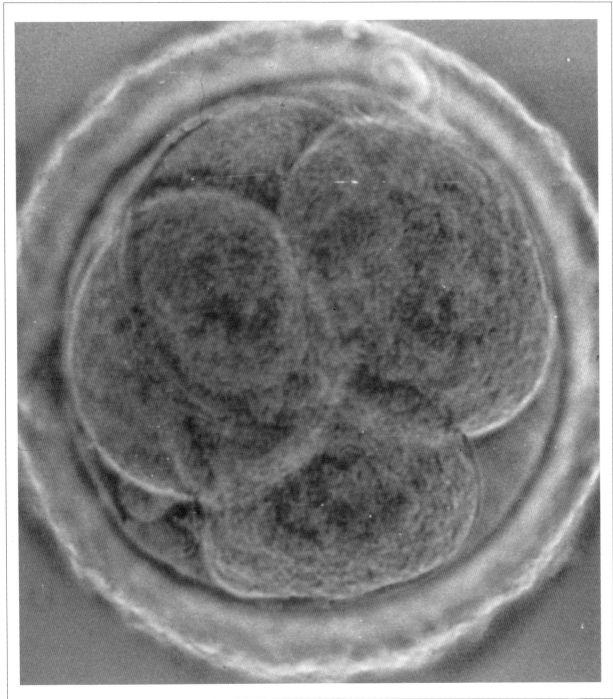

Holo-Ground

The body is such a momentary affair. It exists only for the time being, and, like a rainbow — there's nothing in the hands.

ONE OF THE MOST POTENTIALLY REWARDING hypotheses to date proposes that material existence is actually one of vibrations, analogous to the frequency interference patterns in a *hologram*.

We find that the hologram (Greek Holos-gramma, "the whole message") can offer useful insights into the nature of what is felt to be the undivided wholeness of reality. This analogy allows us to comprehend a single, coherent and flowing whole which contains both consciousness and the external reality as we experience it. Holography can use any wave form, although the best known form is that of the modern photographic hologram.

A hologram encodes information which creates the illusion of a *three-dimensional* image when re-illuminated through a holographic photo-plate. While this is a static model, at least at this stage of development of the hologram, it is a useful analogy to show the encoding potential of all such patterns.

It is suggested that the undivided wholeness of existence is a holographic pattern of matter, energy, movement and space-time. Each locality of space, however tiny, contains as does every fragment from the static holographic plate — the pattern of the whole.

As we have been brought up on the mechanistic idea of a clockwork universe, this is all rather a large pill to swallow and shattering to our previous view of the world.

Central to the whole theory is that even the smallest particle carries all the past (and some maintain the future) with it. This is the underlying stuff of existence, the "holo-ground" of reality which is encoded in patterns, somewhat in the manner of the whorls on a holographic plate. We are simultaneously local fragments and the *totality*.

However, the "all in one — one in all" concept is not as simple as it first seems. What we can establish, however, is that within each level there is a kind of holographic principle at work and that between each level there is a hierarchy involved. Armed with very rough and ready understanding we move to Level Two.

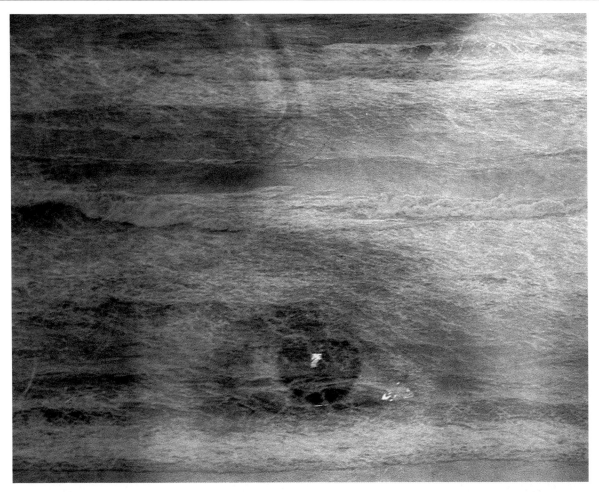

To produce a holographic image the coherent light from a laser beam is split in two. One half of the beam is directed to a photographic plate and the other illuminates the object which is also picked up by the photo plate as an interference pattern created by the two sources of light. To reconstruct the image the holographic plate is simply re-illuminated by the original laser beam and the image of the object appears floating where the original object was.

One of the extraordinary properties of holograms is their resistance to damage or loss of memory. A tiny fragment or chip broken anywhere from the plate essentially holds all the information of the whole plate. When a laser is projected onto the tiny chip the hologram appears with slight loss of detail and clarity but otherwise shows the totality of the image, from at least one vantage point.

The plate can store thousands of images: one only needs to turn it through angles or rotations and record new information upon its surface. This new information in no way disturbs the preceding records. Provided a holographic plate is illuminated by the same light vibrating at the same frequency and the same angle the original image will appear. Change either the frequency or the angle and new images appear.

If the original recording beam is split so that both beams illuminate two different objects then on lighting the exposed plate with one of the illumined objects a hologram of the other will appear.

When a hologram is illuminated with coherent light reflected from the original object, or a similar one, a bright spot appears on the hologram. The brightness corresponds to how closely it resembles the original.

One cubic centimeter of a holographic plate is able to store ten billion bits of information. This is limited to the size of the silver grains of the plate.

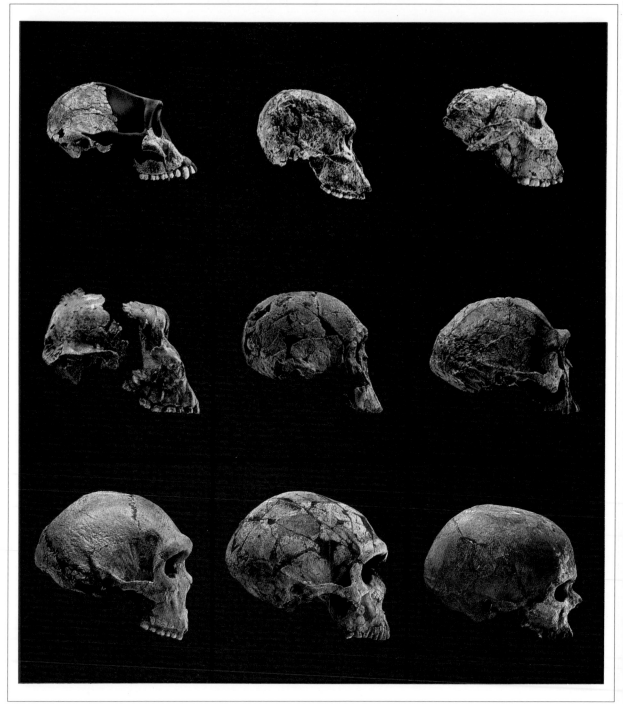

Being and Becoming

"If the design of man is examined he is revealed to be a composite of all previous creatures, environments and experiences. His body below the brows is a machine of animals and elemental cycles... He is not truly unique below the brows. He is rather a summation of all that came before him and everything he already knows.
"But man is also a new stage in the event of time. His newness or uniqueness is hidden in the brain. His lower, or vital, brain including his rudimentary speech and thought, is part of the summary and reflection of the past."
(Da Free John)[5]

Opposite: An orthodox view of the evolutionary line of *Homo sapiens.* **Using the most sophisticated dating technology available, modern man is seen to have appeared alongside his Neanderthal cousins about 32,000 years ago. However, there is substantial conflicting evidence that there were highly advanced civilizations long before this time. Evolutionary theorists remain a speculative profession and largely a science of opinions.
The dates are approximate. Reading from left to right:
A. afarensis 3 to 3.6 million years
A. africanus 2.5 to 3 million years
A. robustus 1.5 to 2 million years
A. boisei 1.8 million years
H. habilis 2 million years
H. erectus 1.5 million years
H. sapiens (archaic) 250,000 to 500,000 years
H. sapiens (neanderthal) 40,000 to 50,000 years
H. sapiens (modern) 32,000 to 28,000 years**

To call a human a being is misleading; he is more a human *becoming.* Man exists in a twilight zone between a beast and a Buddha, for he is in a constant process, knowing that he *is*, but not *who* he is.

In a beast, in an animal, *essence* comes before *existence.* Essence is the whole blueprint of a being partly programmed by the coding of the genes and possibly by fields which determine the collective form, habits and memory of a particular species. For an animal, essence heralds existence. The essential blueprint precedes the living organism. The complete program of the life form, its habits, lifestyle, tastes, its manner of reproduction and its manner of dying all come with the original package at birth. Our first hominid ancestors, A. afarensis, roaming the savannahs three million years ago, carried their essential blueprint with them. They followed the strict regime of that inbuilt genetic program which cast them as clever but simple beasts.

Let us suppose that somewhere along that long hominid line a critical threshold appeared and the line split in two. The beast took the terminal path to extinction and the first true man stepped across the biological barrier which was to profoundly alter the evolutionary process. For now man *existed first* and his whole program followed. The beast had remained a closed being, pre-programmed, dependent upon biological evolution for any change. The new being, however, was suddenly an uncertainty — a becoming. *Homo sapiens* remains that question mark, a movement towards a quest of who he is. In biological terms this situation is created by the vast areas of the cerebral cortex which remain uncommitted. In most animals virtually the whole brain is taken up by particular sense or survival functions, but in man there are large unused areas which are available for other processes, such as learning and thought.

The biblical story of the expulsion of Adam and Eve from the Garden of Eden takes on a new and poignant significance. Both Adam and Eve lose their beast-like innocence and yet pay for their new-found self-reflective consciousness by being perpetually uncertain of who they are and whether they will continue to be. As far as is known they become the first animals to recognize and be afraid of death.

Now we have reached Level Three in our evolutionary panorama.

Mirror

Conscious: *Aware, mentally awake or alert; not asleep or unconscious; known or felt by one's inner self.*

THIS SHORT STANDARD DICTIONARY DEFINITION seems a miserly description of the essential state of man. It does, however, underline the simple fact that we neither know what consciousness actually is, nor do we have any way of observing its nature objectively. We appear to have it, and yet we don't know what it is!

Neurologists can attempt to chart where this mystery might reside and trace some of its favorite pathways in the brain with chemicals and electric pulses, but so far any reductionist approach has proved an inappropriate tool with which to explore this miracle.

Consciousness is not a simple matter of EEG (electro-encephalograph) readings of the electrical frequencies of the brain. There are a myriad of different levels at which consciousness operates in dream states, under anesthetics, waking from sleep, out of the body experiences of meditators or those who have experienced paranormal states in near death situations and accidents.

Primal consciousness is the ultimate mystery, unbounded and unlimited by any experiential or conceptual phenomena. It existed before and will exist after any sense of "I." It is the ground of reality, the holo-cosmos itself, and the awakened consciousness of man in his natural state.

Self-reflective consciousness is the identified consciousness of the normal state of everyday everyman, conceived as the subject and center of experience. Mystics insist that it is the grand illusion of an awareness which is totally identified with experience, with memories, and includes all sleeping, waking, dreaming and autonomous states.

Any mirror can be the agony or the ecstasy of the viewer. On one hand there is the fall of Adam and Eve in their self-consciousness, or the Greek mythical figure of Narcissus who is condemned to contemplate his own reflected image in a pool suffering eternal separation and loneliness. On the other hand there is the ecstasy of the penultimate mirror of consciousness, that moment when existence gazes upon itself.

"If the human brain were so simple that we could understand it, we would be so simple that we wouldn't."
(Emerson Pugh)[6]

Neo-Cortex

Mammalian

Reptilian

Neuro-scientists have many differing explanations for the intricate workings of the brain. Some advocate a division of hot and cold brains. The hot core and mid-brain is impulsive and wants immediate action or gratification, while the cold cortex looks ahead, evaluating the results of past action. Here we can see the great Freudian battle-lines drawn up between the hot ID and the cold Super-ego.
Other accounts present a picture of three evolutionary brains, three levels as it were in time. The brain-stem is thought to be the early instinctive, reptilian brain with the accumulated wisdom of the whole evolutionary stream. There is then the mid-brain, or the early mammalian zone, which reacts in the immediacy of the moment; whereas the last layer is the neo-mammalian cortex which plans ahead, assessing any situation using past experience and acquired knowledge. This cortex is the site of past, present and future.

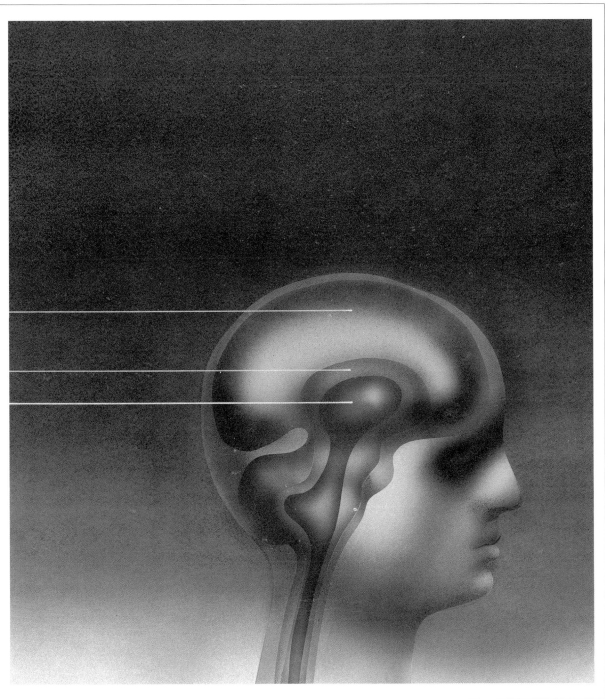

Brainwave

The old idea that memory is recorded and stored physically in little boxes in the head is rapidly giving way to the concept that the brain is a tuning mechanism which tunes to a memory "field."

Brain waves can be grouped into four main types according to their frequencies.
Beta: Normal awake mind. Faster than 13 cycles per second. Normally apparent in the middle and front of the head, an area related to sensory motor functions.
Alpha: 8-13 cycles per second. Found mostly in the back of the head. Associated with deep relaxation, when the activity of the mind is slowed down, in meditation or when listening to music.
Theta: 4-7 cycles per second. Mostly occurs very strongly between the ages of 2 and 5. Often found as powerful fluctuations in adults exhibiting frustration and psycho-pathologies. When maintained, can reflect blissful states of deep meditation.
Delta: 1-3 cycles per second. The mind is almost non-functioning. Occurs during dreamless sleep, early infancy, brain tumors and, most mysteriously in Samadhi, the mystical state. Patanjali, two thousand five hundred years ago, called this state the *"deep sleep with awareness."*

THERE ARE AS MANY THEORIES as to how the brain functions as there are neuro-physicists. The conventional approach is that of the materialistic and reductionist attitude that the brain is composed of highly organized and interconnected units with specific functions and zones.

Scientists have managed to somehow count over 100 billion glia cells, 10 billion neurons and over a trillion synapses. The almost immeasurable interconnections between these microscopic functions are now also being painstakingly assessed.

Yet according to the mystic this is still like someone who has never seen television taking a television set apart and tracing the circuitry in order to see what a broadcast is like, when all he had to do was plug the machine in.

One hypothesis suggests possibilities that memory may be stored in the brain by processes similar to holography, which would mean that memories are not actually stored at specific sites but are distributed throughout the whole brain and even within the cells of the body. But however persuasive the holographic model might be it remains firmly anchored in the mechanistic view of life. The memory traces are still seen as physically located *somewhere* in the brain fabric. And up to the present moment no one has managed to find where.

Rupert Sheldrake, in offering an alternative and revolutionary hypothesis, points out: *"Spoken softly, the possibility is open that the phenomenon of 'life' depends upon laws and factors which have not been recognized so far by scientists."*

He proposes that there is a kind of memory in the organizing fields of nature which determines the form of everything — from the structure of crystals to the form of embryos slowly developing into a human being. He suggests that there is a resonance whereby forms are influenced by the memory of similar forms which have occurred in the past. The collective memory of a species determines what becomes the habitual shape of that particular species. The organism is not only influenced by the collective memory of the species, the biological memory of how to build the phenotype, but it is also influenced by its former states of being.

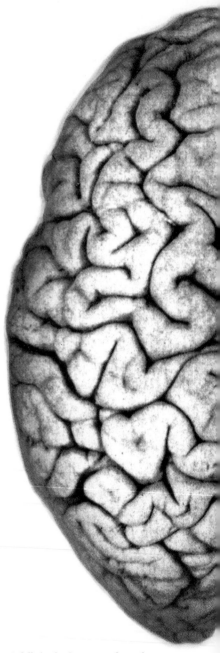

The caterpillar is influenced by the larval memory just as the butterfly is influenced by the trace of being a caterpillar. These memories are held to be within "form fields" having particular morphic (form) resonances in this hypothesis of formative causation. The function of the brain is seen not as a recording mechanism with physical memory traces, as in a computer, but as a tuning system which can tune into both past and present patterns of activity. Thus it can be seen that a brain and a computer are on totally different evolutionary paths of intelligence. In the case of brain damage due to surgery or accident the memory loss does not mean that specific cells in specific locations are lost, but rather that the tuning system of the brain no longer functions properly.

If memories are not stored in the brain itself maybe we can pick up another's memories if we hit the right frequency. Tuning into the memory fields of past individuals begins to look remarkably like tuning into Jung's "archetypes" in the collective unconscious. Such a theory might go a long way towards explaining such puzzling phenomena as telepathy, past life memories, psychometry and other paranormal behavior. If memory fields exist outside the apparatus of the physical brain, then presumably they would survive damage or the death of that brain. Of course there would be no access to them once the tuning system had gone. However, if consciousness is not identical to the functioning of that tuning system, but somehow is an event which happens in the exchange between the morphic fields and the brain, then it is possible that the "self" might stay in contact with the eternal form field with its set of memories.

We shall return to this hypothesis later as it is crucial to the whole investigation.

LEFT: processor of the serial mode. A linear analysis of the sequential flow of information. Through cultural and educational pressures, this hemisphere has become dominant in the West, overriding and even filtering the information of the right side.

RIGHT: processor of the parallel or synthetic mode. Holistic, uses mosaic-like patterns of the whole. Is attuned to rhythm, music, spatial dimensions and tends to grasp situations. It is seen increasingly by researchers as the mysterious unknown and inactive partner.

A full size brain, as seen from above.

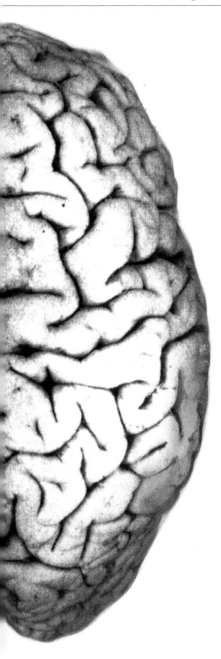

In Two Minds

WE HAVE TWO BRAINS IN OUR SKULLS, two distinct and interconnected hemispheres. However, it was not until the late 1950s that scientists discovered just how different their functions are. In studies of patients who had the dense mass of connecting fibers between the hemispheres in some way either damaged or surgically severed, some very curious anomalies were unearthed. It was found for instance that the two halves are so separate and distinctive that a patient might be struggling to do up his buttons with the right hand, totally oblivious to the fact that his anarchistic left hand was already undoing them.

A healthy and whole human being has a balance of these opposites, for the two hemispheres form a partnership in which certain areas naturally dominate over one another. In a healthy state they can be seen as two lovers both complementing and contrasting one another. As one focuses, the other tunes out to allow less interference.

The great core of cables which connect the brain with the central nervous system does a very neat twist in the *medulla* at the base of the brain-stem, which means that each side of the brain deals with its opposite side of the body.

The two hemispheres of the brain have to be seen as opposing tendencies or preferences rather than fixed and separate realms. The distinctions between the two sides could be summarized as a receptive mode and an active mode. The intaking, receptive right hemisphere contrasts with the projective, outgoing mode of the left hemisphere. The list below illustrates some relevant tendencies for this left-right dialogue.

LEFT: analytical, rational, digital, intellectual, active, convergent, discrete, differential, rational. Concerned with relationships, sequences, serial time, differentiation, inferential intuition. The explicit, analytic, reductionist and successive brain function.

RIGHT: relational, metaphorical, analogical, intuitive, receptive, divergent, continuous, existential. Concerned with intuition, correlation, simultaneous and spatial time, integration. The tacit, holistic, compositional and simultaneous brain function.

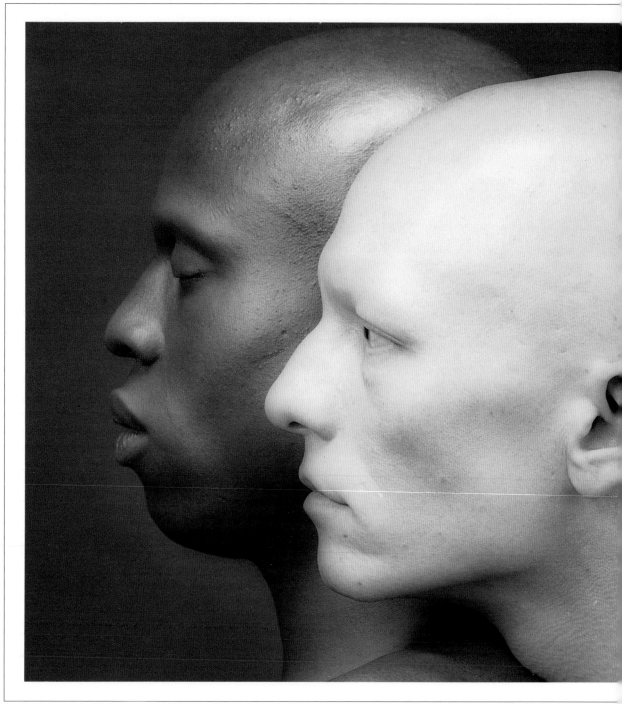

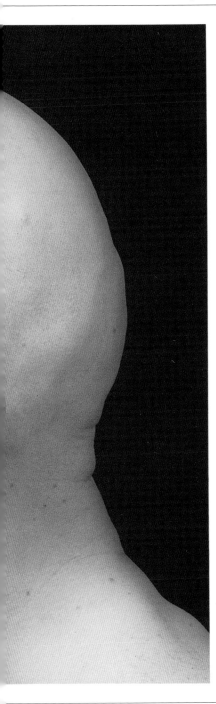

Dialectics

BIOLOGICALLY AND PSYCHOLOGICALLY, man is an ambiguity: a dialectic. The hidden harmony seems paradoxically to be a state of irreconcilable opposites. Yet it is only from the meeting of the male and the female principles that a new child is born. A meeting of harmonious principles has no offspring; it is a happy but sterile union. From the meeting of the right and left eye or ear, each with a very different message, a totally new spatial dimension emerges.

Man has the past heritage of the beast and the future potential of the Buddha. He exists because of these two polarities. The female and the male principle meet within one man or one woman. We each possess both principles: the anima and the animus, yin and yang, the mystic female and the gypsy — all within the single individual. The individual won't exist without them. The duality continues in the two biological motivational centers of pleasure and pain. The brain's arousal system seems to operate on either side of a balance point, like the single control knob of a stereo. Turn the knob clockwise and the system is alert, anti-clockwise and the system is relaxed.

Nature, however, provides two such knobs of *pleasure-unpleasure* which can often be in direct opposition, as we juggle the losses and gains of each system. For instance, a really piquant taste combines sweet and sour, salt and sugar — pleasure and unpleasure. Laughter is both pleasure and pain. It is only in the synthesis of the two aspects that the laughter is exhilarating. The autonomic, self-governing nervous system is also divided in two opposing systems. The sympathetic and the para-sympathetic modes act as a balance of opposites, functioning in stress and in relaxation. Deep within the brain there are two other opposing factions, two quite distinct kingdoms constantly struggling to be on top. These are the kingdoms of the hot and the cold brains.

The hot mid-brain wants everything *now*. It is impulsive, willful, an impetuous animal which tries to impose its needs upon the external world of events. The cool cortex, however, looks ahead, evaluating the results of past actions and carefully projecting likely futures. It attempts to restrict the immediate actions of the hot-headed mid-brain. Action and inaction meet.

Glands and the Heart of the Matter

IN THIS LAST DECADE OF RESEARCH into the workings of the immune system, physicians have been surprised by the diversity of the hitherto mysterious endocrine glands in their regulation of the body.

These are the ductless glands, responsible for secreting hormones (Greek for "to arouse or set in motion") into the bloodstream, sending their messages of balance throughout the whole organism.

Hindu, Buddhist and Taoist yogis and physicians in the past paid a great deal of attention to these glands, recognizing them as primary regulators of both the physical and the spiritual being. They saw these glands as the physical equivalents of the seven "chakras" or energy wheels of the esoteric sciences.

There have been many esoteric explanations for what these glands actually do, but one description does deserve to be mentioned, for it has remarkable parallels with the teachings of Georges Gurdjieff half a century ago. In this description by the channeled entity Ramtha it is said that we are surrounded and bombarded by what is best understood as a "thought field." The thoughts which we claim as our own are really like a continuous universal broadcast. Some thoughts are cosmic in origin while for the most part the broadcasts are what might be described as local stations. The pituitary gland within the brain for instance, can somewhat be seen as a radio receiver channeling all the wavebands, the entire spectrum of frequencies. This gland, which along with the hypothalamus controls many functions of the brain, then secretes hormones appropriate to the frequencies which flow to the pineal. This tiny gland, tucked away in the center of the brain, is supposedly then responsible for amplifying those frequencies throughout the body. In this account the pineal is also responsible for maintaining a harmony of the hormones, determined by whichever collective thought frequencies are being received. The higher the frequency, the greater and the more subtle is the hormone flow. The pineal in its turn instructs the pituitary to secrete its hormones, thus activating the brain to receive ever higher frequencies.

While such an explanation seems far fetched at first glance it does merit careful attention as will be shown later when we explore new scientific theories which view the world as a huge "thought field."

Starting at the top of the endocrine system we find two glands, the *pineal* and the *pituitary*, residing in the brain between the *cerebellum* and the brain stem. These two closely connected glands are intertwined in a region called the *diencephalon*. They share this crucial center with the *thalamus* and the *hypothalamus* which are the egg-shaped masses of grey matter which serve as the major integrators of information that flows between the sensory organs and the higher cortex. The tiny hypothalamus liaises with many areas and controls the pituitary gland. This gland secretes hormones that influence all the other six glands below it, which in turn regulate vital psycho-physical activities. The pituitary is traditionally associated with the "sahasrar," the thousand petaled lotus or female principle in Taoist texts, and is known by Christian mystics as the "Seventh Seal."

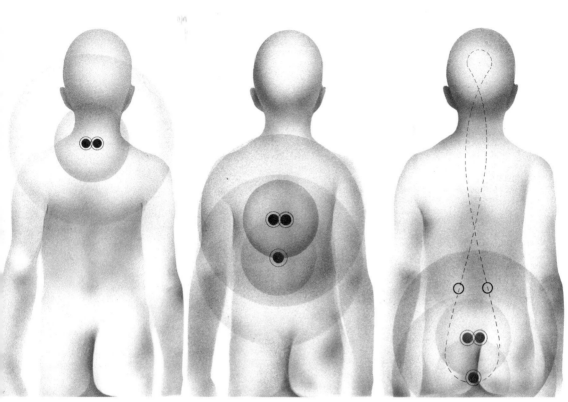

Traditional mysticism locates the "ajna chakra" (or the third eye) at the pineal. By most modern accounts this is both simplistic and misleading. The true "ajna chakra" is said to be the entire braincore which includes the pineal, pituitary, thalamus, hypothalamus, medullar, pons and mid-brain. The "sahasrar chakra," in modern mysticism, is considered to be associated with the whole region which includes the crown, the *corpus callosum*, the upper *lateral ventrices* and the *corona radiata*. As we move down the throat we discover the *thyroid* and its little galaxy of *parathyroids*, these secret but essential hormones which balance calcium and phosphorus in the body. Mystics saw this as the locus of higher creative energies and intelligence. Called the "Visuddha" or "throat chakra," it is intimately linked with the alimentary canal and the lungs.

The thymus sits above the diaphragm, next to the heart. It has a fundamental role within the whole immune system which is linked to the circulatory blood system and of course the heart. This corresponds to the "Anahata" or "heart chakra." Love and the higher states of consciousness meet at this center.

The heart itself is so intimately connected with the glands that it will be included in this diagram. In fact recently it was discovered that it shares many of the characteristics of a gland (see page 218). It is held to be the primary root of all psycho-physical being.

The pancreas lies in the region of solar plexus, controlling the digestive processes. It directs the liver to release stored sugars into the blood for heating and energy. This is the site of the "Manipura" or the "solar plexus chakra" where positive and negative

bio-electrical forces meet. This hara is the center where life and death meet — an orgasmic state of integration when sun and moon, light and darkness conjoin.

Called in India the "Svadhisthana" or "sacral chakra" the next energy wheel is associated with the Gonads positioned at the base of the torso. They secrete hormones related to sexual reproduction.

The last of the energy wheels at the base of the spine is the "Muladhara" or "base chakra." It is the first coherent integration of being, yet it also contains within it the possibilities of all the higher states. It is usually related to the spinal column, the kidneys and the adrenal glands which are located on either side of the kidneys and a little higher. They secrete the "fight" or "flight" hormones, accelerating the heart beat and shutting down inessential functions during an emergency.

The Body Electric

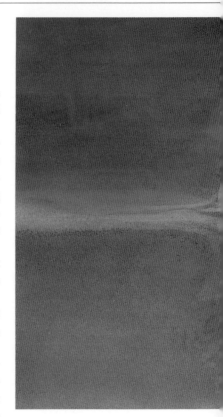

IF WE RECALL THE ORIGINAL MAP of the seven levels with which we opened this chapter, it will be seen that any reductionist, first level tool is really inappropriate to explore the realm of consciousness.

It will be recalled that higher levels of organization embrace lower levels, but lower levels — or their instruments — cannot encompass the higher ones. A billion dollar particle accelerator, howsoever sophisticated, is unlikely to score many hits in its vapor chambers tracking down the experience of love and motherhood! This might explain the failure of laboratory work to pin down even the "simple" mechanisms of memory.

However, modern neurologists have still managed to count virtually all the cells and nerve ends of the brain and have begun to chart all the interconnected neural pathways.

But even with these extensive maps of millions of pathways and cells we are still no nearer to knowing what consciousness is or where it resides.

So we will continue our tour of the body in order to see whether mystics, sages, clairvoyants or mediums have any better methods or clearer explanations. Considering that many of these sources could not have had any corroborating evidence, their findings do seem to have some significance. The following descriptions could derive from almost any of the different disciplines.

The first body is the gross, physical body which is the manifestation of the life current (Level Two). The second is the vital body, the electric field which in traditional terminology is called the "etheric" (Level Three). The third is the psychic body, the emotional field also known as the "astral" (Level Four). The fourth is the field of consciousness, an ovoid, luminous field of colors which is the most subtle of the four, otherwise called the "mental body" (Level Five and Six). And finally there is the fifth (Level Seven). About this nothing can be said. It is the ground of being; the radiance of Primal Consciousness.

The second body is considered as the archetypal pattern from which the first, gross body is molded. It acts as a receiver, an assimilator and a transmitter of bio-energy. It vitalizes all life forms.

Many sages tell us that the soul "holds" the precise "thought

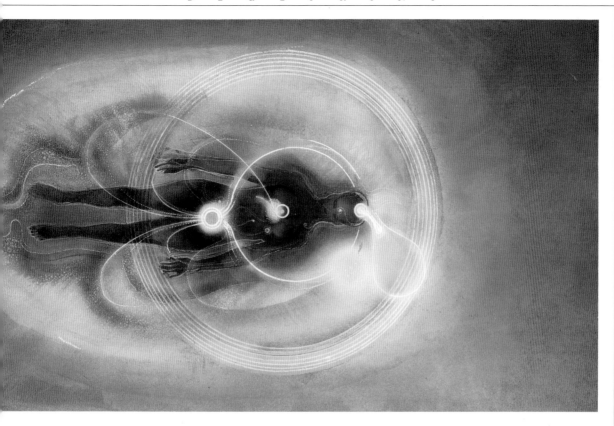

form" of the physical vehicle of the manifest self, i.e. the body. By the time the child is seven years old he or she has become "earthed." The need for an unwavering attention from outside, which was required to "fix" the form, fades. The pineal gland, up until then the main channel through which the soul had gripped the physical manifestation, gradually becomes dormant and in many cases simply atrophies. At fourteen a similar event occurs to the thymus which has been instrumental in grasping the astral body. At twenty-one the mental body has taken shape under the soul's creativity. The glands become active again only when the entity begins the long journey towards self-realization, towards re-establishing his or her self in the primal field of being.

"The entire body became a single, extremely rapid and intense vibration, but motionless. I don't know how to explain it because it wasn't moving in space, and yet it was a vibration (meaning it wasn't immobile), but it was motionless in space. It was in the body, as if each cell had a vibration and there was but a single block of vibrations."
(The Mother)[7]

The True Environment of Evolution

NOW AT LAST WE CAN TURN to the possible existence of the mysterious evolutionary sleepers with which we opened this investigation.

It has been seen that there are many unknown functions within the central nervous system, the brain and the ductless glands. Any of these could well be the seat of the new seed. However, there are higher processes in the brain which have been clearly marked for thousands of years on the esoteric maps and charts of the sages.

For instance one and a half million years ago *Homo habilis* had, it seems, from all the available evidence, a similar strange set of functions which developed long before he ever managed to use them. These were the speech centers around the so-called "Bulge of Broca." It took, it is believed, almost a million years for this unknown center to be triggered.

Evolution often operates with a mosaic-like pattern, certain developments forging ahead of others.

In this particular case there are two current theories for the otherwise unaccountable delay in realizing the presence of these sleepers.

The first proposes that the brain has to be of sufficient size with a critical mass of cells before it is smart enough to use language or symbols; such a magical mass being somewhere around seven hundred cubic centimeters.

From fossil records it would appear that Homo habilis was the first of our ancestors to cross the seven hundred mark, about the size of a modern baby of one year. But this only occurred when the man had grown into full adolescence. So by the time our early ancestor managed to reach his teens, with a brain at last big enough to use language or symbols in anything more than a rudimentary way, he was often a dead ancestor.

In that tough and probably short life any language tradition must have been passed on a very tenuous thread through the few elders who

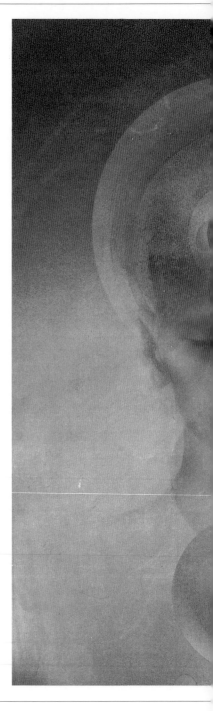

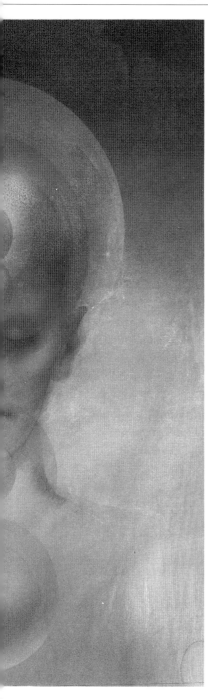

managed to survive. Many times in the last million years or so, language might have flowered only to be lost again as family groups or tribes lost the precious carriers of the sacred spoken word. We shall never know how many Golden Ages and periods of darkness rose and fell during that age — an age one hundred times as long as our recorded history.

The second hypothesis seems a little bizarre at first glance, yet it has a curious ring of truth about it. In this scenario Homo habilis had to wait for a part of his body to catch up with the new speech centers of the brain. He in fact had to wait for the larynx, the speech box, to descend far enough down the throat in order to produce the articulate sounds which are characteristic of human speech.

Immediately these two evolutionary functions worked in consort; the brain size doubled, in evolutionary terms, almost overnight.

It might be argued that we are now at a similar threshold, for what is truly unique about mankind today even now lies unused. What do we know, for instance, of the effect of the new 'languages' of modern technology or that of computers upon these dominant centers?

There are higher functions, new in the scheme of life on Earth, which await our adoption and the subsequent evolutionary jump. So far only a few remarkable individuals seem to have awakened to these higher capacities.

The evolutionary urge is far greater than any individual. It belongs to the species as a whole being far more than is supposed by the scientific dogmas we have been raised on. Beasts, and we are beasts in part, are bounded by the evolutionary urges of the Earth and the environment of the material world. If man's true environment can be seen to be higher consciousness, his place in the evolutionary scheme of things could then surely lie in the exploration of the structures and functions of his own brain, and the self-reflecting consciousness of the whole body-mind. This would then be the realm of true Man.

Flight of the Swan

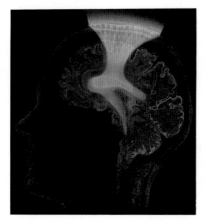

We now embark upon an eso-teric excursion through some of the most clearly documented structures in the brain to discover what higher functions might be there. Here we must depart from the reductionist world of the neu-rologist and use a mystic's map of the inner sanctum as a guide. And in this free interpretation I am indebted to master Free John and Swami Yoganeshwaranand Saras-wati for a modern vision of the traditional view.

"Tell me, Oh Swan, your ancient story,
From which country do you come,
To which coast do you fly?
Where will you rest, Oh Swan
And what are you seeking?

"Wake up Oh Swan, this very morning
Ascend and follow me.
There is a land where doubt and worry
do not reign
Where death is no
There the spring woods are blossoming
And the rich fragrance of "I am He"
Is carried by the wind
There, the Bee of the Heart
has sunk deeply and does not desire
Any other joy."
(Indian mystic, Song of Kabir, 15th Century)

The "caduceus," that ancient heraldic staff of medicine, represents the spinal cord, the brain core and the central nervous system. The single point of the pineal gland stands between the two wings of the lateral ventrices and the corona radiata. below this "swan" the twin coils of the ascending and descending sensory nervous system surround the central core of the body-mind.

We start with the fibrous white conductor material of the braincore which extends like a great fountain into the cerebrum. This material is held to be the mediator of the highest functional aspiration of man, being the primary conductor of the nerve force or bio-energy of the body. The corona of white fibers springs upwards from the corpus callosum, the hard mass of linking fibers which bridges the two hemispheres of the brain, pouring energy into the upper reaches. A whole system of ventricles, or brain cavities, surround the braincore with cerebrospinal fluid which creates a protective watery cushion effectively reducing its weight. That system of interconnected ventri-cles is likened to the shape of a bird with open wings. In the Hindu tradition, a yogi who has managed to stabilize the physical currents in the brain is called "Great Swan" — "Paramahansa." The most famous of the Indian mystics of the earlier part of this century, Ramakrishna, was given this name by his disciples and friends. The wings are thrust out towards the front of the brain while the bird's head extends into the rear part of the head above the cerebellum (small brain). Higher states of the yogi are referred to as the "swan resting on a lake with the bright corona of the sun behind."

As the focus of attention of both hearing and sight withdraw from the outer world they turn inwards along the bio-energy lines into the

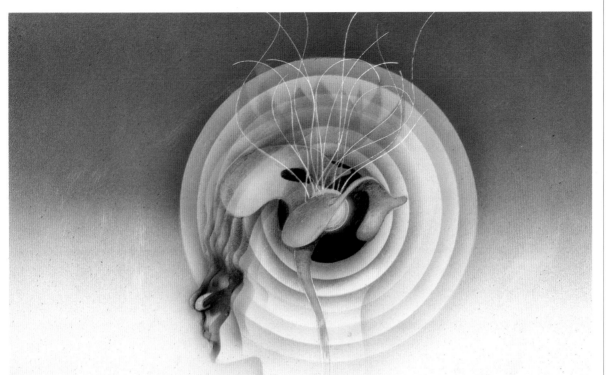

deep interior of the brain core itself. Here the yogi experiences events unique to the core and having no reference to the external world. Here the landscape becomes subtle and, as the whole "swan" is traced, particular visions or sounds appear at each station. Ultimately the psycho-physical currents stabilize in the head of the swan, which is normally associated with the pineal body or the "ajna chakra." This can then be said to be the ultimate center, the final location of the personal self-reflective consciousness.

Still, this is not the final fulfillment. It is beyond this point that an individual really becomes the final flowering of man. We are told that this can only come in the release of consciousness from all links and identification with the psycho-physical mechanism of personal identity. The highest dimension of man which has been awaiting the species is associated with the release of the life current from the brain core, exploding through the white fibrous corona of the total brain. In that penultimate event the life current breaks out of the confines of the body and the psychic structures of the brain and literally "enlightens" the entire body-mind.

Symbiosis

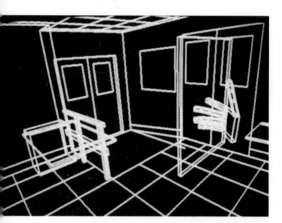

HAVING COMPLETED THIS VERY SHORT inner tour of the species it is necessary to turn our attention to man and his tools. For part of the human mystery lies in the fact that without his tools, his language, his symbols and a collective memory bank which passes from generation to generation, there can be no phenomenon called man.

In the paleolithic Garden of Eden, Adam and Eve tasted the forbidden fruit of language and shared symbols, picked from the Tree of Knowledge. At that moment biological evolution gave way to cultural evolution.

If there is one single medium which might qualify for the real fruit from that Tree of Knowledge it could be the "meme." This term has been recently coined by the neo-darwinist Richard Dawkins and signifies a unit of cultural transmission. It is effectively any idea, word, symbol, sign, theory or code which we use to communicate our thoughts.

Here we must tread carefully. This concept is central to the whole Darwinian scheme while the emphasis within this present text can be seen as its polar opposite. Yet the idea as a provocative metaphor is attractive for just as a "gene" partly determines our biological evolution, so the "meme" in part structures our cultural evolution. An idea like "objective science" could be seen as a meme which caught on three hundred years ago with unprecedented results for the whole species. A meme like "celibacy" could wipe out the entire race if it ever "took." It is proposed that memes jump from mind to mind, just as DNA moves from organism to organism. To some a meme is even considered a living entity, not just metaphorically but in reality. "*When you place a fertile meme in my mind, you literally parasitize my brain, turning it into a vehicle for the memes propagation in the same way a virus may parasitize the genetic mechanism of a host cell. And this is not just a*

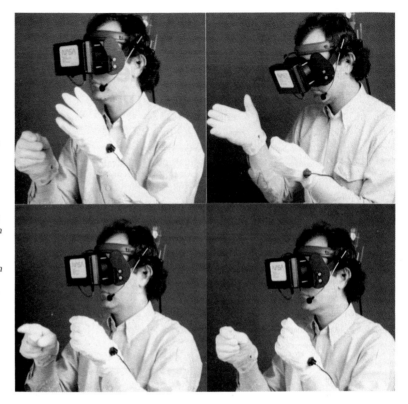

Graphic displays projected inside the helmet provide depth cues by showing each eye slightly different perspectives. The computer generated environment moves as the viewer turns his or her head allowing the user to 'touch' objects within it.

"*Nothing is more striking and more sustained in the whole of human evolution than the two-fold trend towards increase in brain size on the one hand, and, on the other, towards cultural activities, cultural mastery and indeed utter dependence upon culture for survival. These two sets of changes are indissolubly linked. The chain between them may be set forth simply as follows: increase in brain size = gain in intricacy of neuronal organization = rise in complexity of nervous function = ever more diversified and complicated behavior responses = progressively amplified and enhanced cultural manifestations.*"
(P.V. Tobias)[8]

The interacting living organisms which make up the whole colony of life called man contain over 10,000,000,000,000,000,000,000,000 (ten to the power of twenty-five) atoms clustered in 10,000,000,000,000 (ten to the power of twelve) living cells. There seem to be no life forms which have less than one hundred million atoms. Below this threshold life does not seem to occur. It is thought that a "critical numerical mass" of ten to the power of ten nerve cells is necessary to push a brain over the threshold into self-reflective consciousness. The average human brain has ten to the power of eleven nerve cells of which ten to the power of ten are to be found in the cortex.

way of talking. The meme for 'belief in life after death,' for example, is actually realized physically, millions of times over, as a structure in the nervous system of individual men the world over." (Nick Humphrey)

What is remarkable is that one of the first memes to be picked off the tree was time and with the concept of time the idea of death came galloping on its heels. An awareness of death is evidenced even one hundred and fifty thousand years ago by our mysteriously big-brained cousins, the Neanderthals, for they showed careful ceremonial disposal of the dead with flowers, food and the favorite weapons for a supposedly future journey. It remains the major preoccupation of our species and as we have already observed in the original scenario of the seven levels, the fear of death was the prime drive behind the fall and creation itself. With the use of language we come full cycle.

Rainbow on the Seashore of Time

WE HAVE SEEN IN THIS ALL TOO SHORT and limited survey that man possesses a range of talents of which he is only very dimly aware. The list of his talents, however, is almost endless and we have not even touched upon such abilities as psychometry, dowsing, divining, telepathy, telekinesis, precognition, prophecy, intuition, astral travel, out of body experiences, x-ray vision, thought-ography, magnetizing, psychic healing or even the charming of warts.

For man is a rainbow of miraculous para-normal powers and talents, yet an observer must be in the right relative position to be able to see its full spectrum of hues. A rainbow cannot be separated from the environment of the whole; it cannot be isolated from the prismatic water droplets, the clouds, the rain, the ocean and the transforming light of the sun. Consciousness is that rainbow on the seashore of time; it is a potential which is always there, only needing all the elements to come together to reveal itself to the wonder of the onlooker.

Having unraveled some of the mysteries of what makes our species so special, having glimpsed the rainbow over the ocean, we turn to what man has managed to do with this inheritance. So far we have investigated the blueprint of man as if he were in some splendid isolation, set apart from the world in which he finds himself. Now we must investigate what happens to man as a member of a social group, living and creating today's environment.

So many of us are born and die without ever knowing about either ourselves or the earth on which we live. Only very rarely does anyone actually turn their gaze towards themselves or that earth. There are simple objective methods to look inside one's own skull, but who ever finds the time to do so? Everyone has the inbuilt capacity to explore the whole brain core, the great "white swan" of the upper reaches of the brain — or the seven vortices of energy, which govern our psycho-physical selves but who does? Man is a great temple of life, yet we seldom give ourselves anything more than a cursory glance and that only in a mirror to see if it matches the social norm of any peer group. The terrible suffering and sense of separation felt by this first "global" generation, starts with the basic ignorance of who we really are and the universe in which we live.

Mixed Metaphors

IT IS ONE THING TO COIN A WORD LIKE 'SLEEPER' yet quite another to define it in a way which fits either science or mysticism. For a non-scientist it is dangerously easy to fall into the trap of pseudo-science. But we live in an age of mass information and shifting paradigms — a no-man's-land where it is tempting to equate theories and evidence which at first glance appear alike and yet prove on closer inspection to be poles apart. Nowhere is the ground so treacherous as in the field of evolutionary theory.

It was only three decades ago that the world of physics, including Einstein's contribution, underwent a profound reappraisal. We have already spoken of the classical view that the universe was essentially everlasting with unchanging and eternal laws (see page 60.) Until this was challenged in the 1960s, we had two views of the universe, paradoxically living side by side, which were diametrically opposed to one another. There was one conceptual scheme for physics and quite another for the life sciences. Rupert Sheldrake in *The Presence of the Past* succinctly points out, "*In the course of our growing up and education, most of us as modern people have implicitly or explicitly accepted both models of reality: a physical eternity and an evolutionary process. Within the sciences, both models coexisted peacefully until quite recently. They were kept safely apart. Evolution was kept down to earth, whereas the heavens were eternal. Terrestrial evolution is the province of geology, biology, psychology, and the social sciences. The celestial realm is the province of physics, as are energy, fields, and the fundamental particles of matter.*"

Since the 1960s most physicists have accepted that the whole universe is evolving but many anomalies still crop up from the earlier dualistic epoch. Darwin, himself, had to somehow reconcile his evolutionary mode with the dominant classical view and his successors have still not entirely resolved some of the ambiguities of the original theory.

So when we embark on such an ambitious project as a search for the new species, such fundamental concepts as the sleepers or the seven levels, should be rigorously examined.

For, primarily, this is a vision and the author is simply trying to find facts to complement his vision. Its genesis does not depend upon the existing framework of either the traditions of mysticism or science, but upon an all too brief flash of insight. Both the disciplines of science and mysticism seem to be traveling over similar territory so are used as possible explanations for the phenomenon. These will be examined in Part Three. On first acquaintance the whole proposition of seven levels of existence appears to be a perfect candidate for the ambiguity of partly using eternal laws and partly those of evolutionary development. It could be held that if the Prime Consciousness is just playing hide and seek with Itself, then nothing is fundamentally changing. In ascending or descending the levels we use the same ladder and the 'evolutionary' sleepers would be part of the eternal master plan, left like clues in a treasure hunt. There would be no chance for real development for the path is already ordained.

But we are dealing with a metaphor. The essence of the seven levels is an evolving consciousness. Perhaps we might see it as a feedback loop as in the diagram. The descent into the oblivion of matter and the ascent to full cosmic consciousness is the breath in and out of the universe. Each time an individual returns to the Primal State, that Primal Consciousness *changes*. Those changes alter Its next 'descent' in an ever-fluid cycle subtly transforming matter, life, consciousness and the fields which give rise to their varied forms.

Each of us *are* the evolutionary process and every Buddha or Christ or Lao Tzu who struggles up to the Seventh Level adds something to the consciousness of the whole. In this respect the sleepers and the fields which might simultaneously come into being, could be evolving with each new enlightenment.

Here is a model which is firmly rooted in a developing and expanding universe.

CHAPTER TWO   Paradise Lost

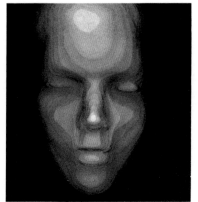

ADAM AND THE PRODIGAL SON are both archetypal figures who appear in cultures throughout the world. There are many stories which intertwine these two figures like the Egyptian Atum, the Mesopotamian Adapa, Tammuz of the Semites, Adonis of the Greeks and Odin of the Norsemen.

The essential story is of a richly endowed hero, like the Syrian prince in the "Hymn of the Soul," who leaves the innocence of his paradise home and enters the world to recover a precious pearl. This pearl (his soul) is guarded by an evil serpent. But in the course of his travels the prince squanders his fortune in debauchery, forgets his family, who he is, and the nature of his quest. It is only when his parents send a letter reminding him of his heritage and his mission that he awakens, recovers the pearl and returns home enriched.

We, the descendants of the hero Adam, have managed to forget our true paradise nature squandering our inheritance like the prodigal son. Yet like so many of the heroes, caught in the grip of a powerful fate, we seem to have had little say in the matter. There always seems to have been some unseen imperative which pushes us ever onwards.

In the Christian myth it was the original disobedience of eating the forbidden fruit that created the irreversible gulf between two animals, otherwise contentedly grazing in the paradise pastures, and a self-conscious man and woman. Up until that moment Adam and Eve had been blindly bound to nature, but once they had tasted the fruit of the Tree of Knowledge their "eyes were opened."

However, this new-found knowledge of separateness irrevocably damaged their link with nature. That noble existential "no" meant there was no going back. Man could only solve the deep unease which such knowledge brought by going forwards through time and evolution until he could find that the Garden of Eden is within himself.

If the prodigal son hadn't gone as far away from his source as possible, he would not have known the benediction of returning totally transformed.

Personally, I see reflected in this parable the whole story of humankind. We have, as species, also traveled far from the original source forgetting our essential nature. But now it looks as if *Homo sapiens* has outdone the Prodigal Son in order to create the greatest possible distance from that true home. Too many of us have effectively become machines, lost automatons. And the danger is that we are programmed from birth to be separate.

The modern hero figure is the "Outsider," the self-divided man whose whole insatiable urge is to become once again unified and whole. He recognizes that somehow he is entangled with the machinery of his own mind and with a loveless type of knowledge but it has all the same become his universal and rigid style of relating to existence. The outsider, like the hero in Hesse's Steppenwolf feels split in two.

Even though the popular image of the two hemispheres of the brain is largely a matter of metaphors rather than scientific facts, it is proposed that the sense of being split in two is intensified if there is an imbalance between the two modes, where one becomes the dormant partner. In our present culture the left-hemisphere, with its linear, reductionist and separatist tendencies, has become master. But in terms of any new development of the species it would seem the wrong half.

We still retain many outdated habits acquired in the earlier scientific age. It was only comparatively recently, in the 1960s, that the mechanistic, scientific view was found to be an inadequate model of the universe. It will take some time before the new ways of viewing the world are adopted and in the meantime the left hemisphere, with its predominantly separatist viewpoint, remains firmly in the director's chair.

However, its function might be seen as a stage of adolescence; full of doubts, fragmented, capable of differentiating the observer from the observed. It is a superb analytic instrument. The right hemisphere, on

Brief Encounter with a Disposable Man

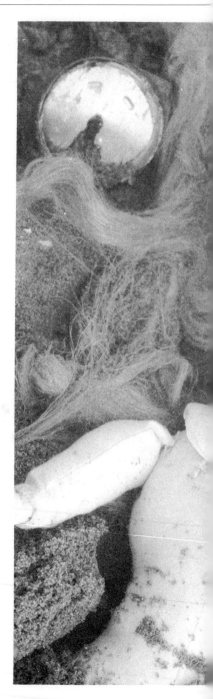

the other hand, while enjoying what seems to be a psychic communion with existence, appears incapable of differentiating itself from its surroundings. It could be said that the left cannot see the wood for the trees, while the right cannot see the trees for the woods.

Complementing one another creates a whole and healthy view of existence, but divided these modes of the hemispheres can point the species to a very dangerous direction. We have seen earlier that humankind is a dialectic and that there are many more examples of dualisms which exist in humankind than just the twin hemispheres. But has some imbalance come about in one of them, thus driving the species down the wrong path?

We now explore some aspects of ourselves which might give an indication of whether this is true or not. It is the dark aspect of the book and can be seen as the journey of the Prodigal Son who lives faraway from his true home and squanders his inheritance.

MAN IS NOW BEING SUBJECTED TO SO MUCH CHANGE, it is almost as though he is in collision with his future. Compared with the solid and stable social norms of only a hundred years ago we have become nomadic strangers in an alien and kaleidoscopic world of instant metamorphosis. In the developed nations of the West the average period of residence in one place has dropped to less than five years. Each year in the United States an equivalent of the entire population of Britain pulls up roots and moves on. Nothing seems to have any permanence in our planned obsolescent and throwaway culture. And the revolutions are speeding up. One hundred and fifty years ago we traveled at a top speed of 20 miles per hour. Astronauts now circle the globe at one thousand times that velocity.

The distances an average inhabitant of the West can now expect to travel in a lifetime has no comparison to a person of a hundred and fifty years ago, who might not even leave the boundaries of his country or shire.

In this fast moving, disposable world, man's ability to form lasting involvements with people, places or things, is greatly curtailed. As the duration of relationships shrinks, so people in effect also become

"There is absolutely no question that one can overshoot the stimulation of the endocrine system and that has psychological consequences that last throughout the whole lifetime of the organs."
(René Dubos)[9]

disposable. Now even the idea of love is packed within a few hours in a brief uninvolved encounter.

By stepping up the whole pace of life, by accelerating the rate of social and technological change, responses are triggered which can threaten the chemical and biological stability of our species. For, biologically speaking, man remains in the late Stone Age. Walking across a road and being narrowly missed by a car sends a surge of adrenalin and nor-adrenalin into our bloodstream, our heart starts pumping furiously and we break out into a sweat just as any of our Cro-Magnon forebears would have experienced when confronted by a charging mammoth.

But we are surrounded by charging mammoths. What happens to an organism when such pressures are maintained? In similar situations of stress and over-stimulation, as in prolonged combat, soldiers at first become angry and irritable with sudden outbursts of uncontrolled violence, confusion and fatigue. If the stress continues for longer periods these symptoms rapidly deteriorate into emotional and in-tellectual withdrawal followed by a retarded, dull state in which they cease to try to defend themselves. Disaster victims have similar experiences. When confronted by the sudden disappearance of everything familiar in their environment, they seem awed and incapa-ble of adaptive decisions.

As we are confronted, daily, by increasingly unfamiliar situations, unpredictable happenings, new environments and cultures, our adap-tive glands and central nervous system often go on overload. At such times we quickly fall into disorientation, fatigue, anxiety, tension and withdrawal. The disturbing increase in crime, violence and insanity, especially in the major cauldrons of change — the cities — can be seen as the symptoms of a soldier constantly under the softening-up barrage of mortars and "whizz-bangs" of the old trench warfare. We are strangers in a fast moving, alien world in which everything is happening too fast. Our position and sense of identity so ceaselessly in flux becomes seriously undermined. Man is the greatest adaptive animal on the planet but we are not infinitely resilient. At some point too many of our thresholds are crossed and we fall apart. And when we fall apart it can be an epidemic.

I Robopath

GEORGE IVANOVITCH GURDJIEFF ONCE OBSERVED that "Man is not Man." He held that we are irresponsible machines, submerged in our own robotic behavior. So long as we remain a machine there can be no psychological study, no portrait, for any such description belongs more properly in a manual of mechanics.

This complication is further compounded by the fact that we are not just one machine but many. Few of us are single, integrated entities with single portraits — we are a crowd. Gurdjieff went on to explain these "many."

"Each of them is a caliph for an hour, does what he likes regardless of everything, and, later on, the others have to pay for it. And there is no order among them whatever. Whoever gets the upper hand is master. He whips everyone on all sides and takes heed of nothing. But the next moment another sees the whip and beats him. Imagine a country where everyone can be king for five minutes and do during these five minutes just what he likes with the whole kingdom. That is our life." [10]

Whilst it is an exaggerated portrait as all caricatures are, the following is a perfect candidate for what Gurdjieff called the "Terror-of-the-Situation." Few of us could deny that many, if not all these signatures, could be our own (or at least our neighbors').

> "For man has closed himself up, 'till he sees all things thro' the chinks of his cavern."
> (William Blake) [11]

"*We are born into a world where alienation awaits us. We are potentially men, but are in an alienated state and this state is not simply a natural system. Alienation as our present destiny is achieved only by outrageous violence perpetrated by human beings on human beings.*"

"*The relevance of Freud to our time is largely his insight and to a very considerable extent his demonstration that the ordinary person is a shriveled, desiccated fragment of what a person can be. As adults, we have forgotten most of our childhood, not only its content, but its flavor. As men of the world, we hardly remember our dreams and make little sense of them when we do. As for our bodies we retain just sufficient proprioceptive sensations to coordinate our movements and to ensure the minimal requirements for bio-social survival — to register fatigue, signals for food, sex, defecation, sleep: beyond that... little or nothing.*

"*Our capacity to think, except in the service of what we are dangerously deluded in supposing is our self interest, and in conformity with common sense, is pitifully limited: our capacity even to see, hear, touch, taste and smell is so shrouded in veils of mystification that an intensive discipline of unlearning is necessary for anyone before one can begin to experience the world afresh, with innocence, truth and love.*"

(Ronald Laing)[12]

Humanoid

THIS MAN-MACHINE LIVES IN PAST PROGRAMS, past events, he is the perfect memory-man. He only feels comfortable in the "non-exist-ential," in memory tapes which are repeatable and not subject to change. Equally this automaton is only happy in that which does not yet exist, in the future.

In the present, in the actual existential moment of *now*, he is very ill-at-ease and feels powerless, for of course anything might happen which is not expected or rehearsed. He fears his programs might not be adequate in dealing with the new situation. He has no ability to adapt. He has lost it.

A Humanoid is a perfectionist, he wants things to conform exactly to his program. The trouble is that he hates to make mistakes and so is forced to live at the minimum. Only in the simplest of routines, rituals and undemanding situations can he remain perfect.

Even so he is in a perpetual state of anxiety. He cannot live totally at the maximum for there are so many dangers in such a state. So he chooses a small impoverished life in order not to make any mistake. Thus he misses any opportunity to live life to the full or allow himself to open to the rich multi-dimensionality of his human potential.

The humanoid hates those who are able to enjoy. Whenever he can, he destroys all possibility of ecstasy. He becomes self-righteous and critical of any form of celebration. Dance, song, laughter, delight and joy all require the whole energy of the being, while the humanoid resides only in his mind. That energy goes sour and becomes, with no other outlet, the disease of *seriousness*. There is an old saying "Beware the man who does not laugh!"

A humanoid sleeps while thinking he is awake. However, he manages to be highly efficient at maintaining his life support system even while being asleep to his true surroundings.

He hates change or any new way of looking at things or doing things, as this is always seen to be a threat to the repetitive pattern of his routine. He dreams twenty-four hours a day regardless of what the real world is relaying to his senses. His thoughts are in perpetual motion but any openness to receive new experiences has been

Gnostic Story of the Birth of Man:
The reflected light of the True World of eternity shone down into the darkness of the Abyss. It cast a pale and distorted shadow of the archetypes above upon the darkness of the waters and the Demiurge, God of the Blind, engulfed the light and called it his own. He was enamored of the primal source and endeavored to create a replica of his own. He created time as a moving image of eternity under the illusion that sheer numbers of temporal units would create the same effect. The objects and creations of his sphere were caricatures of the real archetypes of the realm of light, beginning part of a counterfeit world of the Ape of God. One of those archetypal patterns he tried to copy was of *Anthropos*, the androgynous *Adamel*, who was beloved by God the Father and who was given dominion over heaven, earning Satanel's everlasting enmity by doing so. The Demiurge fashioned a physical image, a replica from clay but this primitive android, or shapeless clod (Hebrew Golem) was unable to stand. The Prince of Light, seeing this misshapen horror, sent forth a spark of energy so that the man-plasma could stand upright. Jehovah-Satanel had seemed content with each of his creations having looked and seen it was good. But in the case of man he said nothing. For man was unfinished.

replaced by the closed mechanism of the mind which edits and re-edits the same past programs.

The humanoid's activities are pre-programmed by society, the nation, the parent and the priest. Rituals of politeness mask whoever might have once been inside. Spontaneity is lost. There is constant rehearsal in a mind which is perpetually in a state of *preparation* of what to do, of what to say and to whom it is to be said. He can never be in the present because his thoughts have rushed on to the next place and the next time. His attempt to be like the rest of the crowd, always trying to gain the approval of others, re-inforces the need for ritual conduct. He lives for others' opinions, acting out his assigned roles efficiently and properly.

A humanoid is dogmatic and a believer. Once an idea is accepted, once a belief, a faith, or any other piece of borrowed knowledge is taken in as a truth, then there will be no further change or any desire to explore the subject for himself. (This is of course as true for writing this book as for reading it.)

And so a humanoid loves experts to whom he can delegate the responsibility of discovering truths which he can then claim as his own, thus relieving him of the burden of having to find anything out for himself. To such a robopath, "once a truth always a truth."

A humanoid, once he has been programmed in even the most absurd belief, will be prepared to go through the most terrible privations and even death, rather than doubt or re-assess that faith.

The most tragic characteristic of the humanoid is that he is alienated, both from himself and from others. The hell of this half-man is that he has become a shadow, a mere functionary of ritual and has lost his intrinsic self-definition. He simply has no idea of who he is and only knows that he exists by what others say about him. He needs the constant mirrors of others' opinions to know who he is. He has lost all sight of himself. He has lost contact with his own resources.

"Man as he now is has ceased to be the All. When he ceases to be a separate individual, he raises himself again and penetrates the whole world."
(Plotinus)[13]

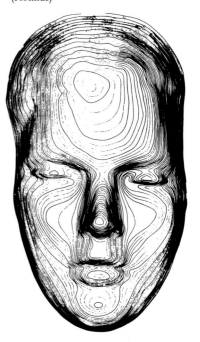

Divided Within

EARLIER IN THIS CENTURY MANY PSYCHIATRISTS lumped a number of severe mental disorders under the general heading of schizophrenia. The popular idea of a split personality derives from the Greek words "skhizoin" (to split) and "phren" (mind). A more poignant and compassionate translation might be "schiz" (broken) and "phrenos" (soul or heart). A schizophrenic can then be seen simply as one who is broken hearted.

When we speak of insanity or use a term like schizophrenia, the very first question which arises is just *who* determines *who* is mad. Almost a quarter of the patients in mental hospitals are diagnosed as schizophrenic. But increasingly psychiatrists such as Ronald Laing are recognizing that the classic behavioral pattern associated with this form of mental disorder is what has been described as "a special strategy that a person invents in order to live in an unlivable situation."

In his or her attempt to deal with the contradictions of what seems to be a mad world, the patient's internal world is projected on the external and the external projected upon the internal. Many schizophrenics would be worshipped as saints and visionaries in more sympathetic cultures. Many of their so-called hallucinations and insights match, by many mystic accounts, the difficult esoteric terrain of the spiritual seeker. The great Eastern mystic Meher Baba visited many asylums throughout India, searching for the so-called insane visionaries, whom he called "Masts," who were found to be very near the mystic state of self-realization.

Gregory Bateson comments in the introduction to an autobiographical account of a patient: "*It would appear that once precipitated into psychosis, the patient has a course to run. He is, as it were, embarked upon a voyage of discovery which is only completed by his return to the normal world, to which he comes back with insights different from those of the inhabitants who never embarked on such a voyage. Once begun, a schizophrenic episode would appear to have as definite a course as an initiation ceremony — a death and rebirth... What needs to be explained is the failure of many who embark upon this voyage to return from it.*"[15]

"Mystics and schizophrenics find themselves in the same ocean, but the mystics swim whereas the schizophrenics drown."
(R.D. Laing)[20]

An American attempts to commit suicide once every minute of each twenty-four hour day; thirty thousand actually die each year. This truly is the Age of Anxiety. It is hardly comforting to know that an American is more likely, by three to two, to die at his own hand than from that of someone else. The incidence of suicide amongst the young has tripled over the last thirty years until it is now the third leading cause of death in the U.S.A.

Here, surely, is the Prodigal Son, the hero who travels far from his familiar shoreline, losing himself only to return transformed. In our strange world it is often the elder brother who "treats" him, the one who has never left the father's house and has no idea of the world outside those tight confines. How could such a man be able to help when he himself has never experienced the terrors and the ecstasy of the road?

Can this scenario indicate something of our collective condition? Are the schizophrenics merely the vanguard of travelers attempting to solve the contradictions of a seemingly crazy society?

The Other Half

ONE EVOLUTIONARY MYSTERY which has been largely ignored until quite recently is the unique role of sex in the higher primates. Virtually all mammals have an oestrus cycle, which is the specific period in which the female is receptive and both she and the male become sexually aroused prior to breeding.

However, with old-world monkeys, apes and human beings an extraordinary evolutionary jump occurred. This was the development of a menstrual cycle. In oestrus the female comes "on heat," giving powerful mating signals as the ovaries ready themselves for impregnation.

But in the human menstrual cycle this period becomes the monthly shedding of the wall of the womb and it is the one time in which fertilization will not happen. Now, we might ask, what possible evolutionary advantage can this state of affairs give to the species? What benefit to survival? We may even conclude that it is there just for fun!

One explanation could be that it is evolution's way of creating a shared experience of unusual intimacy and intensity for any pair of individual animals. Whatever the reason, *Homo sapiens*, as a species, is fascinated by sex on a twenty-four hour basis. What is a single, shared function in most of the animal kingdom splits in two: ovulation and reproduction on the one side and menstruation and sexual drive on the other.

Strangely we find these two principles clearly differentiated in the Old Testament of the Christian Bible. One half as Lilith, the lusty and wild first companion of Adam, and the other as Eve, the mother of his children. In the New Testament the distinction is even more pronounced. As Penelope Shuttle points out in "The Wise Wound," "*Mary Magdalene is the prostitute who had sex but no children and Mary, who, as the Virgin, has a child but no sex.*"[16]

What this unique function of sex without reproduction actually does is to create a dominant factor in the forming of societies. The powerful, non-stop sexual urge stimulates a constant flow of hormones to and from the brain, accompanied by a greatly enhanced electrical activity. This in turn stimulates a whole sense of inquiry, curiosity and

alertness. Pair formations which lead to lasting relationships, groups and social structures, are also more likely to occur.

The non-stop erotic behavior is evolution's stroke of genius to create conditions for curiosity, excitation, stable groups and co-operation. What evolution perhaps did not foresee, however, was Homo sapiens' unique logical behavior which manages to distort many a good thing into many a "worse" thing. It could not have predicted that the female initiator of the sexual revolution should suddenly find herself an inferior species and that the ingathering of energy of the monthly cycle would become a "curse." This was another of evolution's gifts which confers upon the woman a natural entry into a receptive and insightful space. She actually has no choice as Nature renews her connections with the creative rhythms of birth and death. Yet we find that over 30 million prescriptions are issued in the United Kingdom each year for tranquilizers and anti-depressants of which more than half are to relieve premenstrual tension and distress. Even the hormonal activity which is responsible for the real physical distress can be laid on the doorstep of psychological stress.

How is it possible for women to have become so estranged from themselves as to feel so much pain and anguish and in many cases a sense of inferiority?

It is easy to forget that it is only in the last two decades that the revolution of the "Pill" and other birth control devices have at last freed the woman from her historic role in the family.

Overnight there has been an avalanche of re-appraisals of natural female processes. The social acceptance of breast feeding, sexual freedom, the understanding that women can and do have multiple orgasms, childbirth without pain and a menstrual cycle without any distress, have created a revolution which only now is being felt by men and society as a whole. Women may always have known this secretly, but now men have been made aware of just what a rich and fertile sexual landscape a woman lives in. She is capable of an abundance of powerful insights into the lunar and Earth cycles, organic creativity and feelings of motherhood which have no comparable experience in man. It is small wonder that man has both worshipped the Mother

Goddess and at the same time has feared, and been profoundly jealous of, those potent female powers.

What else could prompt Tertullian to describe the mouth of the womb as "the Gate of the Devil" or Sigmund Freud to insist that in menstruation a woman obviously felt the castration of the highly prized male genitals? Freud's attempt to relegate the mystic power of the vagina to the second class status of an inferior organ tells us far more about Freud and the male attitude than about the female experience.

FIVE HUNDRED YEARS AGO the Christian Church published "The Hammer of Witches," *Malleus Maleficatorum*, an infamous manual of an inquisition which was responsible for the systematic slaughter of hundreds of thousands of women and girls in a dark and gruesome Europe. This most terrible of documents, written in 1484 by two Dominicans, singled out women, as a category of evil to be persecuted. It defined what witches were, what they were supposed to do, how to try and how to execute them.

And what was the reason behind burning? The church of the time needed a scapegoat to divert attention from the scourges of famine and plague which the priests were seemingly powerless to prevent or control. Who better fitted than women to be the cause of the sin which warranted such wrath from the Almighty?

The church had long identified women with sin, "the terrible worm in the heart of men." Sin was often equated with sexuality and Eve was its originator in offering the apple to innocent Adam.

The Devil's Gate

It is revealing to compare such a male dominated view of the world with that of the supposedly uncivilized aboriginals of Arnhem Land in Australia. *"We have been stealing what belongs to the woman. Men have nothing to do but copulate."* **In their creation myth two Wawilak sisters initiate the whole cycle. One gives birth while the other menstruates.** *"All that belongs to the Wawilak, the baby, the blood* **(which falls in a pool and gives rise to a serpent),** *the yelling, the dancing, all that concerns the women — we have to trick them...In the beginning we had nothing."*

The Malleus supposed that women were more "credulous and susceptible to witchcraft," "impressionable," had "slippery tongues" and "were of feebler mind and body," which allowed the devil to make them the "advance guard of hell." But above all, witchcraft came "from carnal lust, which is in women insatiable!" Any woman with a natural sexual potency could immediately be suspect of witchcraft. It is quite possible that many of the so-called "witches" in the past were not witches at all but confused and terrified women.

The female style of consciousness seems profoundly attuned to the subtle movements of the Earth and her lifetides. Her sense of time is periodic, waxing and waning in a mysterious tidal communion with the moon. Events flow within the female awareness like birth and death and rebirth. Male time can be seen more like a series of sequential, uniform and equally divided moments.

Such natural differences in these modes of experience have, so far, been unbalanced and when we speak of humankind it must be remembered that in many parts of the world it almost means the division of two species — man and woman.

Divided Without

Above: **Incident at the Berlin Wall in 1971. An example of how human feelings give way to rigid and divisive belief systems. A young East German was shot while attempting to cross the no man's land between the two countries. Despite his dying screams which continued for almost an hour no one from either side dared to approach him. Only when he died did the East German border guard collect the body.**

Opposite page: **Berlin, 1974. If there is one material proof which confirms the divisive strategies of our mind it would surely be the invention of barbed wire**

DIVISION AND SEPARATION must surely be the major disease of *Homo sapiens*. There are over three hundred religions, cults, subcults and sects throughout the world. There are over three hundred Gods of all different colors who range from the jealous and vengeful to the Lover or the Indifferent. The priests of these various Endlessnesses have exacted a terrible toll in human suffering and life. Hundreds of thousands of Buddhists were killed by Hindus in India, who were, in turn, slaughtered by Muslims, who were then decimated by Christians.

The world is divided by over two hundred borders and languages. It masses lethal troops and weapons of destruction in support of abstract ideas such as Capitalism, Socialism, Fascism, Communism, Democracy or Totalitarianism. We fight for someone else's ideas and belief systems and watch crimes of genocide under the various divided flags. We watch as whole populations, or whole peoples die of neglect or systematic starvation as if these were human norms of behavior. We are able to treat other "teams," nations, races or groups as inhuman objects or as a collection of numbers. We can so easily be over-whelmed by horrendous crimes which transcend all our known human values.

Heinrich Himmler proudly told his SS commanders in 1940 of their noble sacrifice by "assuming the painful burden of making Europe 'Jew-free' and fighting battles which future generations will not have to fight again...." In order to carry out the genocide of the Jewish race his troops had to be "superhumanly *inhuman*." And tragically, in our sleep, we almost let them.

"There is infinite hope, but not for us."
(Franz Kafka)[17]

Contemplating Earth from a hundred thousand miles away comes this new consciousness.
"You become startlingly aware how artificial are the thousands of boundaries we've created to separate and define. And for the first time in your life you feel in your gut the precious unity of the earth and of all living things it supports. The dissonance between this unity you see and the separateness of human groupings that you know exist is starkly apparent."
(Russell Schweichart)[18]

Slaughterhouse Planet

A MASS MADNESS RAGES across what Georges Gurdjieff called our Slaughterhouse Planet. In the last eighty years alone the inhabitants of this planet have enthusiastically exterminated over one hundred and twenty million of their fellow men. This is the equivalent of killing the present combined populations of England, Wales, Scotland, Ireland, Belgium, The Netherlands, Norway, Sweden, Denmark, Finland and East Germany.

If this fails to strike a responsive note it could be otherwise said that this number is the same as the entire population of the United States in the 1930s, just before World War Two. Can this be considered as sufficient evidence that our species have taken a wrong turn? One hundred million dollars are being spent each hour over the whole world on death machines for a military which only exists to maintain a divided world. The world is spending almost two million dollars a minute to keep the people of our planet apart. Astronauts return from space with a message that the Earth is a whole undivided organism. Divisions only exist in the minds of men and on pieces of paper.

Conflicts
Major Conflicts in the Twentieth Century

1904	Russo — Japanese War
1904	Chinese Civil War
1911	Turkish — Italian War
1912-13	Balkan War
1912	Mexican Civil War
1014-18	World War I
1915	Irish War
1917-20	Russian Revolution
1926	USA in Nicaragua
1931	Japanese — Manchurian War

1932-35 Bolivian — Paraguayan War
1936-39 Spanish Civil War
1939-45 World War II
1948-49 Palestine War
1947 Chinese Revolution
1950-53 Korean War
1950-75 Vietnam War
1954-62 French Algerian War
1956 Suez War
1956 Polish and Hungarian Revolutions
1959 Cuban Civil War
1959 Chinese Tibetan War

1967 Israeli 6-day War
1967 Russian Invasion of Czechoslovakia
1968 Biafran — Nigerian War
1970 Cambodian War
1971 Ugandan genocide
1973 Yom Kippur War
1979 Nicaraguan Civil War
1979 Iranian Civil War
1982 British — Argentinian War
Since this, terrorist activities from 1970 to 1987 have claimed 60,000 lives with

35,000 seriously wounded. The divided city of Beirut has already claimed 30,000 victims.
Genocide, (the attempted extermination of an entire people, tribe or ethnic group):
1915 Armenia 600,000
1939-1945 Jews 6,000,000
1939-1945 Others (gypsies, Slavs etc.) estimated 10,000,000
1923-1953 Russia (Stalinist regime) estimated 11,000,000
1971 Uganda 700,000 estimated

Flanders 1914-18 War: Repeated shelling and vicious trench warfare reduced a once beautiful landscape to this desolate state. Over 8 million men died with 20 million wounded during the four years of that "War to end all wars."

Misanthropy

"The number of suggestions one could call 'defeatist' within the earth's atmosphere is simply overwhelming! It's so surprising that everything isn't crushed to death, it's so... so... Everyone is constantly creating disasters: expecting the worst, seeing the worst, observing only the worst....And it's down to the smallest things, you know (the body observes everything.) When people react harmoniously, everything goes well; when there is the reaction which I now call defeatist: if the person picks up an object, he drops it. It happens all the time, without any reason whatsoever; it's the presence of that defeatist consciousness. And I've seen this: all the wills or vibrations (for in the end, it all boils down to qualities of vibration) that bring about everything, from little nuisances to the greatest disasters, all have that same quality!"
(The Mother)[19]

In the last two decades there has been a dramatic change in awareness of how we mistreat the globe and ourselves. Increasingly, there are well-organized protests, as in this example in the Netherlands, against how others — the State, industry and the huge multinational corporations — determine and manipulate the way we are to live.

THE SPECIES SEEMS TO BE EATING ITS WAY across the planet, gobbling up in a few short decades resources which took millions of years to accumulate. We have introduced entirely alien ecosystems into the organic totality of the planetary system and are threatening to destroy the whole biological framework by doing so. Rivers and lakes are stagnant or sterile, even the once alive and nourishing mineral waters in Europe are dead and flat, soured by continual acid rains and chemical soups seeping deep into the soils. Forests are vanishing as the surface of the Earth is stripped bare. Concrete continues to spread out over the Earth's surface like an alien and malignant cancer. New macadam highways continue to cover the meadows and grasses at an appalling rate. We eliminate wild life that competes with us for this space. In the United States alone two hundred miles of road are added each day to the network. Urban areas are listed as deserts in world maps and are accounting for huge tracts of once fertile and arable land. Already almost one third of the Netherlands is designated desert and the urban sprawls of every European town and city threaten to engulf the land in a concrete spider's web of developments, which sour the earth beneath them.

We kill billions upon billions of creatures every day. We treat them as disposable, throwaway animals, which come from unknown sources anyway. We have ceased to know what we eat, or what has been injected into the factory-bred animals, or what toxins are released by those terrified animals as they die in a mechanical steel box. All we know of the dead flesh is that it comes in clean plastic packs, nicely, and for us, *emotionally* sterilized with a guarantee that we have no responsibility whatsoever for taking that animal's life. We have lost touch with our reality. This is the world in which we live and our style of life.

Economics of Starvation

"Work that produces unnecessary consumer junk or weapons of war is wrong and wasteful. Work that is built upon false needs of unbecoming appetites is wrong and wasteful. Work that deceives or manipulates, that exploits or degrades is wrong and wasteful. Work that wounds the environment or makes the world ugly is wrong and wasteful. There is no way to redeem such work by enriching it or restructuring it, by specializing it or nationalizing it, by making it 'small' or decentralized or democratic."
(Theodore Roszak) [20]

FEW MODERN INDUSTRIAL WORKERS HAVE MUCH SENSE OF PRIDE and achievement in what they do. The article he or she produces, or helps to produce, is of little consequence in their lives. The purpose of such work in the first place is to earn a living so that another part of life can be spent in leisure. The main purpose of the work for the employer is to increase profit. In such a situation both work and worker become depersonalized as the job becomes an activity without love.

Any technology which achieves such production is likely to be fragmented, hard and manipulative, as opposed to being co-operative. It tends, like nuclear power generators, to be centralized and in the hands of a small élite power block. Invariably such an enterprise finds itself connected to the military or to the national security with all the political super-structures. Almost by definition a centralized hi-technology activity is secretive, anti-ecological, anti-social, anti-human and anti-health.

Five percent of the world's population consumes over thirty-five percent of the planet's resources. Most of these resources are handled by a few huge multi-national organizations. Many of these corporations are economically obsolete and block the flow of currency. Their very rigidity determines an over development of hard and centralized technologies like the major power agencies or the huge chemical and pharmaceutical industries. In the United States and increasingly in Europe, excessive consumption and waste have become a way of life, relentlessly altering our attitudes towards nature and the delicate ecosystems of the planet. Our glossy magazines and newspapers give madly conflicting views of life. On the one hand they report the horrors of war, of murder, of violence, greed, corruption and starvation, while on their advertising pages we see an Arcadian world where everyone is well fed and totally happy. Cigarette advertisements paint nostalgic cowboy scenes in the idyllic West while the page opposite reveals that half a million Americans die each year from tobacco poisoning.

In such an environment it is small wonder that twenty-five percent of the population needs psychiatric treatment at some time during their lives.

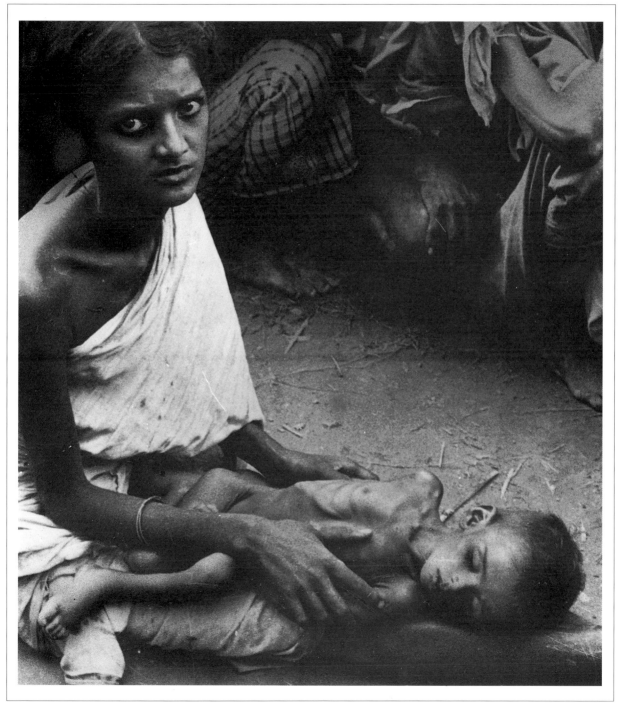

Immune to Life

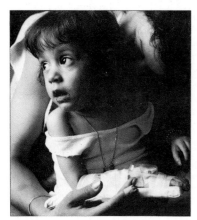

AFRICA IS THE MOST LIKELY CANDIDATE AS THE WOMB OF HUMANKIND. Now by a tragic quirk of fate it is this continent that has again become an incubator, but this time of the greatest pandemic of this century. We are witnessing the first plague which could well overtake, in terms of a death toll and of human suffering, the bubonic plague of five hundred years ago which claimed the lives of over thirty million people in Europe, over one-third of the total population of Europe of that time.

Acquired Immune Deficiency Syndrome began during those fateful "turning point" years of the 1950s. There are many scenarios as to how it started, but at some time a virus mutated, turning into the vicious pathology of HTLV III, the third human retrovirus. As far as is known, the virus continued to spread throughout Africa unchecked during the 1970s, crossing the Atlantic to spread through the Caribbean and then pass on to the United States and Europe. By the end of 1987 the worst estimates revealed that five million were infected in Africa, three million in the Caribbean, two million in the United States, while in Western Europe, which caught the plague later, this figure is just over one million. While estimates are difficult to assess, it is possible that ten million people were infected, worldwide, by the end of 1987. This includes AIDS, ARC (Aids Related Complex which is deadly in its own right and, a frequent precursor of AIDS proper) and Sero-positives, those who have come into contact with the virus but have not actually contracted the disease. Sero-positives can, however, pass the virus on to others.

There has never been anything like AIDS before. It attacks the whole ability of the immune system to respond to infections. This apocalyptic scourge touches the whole species at its very soul, for the virus is transmitted sexually. The whole will to live is rooted in the sexual drive. As we have just seen (page 100) one of the unique bonding mechanisms of human society could be the evolutionary initiative of giving mankind sex just for fun, unconnected with the survival factors of reproduction.

If that will to live disappears, due to prolonged stress, then sex will be the most vulnerable area of life to invite death. It has been

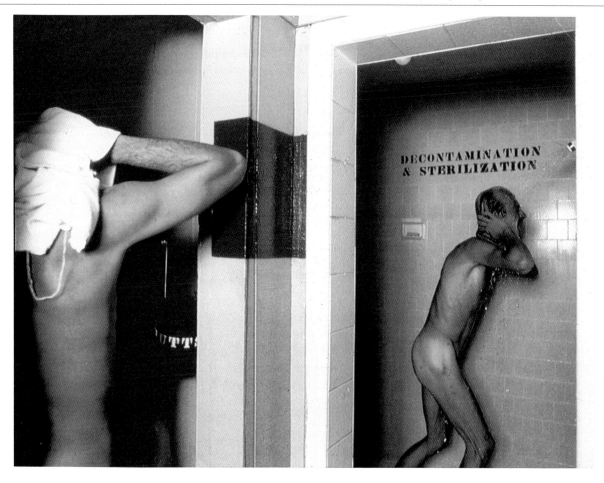

conclusively demonstrated that repeated and unremitting stress lowers the resistance of the immune system. Bio-feedback experiments also show that the action of the immune system can be altered by conscious effort. An AIDS victim who is told of his condition frequently slides into a helpless despair. The very knowledge of impending death accelerates the death process.

Does the species as a whole unconsciously feel a kind of existential despair? Are we caught in the momentum of a collective suicide, or have many of us just lost the deep lust for life?

An Insane Species

I ONCE VISITED THE "DANGEROUS" REFRACTORY WARD of a mental hospital in Southern England. The very first things to be noticed in the bleak and barred institutionalized rooms were huge bunches of hideous artificial flowers in cheap plastic vases. On suggesting to the Chief Psychiatrist that perhaps this might tend to give the patients an even greater sense of alienation and lack of reality, he replied rather reprovingly: "You don't understand: the patients don't really notice, they are for the staff."

Now full-scale artificial reality is becoming a reality with present day electronic simulators. Artificial flight simulators have been around for decades but the new generation of simulators have helmets which fit completely over the head, covering both eyes with 3-D television screens and stereo speakers for both ears. Sensors in the helmet detect whenever the head is inclined or turned and the corresponding image matches the new position. In one demonstration the helmet wearer experienced a computer "space walk." As he looked over his shoulder the picture followed his full 180 degree turn to reveal a huge spinning space station behind him. These simulators are so real that even hardened city cops feel their pulse quicken and their hands sweat over an artificial encounter with a "villain" in a simulated robbery sequence. Packaged artificial reality is as an inevitable future product as our present tape recorders, computers or home TV.

It is the logical outcome of steel and glass environments, air conditioning, concrete paths and plastic grass. Soon we need not even venture outside our high tech apartments to stand under a starry night sky, lit by a full moon and with the sound of a nightingale close by. It will all be taped. A child might even go for years before experiencing a "real" night sky and this is the plight of many urban children now. But this image of the near future is with us now, and the state of many city dwellers today, bombarded as they are with the artificial realities of radio, advertisements, TV and films.

We have now touched upon just a few of the symptoms of an increasingly robotic existence, in which alienation seems to beckon around each and every corner. It is time to move on to some of the underlying causes of our collective distress.

It was a slow day
And the sun was beating
On the soldiers by the side of the road
There was a bright light
A shattering of shop windows
The bomb in the baby carriage
Was wired to the radio

These are the days of miracles and wonder
This is the long distance call
The way the camera follows us in slo-mo
The way we look to us all
The way we look to a distant constellation
That's dying in a corner of the sky
These are the days of miracle and wonder
Don't cry baby don't cry
Don't cry
(Paul Simon, *Boy in the Bubble*)

"The ordinary consciousness lives in constant state of fidgeting, it's frightening when you realize it! As long as you are not aware of it, it's perfectly natural, but when you become aware of it, you wonder how people don't go crazy, it's a grace! It is a kind of tiny microscopic trepidation. Oh, how horrible!"[21]

"...And it's the same for everything: for world events and natural cataclysms and mankind, for earthquakes and tidal waves, for volcanic eruptions, floods and wars, for revolutions and people who take their own lives without even knowing why — everywhere, they are all impelled by something; behind that 'fidgeting,' there's a will for disorder seeking to prevent the establishment of harmony. It's in each individual, in each group and in Nature."[22]

CHAPTER THREE

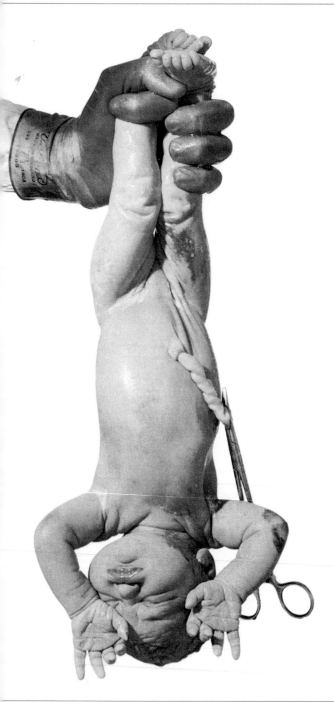

"It is like an image reflected in a mirror, it is seen but it is not real; the one Mind is seen as a duality by the ignorant when it is reflected in the mirror constructed by our memory... the existence of the entire universe is due to memory that has been accumulated since the beginningless past but wrongly interpreted."
(Lankavatara Sutra)[23]

The typical entry into the world for many of us. To the hospital staff it is another birth. To the child it is a death. One moment there is the paradise womb, a soft floating security, and the next moment there is an heroic struggle to move through a tiny constricting birth canal. Suddenly there are blinding lights, the pungent smell of antiseptic, a frightful noise, cold and an alien rubber hand holding him upside down in the new and dreadful gravity so that the blood rushes to his head flooding the delicate brain. To complete the trauma he receives a sudden painful smack on his buttocks to help take that first panic gulp of oxygen. Then comes the severance of all ties with the old life as the umbilical cord is cut.

And this is only the first step in a long line of programs which are thought to be good for him.

We are like the little Chinese girls who had their feet bound at birth. The fact that the poor children couldn't walk was hardly compensated by their feet being highly prized as status symbols.

Stranger in a Stranger Land

OF THE LITTLE WE KNOW OF THE EVOLUTION OF OUR SPECIES it seems that as intelligence increased in our distant ancestors, nature found herself with a design problem. In order to walk vertically the wide ape-like pelvis of the earlier Australopithecines gave way to smaller, more graceful hips. However, the brain was becoming far bigger which could have made childbirth painful and a hazard to both child and mother alike. Nature came up with a compromise juggling the losses and gains. Her highly novel solution changed the whole direction of our species. The gestation period in the womb was drastically shortened which allowed a less developed brain of bearable size.

This ingenious evolutionary device had the unavoidable side-effect of a prolonged period of infant dependence which was unparalleled in the animal kingdom. It is almost as if nature washed her hands of the genetic evolution of the species and from the very moment of birth abandoned the responsibility for the programming of the half-made-up "embryos" straight into the human lap.

We arrive at birth in a way incomplete and the group into which we are born has the freedom to complete the job. The rate of growth of the brain is kept to a minimum in the last months of pregnancy. However, once the organism leaves the confines of the womb the brain enlarges to three times its birth size within the first year of life. This is unique also within the animal kingdom even including our nearest relatives, the great apes.

However, the rest of the body remains infantile by comparison and often stays that way into adolescence. It may be seen then, that perhaps we are born too young and too soon. From the moment of birth a cultural programming begins its relentless re-designing of the vulnerable little animal, over-riding nature's original program. We are all so open at that age that anything can be put into the soft computers in our heads — any program or any imprint. To many it would seem that our brains and minds have been tampered with. The disquieting part of this is that we are not aware of the corruption.

We are fish in the ocean who don't notice the water. We are unconscious of the continual linguistic ocean which shapes our perceptions, our experience and our actions within the phenomenal

Let There Be Two

world. We remain unaware of the role of language in molding our experience and giving that experience significance and meaning. The child is not protected in any way against the ideas which man passes down as normal behavior from generation to generation.

And the most inhibiting idea of all is that of the *ego*. Almost every historic culture, in its own way, has managed to give birth to that monster. Most social groups on the planet encourage the fabrication of a false identity — an ego, a persona, and a separate sense of an "I."

We now therefore set out to explore why this is so and who the principal programmers are.

THERE HAVE BEEN RARE VOYAGERS THROUGHOUT HISTORY who have returned from the frontiers of their consciousness with the message that the reality which we take for granted, the one we think we know, is not the real world at all.

These adventurers in consciousness tell us that we are all fast asleep in a shadow world projected on a twilight screen which is not there. There have been enough of these disquieting individuals to make us suspect that perhaps they may at least have a point worth listening to.

The message they bring is that the real is ONE. It is a unity, non-dual and whole. Many of these visionaries ominously add that we have been duped. For as a result of our various programming we have divided life into subject and object, observer and observed. We no longer say to ourselves "Am bodying" but "I *have* a body" and it is this sense of separation which is giving the species most of its headaches.

This "I" is the elusive and imaginary entity called *ego*. And here we stumble across the central issue of our dilemma. The moment a line is drawn on a piece of paper a world comes into existence.

Universes come into being the moment there is any act of division or separation. The very moment past is separated from future we enter a new world called "time." The moment our one undivided consciousness is reflected upon by our identification with the memory, then two worlds appear where once there was only one.

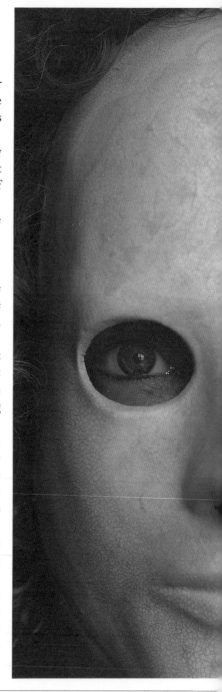

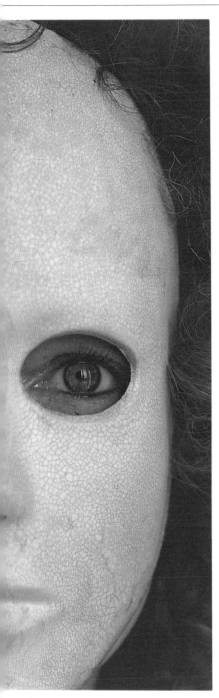

Memory is that mirror which creates two worlds from one. Memory has an intimate relationship with language and the whole socio-system from which it arose. Yet any of those who have entered higher states of 'Oneness' or the scientist who sees the universe as a holo-movement are right, nature is not separate or segmented in any way: it is a seamless and continuous totality. But language, and the whole collective socio-agreement based on language, divides and slices it up, creating such dualisms as hard and soft, hills and valleys, good and evil which we fondly imagine must always have been there.

Nouns and verbs which are useful tools of survival when it is necessary to distinguish between "big fish eat me" and "me eat big fish," are inappropriate instruments with which to explore the rest of the universe. If the only tool you have is a screwdriver, then everything becomes a screw. A word which designates any phenomenon freezes that event into separate objects and actions, each having a status, a quantity and a quality quite independent of the whole reality. It happens that virtually all the languages of the West are noun oriented, which means that we have effectively fixed the experiential world into static solid boxes.

A noun is a fixed box, static, consistent and someone else's. It is by its very nature second-hand but once such words and ideas have entered into the soft memory machine, our derived ego-selves identify with these as if they are real.

As we have already learned (see page 88), Richard Dawkins coined a word for such an idea. He called it a "meme." These are supposedly just like their biological counterparts the "genes." They are codes with which we build up our view of the phenomenal universe but they only *apparently* exist. The memes which make up this book are non-existential. They are illusions of the real.

The great leap forward, when our ancestors became self-aware, happened about five hundred thousand years ago. It appears that it was simultaneous with the rise and growth of language and the use of shared symbols. In that garden of Eden, man and woman tasted the forbidden fruit of "good and evil," of borrowed knowledge and started using it *as if* it was their own direct experience. Collective social

False Identity

language made it possible for them to be both the subject, the center of activity, and the objects of their own thought. The premature birth of the huge-headed-child meant that the "meme" took over from the "gene" as an evolutionary building block.

Ask yourself: "Who Am I?"

Invariably the internal answer will be autobiographical — an identity based on the past. It will be a description of a continuity from childhood through adolescence to adulthood which is all past memories and no longer exists. Memory is the mirror and we live on the wrong side. Seldom will anyone answer the question of "Who am I?" with: "I appear to be the process of reading this page."

How did the sense of a continuing "I," the *ego*, arise?

Consider the brain as a memory machine, either storing the memories physically within itself or acting as apparatus which tunes into a memory field.

The very first moment consciousness identifies with even one memory in the brain machine the floodgates swing open and the entire contents of memories pour through. This is the moment when there is a sudden awareness of "past." A moment before there was an absolute *Here* and *Now*, a "birth with no past" and a "death with no future," then suddenly those twin aspects of one unity divided. On one side was a memory of a "being" in the past and on the other was a future with the possibility of that continuity of being "ceasing to be."

When past is separated from future we enter a new world of time. We have sprung the trap upon ourselves. It is the panic recoil from the terrifying possibility of a "death without future" which splits the here/now, severs man from the unity of the whole and sends him hurtling into a false mirrored world of illusions.

Man becomes a *historical animal* preoccupied with the past and the future, and here we encounter the strangest of paradoxes. From what we hear from the sages we exist out of time. When asked what heaven would be like Christ replied, "There shall be time no longer." We exist in eternity, but our new false identity can only exist in time. The historical idea of self, the ego, requires a constant re-living of

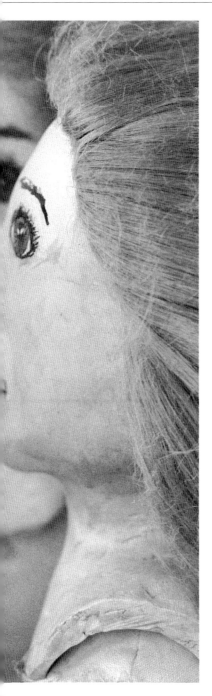

memories in order to sustain a continuity of its own. It is only aware of itself as a repeatedly up-dated autobiography. The ego does not actually exist — it is an illusion of continuity.

You cannot smell, see, taste, hear or touch either the past or the future. In order to create a sense that it does exist, however, it is first necessary to forget the here and now. We all do this with the full approval of the whole social structure. We have managed to set up an ego image of ourselves to adore and cherish. This Narcissus is molded from the memories. These non-material ideas are of course immune to death for they are abstract and therefore incorruptible.

So the conventional ego, the false passport, is built up from an edited picture album of our past. That version often seems far more real than we are in the present moment. That is because here/now we are in a constant flux and flow, but what we *have been* is nicely and securely fixed. The false identity is frozen throughout time, a final static noun. And just because it is unchanging we become more clearly identified with that identity card than we do with the real living, moment-to-moment entity.

In order to support the new false self we have to become more and more identified with the past, with old knowledge and fixed belief systems which continue to bolster up our historical selves. And we forget there was ever anything else.

"This incapacity to die, ironically but inevitably, throws mankind out of the actuality of living, which for all normal animals is at the same time dying; the result is the denial of life (repression). The incapacity to accept death turns the death instinct into its destructively human and distinctly morbid form. The distraction of human life to the war against death, by the same inevitable irony, results in death's dominion over life."
(Norman O'Brown)[24]

Blind Belief

"I sell mirrors in the city of the blind."
(Kabir)[25]

"Every time a thought is born, you are born. When the thought is gone, you are gone. But the 'you' does not let the thought go, and what gives continuity to this 'you' is thinking. Actually there's no permanent entity in you, no totality of all your thoughts and experiences. You think that there is 'somebody' who is feeling your feelings — that's the illusion. I can say it is an illusion but it is not an illusion to you."
(U.G. Krishnamurti)[26]

"Who made me?" asks the child. **"God,"** comes the ready answer. That's that. Finished. The quest is over. But the parent, the teacher or the priest who reply may have had no direct experience of that God, yet most act as if they have. Few individuals are honest enough to admit both to the child and to themselves that they just don't know. Or that God might be just an abstract idea which has been passed down from generation to generation. There may not have been one person in the long line of believers who had actually experienced "God" face to face, but the very fact that the belief has a long tradition gives added weight to the idea as a truth.

WE ARE CONSCIOUS OF OURSELVES THROUGH A CONSTANT FLOW OF THOUGHTS. These thoughts might not even be our own; we have picked them up from someone else. And they had picked them up after they had been well-used before. All questions of belief are programs of pre-set, ready made, answers. They can never be a real quest for truth.

The paradox of the human mystery is that without a storehouse of knowledge in the form of language and symbols there can be no human phenomenon. Yet when that knowledge is used *as if* it is the actual direct experience of the individual, that selfsame storehouse becomes a graveyard turning humans into humanoids. When beliefs and symbols are identified as if they are the experiential world itself, then man becomes alienated from both himself and the world about him. Not only does he then live in a plastic universe, but he feels he does not need to explore it for himself. All a child has to do is to look up his question in the answer book of the species and no further personal responsibility or curiosity is needed.

But truth is not so cheap. It needs courage and intelligence to explore unknown frontiers. Beliefs are cheap and they do seem great bargains at first. Ready-made answers are free. However, there is one small problem — there is no room for doubt. Doubt is the worm in the apple.

It is always the fear of a true believer that somewhere, somewhen, someone will come along to disturb his cherished and borrowed ideas. Believers have to burn books, or heretics. At all costs they must repress that threat to their belief. If you have experienced the sunrise in the morning you don't announce, "I believe the sun." You have seen it. You *know*. Knowing is a direct experiential understanding, vibrant with life, authentic and individual. How can there be any doubt? You have seen the sun rise. But belief and knowledge can never be quite so sure; there's always a niggling doubt.

Beliefs are rigid, dead and frozen fish. If they ever did swim with life it was in the mind of the original innovator, who *knew it*. It was truth for him, without doubt or belief.

Truth is always individual, anyone else's truth is worthless. Truth is a non-transferable ticket which only bears one name.

The Priest, God and the Hereafter

THE PRIEST'S PROGRAM IS SIMPLY BELIEF; for example, "Belief in God." The 'true believer' identifies with a set of mythic stories which were invariably created in the distant past. Each belief system tends to exclude all others from the right path to truth. The beliefs of the popular religions require little more of anyone than to dutifully purchase the "product." *"To actually use the "product" is not demanded in any profound sense. Just buy it, praise it, own it, believe it and glamorize yourself by association with it."* (Da Free John)

The popular church of almost any denomination appeals to the child in us. Religion rekindles those lingering feelings of dependence in the form of the God-Parent strategy. There seems a great desire in us all to be reunited with a principle which is safe, caring and which as such carries no real personal responsibility. Such feelings are instantly gratified by any belief system which touches the longings towards a womb-like parental existence. Consoling beliefs create a sort of vaccine against fear and vulnerability. The cost of such a vaccine is obedience.

In the Judaic, Muslim and Christian traditions the original guilt came from the sin of sex and disobedience in the paradise gardens.

"Behold I was shapen in Iniquity; and in sin did my mother conceive me."

Seriousness, control and life negation are unaccountably the bedrock of most expressions of a religious life.
One common theme shared by the popular world religions is that of Paradise, the Promised Land. Heaven can only be enjoyed after this life of suffering and misery. It would seem almost that to believe in Heaven is, by definition, to live in Hell.

In most popular Western religions there isn't even the chance to sin. You are already born a sinner.

In the past you were in sin; in the present you are in sin; it is only in the future that there is the possibility of redemption and a chance of heaven for the obedient. This is the priest's Promise. Heaven is never *here/now*, but always and ever *here/after*.

Whenever a God is seen as all powerful, omniscient and omnipresent then the only necessary action we need to take is to be obedient. For He is ultimately responsible for all and everything so no personal responsibility is required from the worshiper. All you have to do is believe — in Jesus, Jehovah, Krishna, Mohammed or whosoever, and your place is assured in the promised land of the hereafter. This strategy ensures that man remains childish, irresponsible and dependent on the particular cult or belief. In return for faith and obedience you are given an assurance against the fear of death of the ego. The priest feeds us hope of salvation and a sense of superiority in knowing that not only are we on the right path but also that we are the chosen people. Sadly the cost is to lose the real possibility for transformation or for discovering the truth of who we are.

"Your religion was written on tablets of stone by the iron finger of an angry God...
"Our religion is the tradition of our ancestors — the dreams of our old men, given to them in the solemn hours of the night by the Great Spirit — and it is written in the hearts of our people."
(Chief Seattle)[27]

Four Horsemen of the Apocalypse

THE PRIEST, THE PARENT, THE PEDAGOGUE AND THE POLITICIAN in general terms, can be viewed as four unconscious conspirators who are responsible for the programs which have been fed to every one of us. And we carry all of them within us unknowingly.

As children we are fed old programs which have been made by someone else. Any intelligent child who rebels against such treatment is invariably regarded as an outcast or has to adopt another competing belief system. The son rejects his father's Fascist beliefs, yet promptly picks up a borrowed Socialist stance.

Neither of these belief systems is his own inner vision or experience.

The imposition of acquired knowledge on the small child is often done with the very best of intentions. The aim of most of the programmers is that the child should follow their particular belief and world view so that they are able to fit into the surrounding society.

It was pointed out by Bertrand Russell that all the supremely gifted polymaths, scientists, inventors or eccentric adventurers had childhoods which had little or no pressure towards conformity. They were allowed and encouraged to experiment and pursue their own interests, whatever they might be.

We are engulfed by ready-made, easy-to-serve concoctions on Capitalism, Communism, Fascism, or New Age Consciousness. The wrappings become even more exotic when the questions are spiritual, or on the nature of the universe, God, or our place in the scheme of things. But the programmers seldom admit that they just don't know anything. It is important, in the context of what you are reading at this moment, to remember it applies to this text as well.

Dionysius, an early Christian mystic, once said: "*Not* knowing is the most intimate." The state of innocent questioning has been lost and with it the capacity to ask questions of who we really are. Knowledge and belief get in the way, and unless we undertake the grueling task of de-programming ourselves — of breaking out of the rigid frames of other peoples' belief systems — we face the coming apocalypse as irresponsible and blind as the programmers themselves.

Whenever the status quo is threatened the establishment of priest, politician, parent and pedagogue generally gang up to maintain their old ways, often long after the foundations of that world have crumbled.
The ensuing clash between old and new belief systems is often bloody and yet such revolutions substitute one belief for another equally rigid system in an unending vicious circle.

The Prisoner of Knowledge

RELIANCE UPON BORROWED KNOWLEDGE is one of the fundamental characteristics of our western culture. The handing down of a collective heritage is the dynamic engine which has produced the whole technological culture of our time. Science, for instance, required many generations of innovators succeeding one another to pass on discoveries which could be developed further. But this passing on of shared and second-hand knowledge has an unhappy side effect. Both teacher and scholar are liable to fall into the persuasive trap of believing that knowledge is their direct, firsthand experience. Ideas are expressed in words and symbols, and these are necessarily static and unvarying.

The existential world of this moment is not like a static black and white photograph, shot in one flat lifeless foreverness. Yet many programs we pick up from a teacher inevitably are like that — a past and fixed idea, time honored and verifiable.

Education is often built upon a uniform class system where each unique individual is expected to learn exactly the same programs as everybody else. Logic and linear thinking are favored as the best basis for any examination, or test of abilities. The whole process heavily favors the workings of the left-hand hemisphere of the brain, so it is small wonder that we find this thinking mode so dominant in our times. Such imbalance is compounded by the use of language itself. The inherent mechanism of language is that of separation. A child learns to use nouns to distinguish things and verbs to separate actions, as if these ideas are real in themselves. The wondrous kaleidoscopic flux of living has no such static divisions. The grammar of language, those linear chains of ideas which we know as reason, cannot express cyclic events, paradoxes and the total network of holistic relations which are the rule of life rather than the exception.

Parent and the Family

We join a classic double-bind family case as the psychiatrist asks a boy, who had just emerged from a serious schizophrenic episode, what he meant by the word "selfish."

"**Son:** *Well, when my mother sometimes makes me a big meal and I won't eat it if I don't feel like it.*
"**Father:** *But he wasn't always like that you know. He's always been a good boy.*
"**Mother:** *That's his illness isn't it Doctor? He was never ungrateful. He was always most polite and well-brought up. We've done our best by him.*
"**Son:** *No, I've always been selfish and ungrateful. I've no self respect.*
"**Father:** *But you have.*
"**Son:** *I could have if you respected me. No one respects me. Everyone laughs at me. I'm the joke of the world. I'm the Joker alright.*
"**Father:** *But, son, I respect you, because I respect a man who respects himself.*"
(R.D. Laing)[29]

OF ALL THE WELL-MEANING AND LOVING PROGRAMMERS, parents are surely the most formidable. In an attempt to give the child what they think is best, they manage to project all their hopes and their fears. The child finds himself in the double-bind of wanting to live his own unique and individual life while being programmed to live someone else's.

Before he knows it the child is living a borrowed existence, fulfilling the parents' unconscious ambitions howsoever lovingly manifest.

Many serious psychological disorders can be traced back to the well-meaning nuclear family unit. A child is helpless and dependent upon affection and the need for a sense of self-worth and acceptance. All these natural human requirements can easily become distorted within the family, for nowhere are the interactions of intimacy and power so intense and passionate.

A mother speaks lovingly to the child as she boils with ill-concealed irritation over some misdemeanor. The perceptive child can either interpret the annoyance as love or see that the mother is lying. If he acts upon either of these assumptions he loses: if he approaches her for love when she is angry he is likely to be rejected and yet if he confronts her lie directly she will probably lose her temper, telling him that he should know that all mothers love their children, *always*, however bad they might be.

Now the child feels guilty but cannot understand why. He resents the feeling but begins to suspect that he is worthless and full of blame. Such normal misunderstandings and the contradictory network of lies are passed from generation to generation as norms of behavior. But if a child is both sensitive and honest, and the contradictions are prolonged and extreme, then he will suffer a chronic confusion which can result in more serious complaints later in life. While most of us are fortunate enough to be more resilient and more pragmatic in such no-win situations we have all learned complicated strategies to minimize and avoid such intolerable confrontations. These strategies later form the basis of our normal dealings with others, with often unhappy consequences.

The Politician and the State

JUST AS THE PRIEST IS THE PROGRAMMER OF A FUTURE IN HEAVEN, the politician is the programmer of a future on Earth. Both offer a better time to come than that which is actually happening to us now.

In order to achieve that future which "does not yet exist," both priest and politician are prone to believe that any "means" are justified. In order to achieve peace one must go to war. In order to achieve the golden future we must get past the present (make the present the past) as soon as possible. Both programmers find their main leverage to accomplish those aims, which may in fact be both benign and well-intentioned, in the manipulation of the *ego*.

As egos we derive a sense of identity from our social group and peers. We need others as mirrors to reaffirm our existence. We need recognition and attention. It is estimated that most of us spend as much as 90 percent of our lives seeking such personal reinforcement or what are popularly known as psychological "strokes."

We use many strategies to maintain our constant sense of identity. One of these is the acquisition of material possessions. *Who we are* is often seen as *what we have* and most advertising campaigns, for example, are directed at that need to reaffirm our sense of status. One such reinforcement of a sense of ongoing self and a strategy for bolstering up a sense of ego importance is the joining of a group which gives a sense of belonging to a shared belief system.

There is a constant need for such supporting enterprises as family, material possessions or the security of a "belonging identity." A politician, on his campaign staff, might, for example, play upon the ego's passionate reactions to any threat, real or imaginary, to any of these "crutches."

Any other group which threatens these beliefs, possessions, or any mirrors of self-esteem, will be subject to mindless, irresponsible and often violent reactions. And this is where both politician and state can exploit our worst motivations rather than our best.

In the worst situations, the authoritarian, parental state appeals to our childish dependence. Once a community is fed ersatz and materialistic reasons for living it weakens and collapses, leaving only the state as the one sense of sanity, security and identity.

Blind Alley

"If Man had originally inhabited a world as blankly uniform as a high rise housing development, as featureless as a parking lot, as destitute of life as an automated factory, it is doubtful that he would have had a sufficiently varied experience to retain images, mold languages, or acquire ideas."
(Lewis Mumford)[30]

"We shape our buildings, and afterwards our buildings shape us."
(Winston Churchill)[31]

LIVING IN OUR CONCRETE SAVANNAHS we are as displaced as wild animals in a zoo. There might be comfort, food, reasonable security and good sanitation yet the surroundings are often bleak, sterile and dehumanizing. Young children, brought up in featureless, soul-less environments are more likely to have limited experiences, which affect both intelligence and the ability to enjoy the full spectrum of life. They can so easily become intellectual and emotional cripples.

Experiments with rats exposed to featureless surroundings and others enjoying rich and stimulating environments show marked differences in the actual size and mass of the cortex of their tiny brains. Those who enjoyed the "rats' paradise" even underwent dramatic changes in their brain chemistry.

While we still don't actually know which parts are stimulated or repressed in human beings having such differences of background, we do know that children who are lucky enough to have varied and stimulating environments in early life have quite phenomenal advantages over their less fortunate brothers and sisters in featureless dull surroundings.

One of the historical reasons for many great cultural leaps has been the development of the city. In a large metropolis the full spectrum of diverse peoples and creative cultural ideas can be experienced. But an equivalent richness and diversity has sadly not been matched in modern times by the physical environment. It has, if anything, reduced life to a standard dull uniformity. The planning of cities now is almost entirely based on speculative growth by standardized units. In terms of human values there are few buildings which exuberantly celebrate the lives of those who live and work in them. Production and efficiency have no intrinsic life enhancing value in themselves — they merely serve as means to an end.

It is recognized that animals who have experienced abnormal laboratory environments from birth, such as extreme deprivation, loneliness or dull repetitive surroundings, tend to seek the company of others who have had similar treatments. Urban ghettos increasingly fit this sad description. When such trends of urbanization continue in our cities, it cannot create whole and mature beings.

The New Priesthood

OVER THE LAST CENTURY "SCIENTISM" has become the popular world view of the modern cosmos and the favored way of relating to the natural world, to others and ourselves. It has managed in many parts of the world to depose religion as the official and popular form of relating to the universe. Yet the mood which scientism has created is one of separation, doubt, questioning, analysis and emotional disassociation.

Scientific materialism is a special form of relationship, to specific events, specific moments, specific places and for specific purposes. At worst it is knowledge without love. If this becomes the dominant mode of viewing the universe and ourselves and the standard form of relationships, then any appreciation of the holistic and wondrous nature of the flow and play of existence becomes submerged. We then lose the ability to respond to the phenomenal world as a mysterious and magical whole. We find ourselves living in a substitute world of ideas.

The old mechanistic, intellectual approach requires the separation of the observer and the observed. Francis Bacon, one of the major founders of modern science, even went so far as to exhort the scientist to "torture nature's secrets from her." We are witness to such tragic attitudes and the victims of this mechanical approach to what was once known as "Mother Nature." The material successes of scientific methodology have most effectively deposed intuition and spirituality and we are the inheritors of this spiritual vacuum. It is reflected in the whole form of our world view and culture. There is little sense of love, no point to our lives. Science can give facts but is unable to impart meaning and significance. The new priest still cannot answer these fundamental questions: "Who are we?" "From whence do we arise?" or "Where are we going?"

He cannot even define what life is, while at the same time many of his kind are so enthusiastically trying to reshape it. Thus we blindly follow the blind.

"Science probes; it does not prove."
(Gregory Bateson)

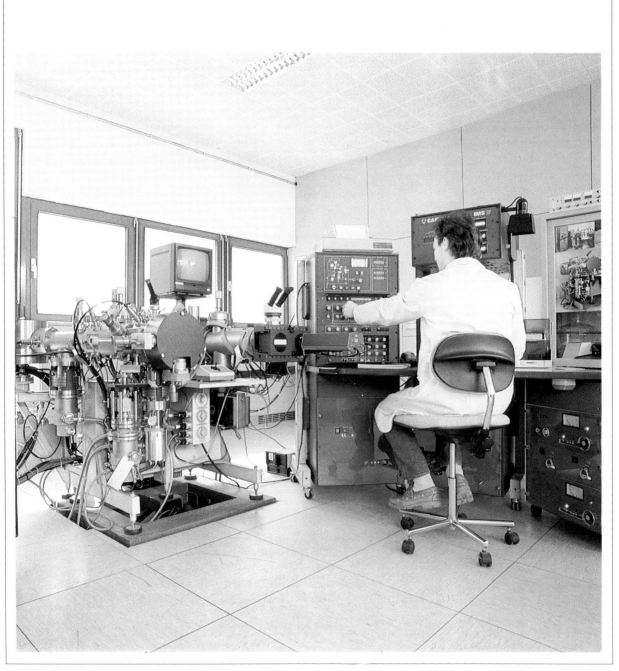

Tapes of Belief and Tapes of Doubt

"Scientists in their quest for certitude and proof tend to reject the marvelous." (Jacques Cousteau)[32]

SCIENTIFIC METHODOLOGY HAS BEEN BOTH A NECESSARY STAGE in the human development and a supremely valuable tool. It is only when it is mistaken for the truth, the only way of looking at reality or the basis for moral or spiritual values, that we manage to get ourselves snarled up. It is only one method of inquiry. It is a system to know *about* existence. It cannot *know* existence. If a person adopts any permanent attitude of a separate and analytical observer then he acts in direct opposition to the prime evolutionary conditions of being human.

Collectively we seem in a chronic mood of doubt and repeated questioning. The questions never end. At the other end of the spectrum are the religious beliefs where only "answers" are given. These older popular religions, formulated in ages of childlike depend-ence, encounter the adolescent separatist abstractions of modern scientific materialism. The old religions of faith with their ready made answers, mostly created thousands of years ago, cannot withstand the scrutiny of our age of doubt. But our culture has somehow lost out on the deal and finds itself alone and bewildered sitting on a pile of plastic trivia.

All the programmers we have encountered so far, whether they sell tapes of belief or tapes of doubt, are still blind — they don't *know*. As the sun rises on their blindfolded eyes one of them talks of the light of heaven and another talks of degrees centigrade.

Yet neither can see the beauty of the sun in the morning mists, and tragically, by the time they have finished with the child, he can't either.

We can now turn from this dark portrait of our age and begin to explore how it might have been and how it can be. We enter a very different world in Part II as we follow how man can mature and step beyond a childhood dependency and an adolescent alienation into an entirely new synthesis. We shall see how an Adam transformed by being sent out from Eden can reclaim Paradise and how the prodigal son can return after traveling far from his home.

Part II

P A R A D I S E   R E G A I N E D

CHAPTER ONE

Ways and Means, Men and Madcaps

An exploration of the evolutionary process as seen through the unique eyes of mystics, sages and individuals in the natural enlightened state. A survey of the various traditional and radical "Paths" and "Ways", which are designed to arouse the evolutionary sleeper

THE WAYFARERS ALL — RAINBOW SLEEPER — GOLDEN PATH — WAYS OF INIDA — WAY OF YOGA — WAY OF TANTRA — WAY OF ZEN — THREE SATORIS — WAY OF THE HEART — WHERE THERE'S A WILL THERE'S WAY — THE WAY OF THE PATHLESS LAND — NO WAY — WAY OF COMMUNION — WAY OF CELEBRATION — WAY OF A WOMAN — COMMON GROUND — NEW EVOLUTIONARY DIRECTION

CHAPTER TWO

Witness

First hand accounts of the natural enlightened state or what is understood to be the penultimate expression of the evolutionary process.

FLIGHT OF THE UNKNOWN TO THE UNKNOWN — FIRST WITNESS — SECOND WITNESS — THIRD WITNESS — FOURTH WITNESS — FIFTH WITNESS

"Now the process by which evolution unfolds through time is understood."
(Patanjali)[6]

CHAPTER ONE

Ways and Means, Men and Madcaps
Evolutionary Journey

WE HAVE NOW COME HALFWAY ON OUR TOUR OF THE PHENOMENON OF MAN. The concept that man is an evolutionary being, perpetually in the act of becoming, has been examined. But what of his future? What might be his next stage of becoming and what are the resulting changes to the species likely to be?

Orthodox theories view evolution as a movement from simple to complex, but do not account for the role of the spirit. Most of our present, established hypotheses of evolution are materialistic. Life and growth are still explained in purely physical terms.

But in speculating on how a new species of mankind might develop, the spirit and the higher realms of consciousness cannot be ignored. As we shall discover in the course of this investigation it is precisely within the realm of higher consciousness that the real evolutionary environment appears to exist and the territory in which any change is likely to take place.

Mankind, as a fluid, ever changing event — *a far-from-equilibrium state* — totters at the edge of a bifurcation point. It will be recalled from our earlier discussion that dissipative structures (and our species can be seen as one such structure) undergo periods of intense instability and chaos, which come to a sudden threshold, beyond which they suddenly jump to a new configuration and organization. Humankind stands at just such an anxious and crucial half-way point — a critical crossroads.

In terms of our original map for all seasons, this point would be the equivalent to the level of the intellect or the third stage of the evolutionary hierarchy. Have we, as a species, remained at this level too long?

We have already examined some of the sour fruits of this dilemma and have seen how much the situation has been exacerbated by too great a reliance on scientific materialism for our present views of both the universe and our place within it. The severely limiting views of old belief systems seem to have further entrapped us within Level Three.

Two diagrams giving an interpretation of the two aspects of Evolution and Involution, according to Meher Baba. The original void at the top of the inverted S *Evolves* through seven stages culminating in God in the consciousness of man. That consciousness then proceeds to *Involve* through a further seven stages returning to the original void transformed. The dual processes are irrevocably intertwined in one whole like an inward and outward breath.

Why has the species as a whole not managed to mature beyond this point? For we appear to stand, like the prodigal son, as beggars, having squandered our inheritance while using the barest minimum of our higher gifts solely for survival.

But, has man ever known anything different? Is there any evidence to show that anyone has walked a different evolutionary path towards the fulfillment of that vast potential?

The Wayfarers

WE WILL SHORTLY BE MEETING with very remarkable individuals. They might best be described as evolutionary explorers — pioneers who have opened up new frontiers of self-transformation. Somehow they have managed to jump across a crucial threshold to entirely different evolutionary territory.

In doing so, they appear to have triggered both the sleepers in themselves and an explosion of consciousness which confronts *Homo sapiens* with its higher potential — *Homo novus*. Yet as we examine each individual case we may be left with the feeling that howsoever remarkable these men and women are, they still remain only fragments of our species, isolated from the main stream. They are extraordinary indications of what might be if the species as a whole traveled down the same evolutionary track as they have done.

These rare wayfarers, however, have provided maps which can be used to help navigate those uncharted areas leading to the next stage of man. Even though many of these charts are now heavily encrusted with the accumulations of cultic and religious legends, they still outline a landscape of breathtaking beauty. Each individual traveler paints the higher human states in widely differing styles, but underlying those differences there is always a recognizable pattern. Buddha once observed that the taste of the ocean is the same wherever you take the sample.

The first chart is only a rough sketch to enable us to take our bearings. This might give some perspective when viewing the many varied ways of reaching the higher functions. But, as it is said: "All paths reach to the top of the mountain."

Exploring some of the ancient tracks made by the "past masters" and some of the new and radical pathways cut by the travelers of our time, we immediately encounter an obstacle. There seem to be those who have "tasted the sugar" and those who have only "looked at the sugar." So that any search is complicated by distinguishing the authentic article.

As a generation we are privileged to have had a number of remarkable pioneers in this field living amongst us. From what we can deduce, they are exceptional by any standards of any previous age. Still more significant is the impact that their combined presences might have had throughout the globe.

Two thousand five hundred years ago, at the time of Gautama the Buddha, there was just such a gathering, with no less than eight enlightened masters living in the tiny state of Bihar in India alone. However, in that time communication was slow and often even centuries were needed before the message of these enlightened masters could spread further than their own small area. Today, the teachings of our generation of masters is available, direct and undiluted through instantaneous media.

The maps, the methods and the men and women we now examine are actually fingers pointing towards those evolutionary sleepers which we seek. Here are the open pathways to the higher functions of the glandular and nervous systems, to the heart and to the brain. Once activated these pathways quite naturally, with seemingly no effort on our part, carry us deeper and deeper into the territory of our true evolutionary environment: to consciousness itself.

Most traditions agree that there are seven planes of life or stages in the evolution of man. As a species, we stand on the threshold of Level Four. As Gurdjieff pointed out this corresponds to the interval between *mi-fa* in the octave where there is a semi-tone missing. Few individuals ever consciously venture across the first borderline into the higher realms of consciousness. However, recent surveys into paranormal experience and behavior do suggest that as many as one in every two of us have at some time in our lives made an involuntary dash across that no-man's-land of Level Four.

The sudden and unheralded glimpses we have at such moments often change the whole direction of our lives or at least leave us with the uneasy feeling that the everyday reality which we take so much for granted is not at all what it appears to be. These transforming sprints across the twilight zone might be "out of the body" or "near death" experiences, telepathy, precognition or an overwhelming glimpse of the underlying unity of all and everything. Once experienced we know beyond all doubt or the beliefs and ideas of others, that there is something more real than that which we have become accustomed to.

Rainbow Sleeper

The true evolutionary journey of man could be said to begin at the border of that twilight zone between Level Three, the intellectual level, and Four, the psychic zone. This is the stage in which most of the known, visible work of the enlightened masters seems to happen. It is here that the would-be seeker needs a good push in the right direction.

Depending on the tradition or the navigator this can be "sweet talking" or a "hit on the head." Once across that initial borderline the seeker enters unknown territory.

However, at the same time the paradox immediately arises that the landscape is vaguely familiar, as if we had traveled this way before but have forgotten it. Most traditions agree that the last time we were in this position we were traveling in the opposite direction, from the innocent and psychic eyes of childhood to the shattered vision of adulthood. The masters tell us to re-trace the journey but this time do it fully consciously. For, like Adam, or the *prodigal son*, man will not return to the paradise garden with the same innocence and un-consciousness as when he left it. As we shall discover, something quite extraordinary happened on the way.

REMEMBER THAT IN OUR ORIGINAL MYSTICAL MAP there was supposedly a "fall" from the highest and most subtle Level Seven to the lowest Level One. According to that vision of "Involution" we have managed, as a species, to bounce back from the first level to the third on the return journey to the Garden of Eden. But things are never quite as simple as they first appear.

Imagine that you are in a deep and sound sleep. You are in the "void" where there are no dreams and there is no consciousness — simply a velvet nothingness. Ancient texts of India speak of an "Original State of Existence" that was once exactly like that of a deep and unconscious sleep. Through some whim there was the briefest of stirrings, a little ripple in the void. In essentially the same way that we begin to dream in normal life when we surface from the deep dreamless sleep of the void so the original "Void of Existence" began its slow awakening.

First it too entered a dream state — the "Divine Dream." The first

dream was of creation and, in exactly the same way as we identify with the impressions of our own created dreams, Existence did likewise.

It is said that the "Divine Dream" took the form of the trinity of: "Sat" (power,) "Chit" (knowledge) and "Anand" (bliss.) But on awakening as a human these divine aspects became Energy, Mind and Body because they existed on the lower levels of manifestation.

Now Existence finally awakens but now the problem is that It only does so at the level of the human. It experiences Itself as us. The Void has gained consciousness in this way, but only in our gross form. It no longer dreams the Divine Dream of Creation, and It now is no longer unconscious, but It has managed to awaken with a false awareness and a false identity. When the Void awakens to ask "Who am I?" the answer is the false: "I am human." The face in the mirror is quite oblivious to its true Reality as the Eternal and Infinite Radiant Void. The evolution of consciousness has been gained at a bizarre cost.

So here we can view the so-called journey in an entirely different light. Only by *re-tracing* the steps of the Divine Dream, consciously following all the stages back to the Original State of Void can we finally understand "Who am I?" For, when last in that state the Void was unconscious and asleep but now the face in the mirror is conscious of its true self and can answer with an ecstatic cry "I am VOID." This is surely the ultimate in both human absurdity and ecstatic cosmic humor. For here is the great joke: the whole quest was a dream and that final recognition is the belly laugh of Existence.

The great paradox of the Original "fall" or "Involution" turns out to be an "Evolution" — the evolution of Consciousness.

When the Void looks into the mirror
    It sees us
    When we look into the Void
    we see the mirror
    When we look in the mirror
    We see the Void
    When the mirror looks in the mirror...
    It laughs.

Golden Path

HAVING BEEN INTRODUCED TO THE CONCEPT of evolutionary sleepers, those functions within man which we proposed hold the key to bridging the next stage of humankind. It might be revealing to examine some of the practical methods which have been used throughout history to *arouse* them. Those who have actually managed to activate the higher functions are perhaps one in a billion and those who have left any record of their exploration are even rarer. The Golden Paths by which the higher functions are reached invariably die with the innovator. What is left behind invariably are a series of maps which have become so layered with other people's interpretations, corruptions and distortions that any seeker would do well to avoid them altogether. As far as possible we have tried to extract just those essential descriptions which throw some light upon the evolutionary process itself. In doing so, of course, I am again adding a further interpretation and you must follow the reasoning at your own risk.

A timely word of warning for those who have never embarked on such a heady journey through esoteric landscapes. Even in the relative safety of abstractions, the paths are none the less minefields. It is usually only the *un*-enlightened who are so keen on assuring us that there are maps in the first place. The enlightened person often maintains, like J. Krishnamurti, the *"Truth is a pathless land and you cannot approach it by any path whatsoever."*

U.G. Krishnamurti is even more blunt, *"There is no path of wisdom, there is no path at all. There is no journey."* Their point is simple and meaningful. Seekers often fall into the trap of eating the menu while forgetting the food before them. It is even easier to get lost in a map as

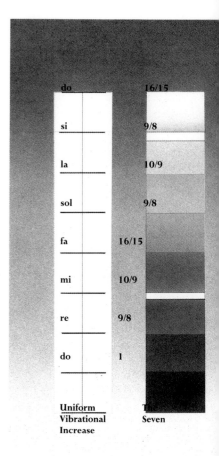

Uniform Vibrational Increase		The Seven
do		16/15
si		9/8
la		10/9
sol		9/8
fa	16/15	
mi	10/9	
re	9/8	
do	1	

Georges Gurdjieff asserted that there exists a cosmic Law of Seven. He saw the phenomenal universe as essentially one of vibrations. Contrary to the views of orthodox science such vibrations are non-uniform. According to Gurdjieff there is a dis-continuity which is the bedrock of the cosmic order. He cites the case of any frequency of vibration which doubles showing there are eight *un-equal* steps in its rate of increase. This period we know as

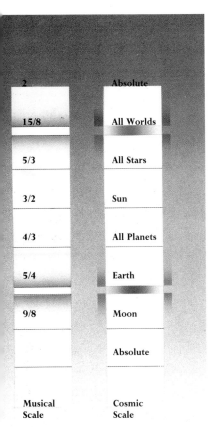

Musical Scale	Cosmic Scale
2	Absolute
15/8	All Worlds
5/3	All Stars
3/2	Sun
4/3	All Planets
5/4	Earth
9/8	Moon
	Absolute

the landscape passes by unseen. Alerted to these dangers and using the following charts and methods only as *indicators* pointing in the general direction of where the species could be heading, we can explore the territory across the border examining a number of paths and super-highways on route to the higher evolutionary states.

Ramana Maharshi prescribed two methods of paths which almost sum up the entire spectrum of methods. These were the path of *self-inquiry* and the path of *surrender* to the master or Guru. He would say, "*There are two ways: ask yourself 'Who am I?' or submit.*" Below is a short list of just some of the polarities we will encounter.

Path of Absorption
Trust
Surrender to a master
Eti-Eti This and this
Positive
Heart, emotional, feelings
Bhakti..devotional
Love, Prayer

External landscape — dry, desert, arid
Internal landscape — luxuriant, abundant, variegated
Popular religions tend to be childlike and dependent on father/mother figures
Unquestioning, surrendering, egoless
Sufi, Islamic, Christian, Judaic, Gnostics, Zoroastrianism, Hinduism

Path of Insight
Doubt
Self-Inquiry
Neti-Neti Not this not that
Negative
Head, intellect, conceptual
Yogi, non devotional
Meditation

External landscape — luxuriant
Internal landscape — dry, calm, clear and desert-like
Popular religions tend to be adolescent, doubting, questioning and 'scientific' and ego-ful
Buddhism, Taoism, Zen, Jainism Yoga, Confucianism, Vedanta

an octave. Our own musical scale is seen as a symbolic representation of the cosmic law. Although it would at first appear that any increase in frequency would unfold as a uniform process, what actually happens is that there are two distinct retardations or shortenings within the seven passages between notes. These retardations Gurdjieff called 'Intervals,' 'Thresholds,' or 'Shocks' and they mark the sudden revolutionary jumps within the cosmos.

It is regretted that there is simply insufficient space to include all the major paths. Notable omissions here include the Judaic and Christian tradition, with such spiritual greats as *Baal Shem*, *St. Francis*, *St. Theresa* or *Master Eckhart*. The purpose of the chapter, however, is to introduce less well-known paths and evolutionary ways.

The Ways of India

HISTORICALLY INDIA HAS ALWAYS BEEN THE SPIRITUAL DYNAMO of the planet. More men and women are known to have entered the natural enlightened state in this land than in all the rest of the world.

The Indian philosophic approach to the Ultimate, Transcendental Reality is not just an intellectual exercise as it has become in the West. It is a prismatic array of practical devices to experience directly what is being described.

Here we find an evolutionary science of the spirit where each level of our higher functions has been lovingly charted and dissected, as clinically precise as in any Western experimental laboratory of material science. But in India the focus has not been on the objective world but the subject or the witness of that world. Experiments are carried out upon *oneself*, upon the subtle inner world of consciousness, which is claimed as the true revolutionary environment of man and the species.

There are five major disciplines in India to activate the higher evolutionary centers. These are *Yoga*, *Nishkana Karma* (Selfless action in the service of the Divine), *Jnana* (Path of Wisdom), *Upasana* (Worship or Prayer) and *Bhakti* (Devotion.) These are the five practical methods which involve the whole being.

Intertwined about these disciplines are what might be termed six philosophic approaches to the Ultimate questions of Reality.

The root of Indian philosophy is not materialistic or object oriented. Its motto is — "*Know the self.*" The whole body of Indian philosophy is known as "Darshan" which roughly translated means "to see a point of view." The system has six distinctive perspectives, each viewpoint being from a different level of consciousness. The views are often contradictory because while there is a "holo-archy" in each level, there are hierarchies between levels, all with totally different views.

In our present search for the higher evolutionary functions of the mind-body of man we now turn to one of the methods of India. This is Yoga.

The six approaches are:

1. *Nyàya:* a dialectic of reason which establishes the correct procedures to understand objective phenomena.
2. *Vaisheshika:* identifies individual objects by those qualities which make them

differ from others. This is a non-theistic approach.

3. *Sànkhaya*: An enumeration of the levels from the gross plane to the highest level. It proposes a cosmic duality of matter and spirit and provides the intellectual expression of Yogic realization.

4. *Yoga*: the practical means of purifying perceptions which enable the "philosopher" to experience reality, directly, face to face.

5. *Karma Mìmànsà*: of Vedic rituals which enrich the universal energies and the field of evolutionary action.

6. *Vedànta*: the fulfillment of *knowing* "Veda-Knowledge." It is the totality of non-dualist Indian philosophy and is considered its highest expression. We have observed much of its central philosophy in the general map which opens this chapter.

The Way of Yoga

ONLY A FRACTION OF THE IMMENSE LITERATURE IN INDIA on Yoga has been translated for the West so it is hardly surprising that many of our ideas on the way of Yoga are fragmented and partial. Yoga is a peculiarly Indian phenomenon, a kind of systematized soaring which comes to earth in two main schools.

Raja (Sanskrit for king) Yoga is the royal path to Self-Realization while *Hatha* (Sanskrit for violence) is a more arduous and often dangerous method. The Hatha discipline uses extreme physical exercises, designed to trigger correspondingly extreme effects in the nervous system and the brain. Its aim is to coerce the higher functions to activate: to force the evolutionary sleeper to awaken.

Raja Yoga on the other hand uses the body postures or "asanas," primarily as an aid to yogis who sit for hours in meditation and who need physical exercise to keep their bodies in shape. Many Yoga practices are extremely ascetic and some extremes of self-torture can often lead to pathological conditions. A seeker just cannot hammer down the door to higher consciousness. This does not seem to be the nature of the game although many try. Such attempts to wrest nature's secrets or rend the veil have parallels in the foundations of Western science but prove both absurd and pointless in the realm of inner space.

Yoga derives from the Sanskrit root "yuj," to yoke or to join. It implies union with the Universal, a state of Oneness with Existence.

The heart of Yoga is the settling of the mind into a state of absolute stillness. The Yoga Sutras of Patanjali were originally chanted or sung and the sounds themselves had a resonating effect upon the minds and bodies of those who listened. They are a hymn of praise with the sophistication of a science incomparable in its complexity. The classic form of Raja Yoga consists of eight interacting "limbs." These limbs grow simultaneously as a whole organic process like an embryo, although in actuality a clear sense of hierarchy prevails. The whole quest ends in *Sahaj-Samadhi*, an ecstatic state having full alertness and consciousness — "ecstasy with wide open eyes."

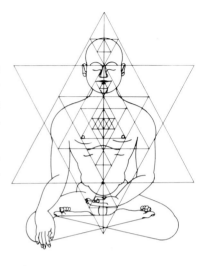

Ashtavangani — **The Eight Limbs**

First Limb: YAMA — *Laws and Nature of Life*
Ahismà — **dynamic peacefulness and loving openness. Living free from fear.**

Satya — **impeccable in thought, speech and action.**
As teya — **integrity laying no claim to what is not ours.**
Brahmacharya — **living in reality, a state of innocent ecstasy and self-sufficient wholeness. Chastity not imposed or sexuality repressed, but a loving awareness.**
Aparigraha — **not grasping, non-attachment, being *in* the world but not of it.**

Second Limb: IYAMA — *Rules for Individual Living*
Shaucha — **simplicity, clear and uncluttered consciousness.**
Santosha — **equanimity, seeing things as they are without judgment or expectation.**
Tapas — **fire of purification.**
Swàdhyaya — **refinement that comes from purification.**
Ishvarapranidhàna — **surrender and devotion to the Creator. The Infinite creates the primordial vibration of life AUM.**

Third Limb: ASANA — *The Postures*
These are the rejuvenating physical exercises which release the energy blocks and stress throughout the body. There are over 80 such postures.

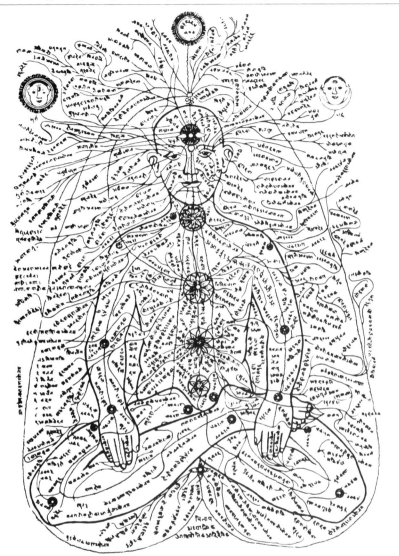

Fourth Limb: PRANAYAMA — Expansion of the Life Energies

This is accomplished by the conscious exercise of the breath.

Fifth Limb: PATYAHARA — Retirement of the Senses

This can be translated as "in the direction of the food." As the mind settles, attention turns inward and the outer senses slowly withdraw. The natural gravitation of the quiet mind is to move on its own accord. No control or restraint is needed now. Here is the cleaning of the doors of perception as the senses become more refined and attuned to higher frequencies of consciousness.

Sixth Limb: DHARANA — Focusing of Attention

Directed awareness, subtle and effortless.

Seventh Limb: DHYANA — Meditation

Consciousness becomes more and more subtle and refined. Here, in the midst of the realm of Yoga, the seeker begins to settle the mind into a state of absolute stillness.

Eight Limb: SAMADHI — The Settled Mind

In this state of unclouded truth the One who has attained complete discrimination between the subtlest level of mind and the self has no higher knowledge to acquire.

"*This Samadhi completes the transformation and fulfills the purpose of evolution. Now the process by which evolution unfolds through time is understood. This is Enlightenment.*" (Patanjali)[1]

That calm confirmation is the first recorded statement upon the nature of the evolution of the species inscribed over 25 centuries ago by Patanjali. It is a timely reminder of what we have perhaps lost in our scientific epoch.

The Way of Tantra

OF ALL THE METHODS OF AROUSING THE EVOLUTIONARY SLEEPER, Tantra is perhaps the most exotic and at its initial ritual levels certainly the most erotic. A Tantrika raises all the latent energies of the body, and channels them into such a sensual and emotional charge that it literally "blasts" its way through to the higher functions of the organism. It is rather like a seven stage space rocket, escaping the Earth's gravitational pull. The first stage is gross, but each subsequent stage becomes more sophisticated and refined.

The first stages of the rocket are raw sexual energy and the seventh is the ultimate subtlety of "Samadhi" (Enlightenment.)

Tantra is perhaps the most richly variegated method of transforming man to be found anywhere on the planet. It is a synthesis of the major devices of Indian religion and philosophy.

But Tantra is also outrageous at its initial levels, shocking its orthodox Brahmin and Buddhist counterparts, for it demands total severance of any identification with the everyday world. Tantrikas often perform their elaborate and sexually based rituals close to cremation and burial grounds. This is a constant reminder of death which destroys everything. For the Tantrika, time is the great illusion. It is time which gives the appearance of birth, death, all objects and all space.

Fundamental to this view is that the world of events and objects is constantly being projected from a present moment which issues forth in all of us. All the Tantrika has to do is to turn around 180 degrees and look back up the projector from which it all comes, to be one with the Source. Tantric meditation turns the mind around, to witness the whole creation of existence continually spewing forth from the mystical cosmic Yoni or the female vulva: a result of the orgasmic and ecstatic union with the male seed.

The Tantric adept focuses on the Female Divine Form as the true creator of all time-enslaved events. In fact the woman is the teacher, the "power holder," who instructs the seeker. It was so for the Tibetan scholar-sage Saraha who was finally instructed by a common arrow-smith woman. It was true for the great Indian religious genius Shri Ramakrishna who was initiated by Bhairavi Brahmain in the last century.

Shri Ramakrishna, one the greatest religious geniuses of the last century, experimented with virtually all the evolutionary paths. He was initiated into Tantric practices when 25 years old. He tried, "scientifically," to explain each stage in the ascent of the Kundalini, but each time he came to the penultimate Samadhi he became lost to the outside world and would pass into unconsciousness. He then tried to explain the experience in terms of Vedanta.

"The Vedanta speaks of seven planes in which the mind moves and works. The ordinary man's mind moves and works only in the three lower centers and is content with satisfying itself through the common appetites: eating, drinking, sleeping and begetting. But when it reaches the fourth center opposite the heart, man sees a divine effulgence. From this state, however, he often lapses back to the three lower centers. When the mind comes to the fifth center opposite the throat the spiritual aspirant cannot speak of anything but God... Even from this state a man may slip down; he should therefore be very watchful. But he need not have any fear of a fall when the mind reaches the sixth center, level with the junction of the

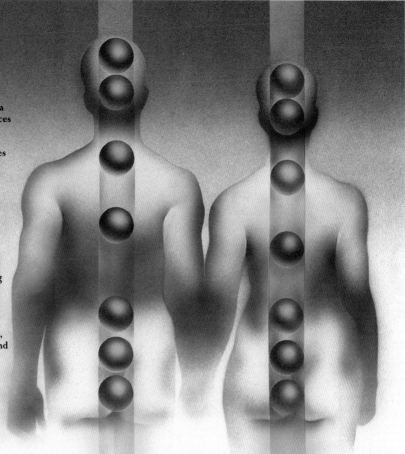

Level Seven: The Unity of Transcendental Reality, Undivided, Infinite and Eternal.

Level Six: The sexual Divine Couple, Shiva and Shakti, are unaware of their differences in deep sexual and ecstatic embrace.

Level Five: The male and female principles have become aware of their distinctions and dance and conjoin in orgasmic embrace.

Level Four: The female "objective" principle separates from the male "subjective" principle.

Level Three: The female objective aspect creates an enthralling dance of illusion, dazzling the male subject into identifying with the objects of her creation in the realm of time.

Level Two: Time and objects, the appearance of life and all things in space, being the result of the dance of power and creation.

Level One: The physical universe of separate particles.

eyebrows. He gets the vision of the 'Paramatman' (Oversoul) and remains always in 'Samadhi.' His mind, however, is not really merged in the 'Paramatman' for there is a thin transparent veil between the sixth center and the 'Sahasrar,' the highest center."

Ordinary spiritual aspirants, the "Arahats" cannot come down from this state. These Jivas remain in Samadhi for twenty-one days and then "rend the final veil." But usually the physical body cannot withstand the release of energy and dies. Only masters come back from this exalted state.

Hindu Tantra
This tradition focuses attention upon the arousing energy of the coiled Kundalini which lies asleep at the base chakra. This snake is the individual's projecting world aspect and is coiled around the inner lingam, covering its mouth with hers. That mouth is the entrance to the bottom of the "Sushuma" at the spinal base. Once awakened the Kundalini uncoils, straightens and in a wild rush penetrates the central canal running along the spinal cord. It enters each of the lotus chakras, activating each in turn, to burst finally through the thousand-petaled lotus at the crown of the head.

Buddhist Tantra
The Buddhist Tantra, both Indian and Tibetan, ignores the Kundalini altogether and does not include the lower chakras. It does, however, identify the ascending energy of consciousness with that of sexual energy.
What is peculiar in the Buddhist approach is the importance given to the heart as a field of energy. Here, it seems, resides the true Self, the Buddha Nature, and while the conscious energy must flow upward in its course to the Sahasrar crown chakra, it then blossoms as a fountain to fall back into the heart for the final ultimate union.

The Way of Zen

ZEN CLAIMS TO CARRY THE INNERMOST ESSENCE OF BUDDHISM.

The story unfolds that Zen was born on one still morning in India twenty-five centuries ago. Gautama the Buddha sat before a huge congregation of his followers who waited for his usual discourse.

Buddha, however, simply sat in silence holding a flower before him. Mahakasyapa, Buddha's oldest disciple, smiled knowingly at the Master and Buddha proclaimed: "*The most precious transcendental treasure I can now hand to you, O venerable Mahakasyapa*" and gave him the flower.

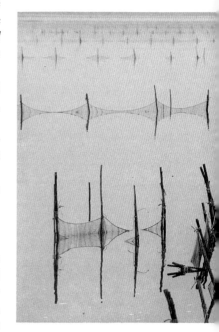

In that one sudden moment of revelation something had triggered the opening of the old disciple's mind and Buddha's true message, which was essentially without words, was understood and realized.

Here is the quintessential message of Zen. It is a *special transmission* outside the realm of the scriptures. If we look here for abstract maps or philosophic words we will be disappointed.

Zen is a direct "seeing into one's own nature" and the realization of one's Buddha nature.

There is a significant story of the sixth Zen patriarch, Hui-neng, when he was still a young man. It is said that he once heard the Diamond Sutra of Buddha being recited in a city street and he was so touched by it that he sought out the master Hung-Jen at the Yellow Plum in Chin-Chou. The master questioned him closely, finally asking: "*Do you want to* know *truth, or do you want to* be *truth?*" "To be truth" came the prompt reply. The old master was well pleased. However, instead of initiating him as a monk the master offered him a job as the rice cleaner for the Zen brotherhood.

Years passed and when Hung-Jen knew he was about to die he was troubled that there might be no one to succeed him. He announced that he was about to select a successor and that whosoever could prove, by verse, that he had understood his teaching would inherit the patriarchal staff and the mantle, being the legitimate heir. Next morning there was a verse written outside the meditation hall:

"This body is the Bodhi-tree.
The soul is like a bright mirror.
Keep it clean at all times,
And let no dust gather upon it."

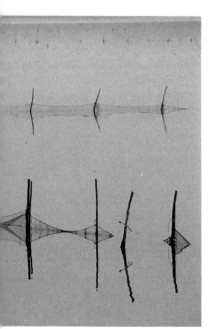

The verse had been written by Shen-hsui, the most learned of the patriarch's five hundred disciples. It was much admired by all the monks, but the rice cleaner was overheard to say that it was rubbish and that the writer was a fool. Two monks passing were astonished and challenged him to do better, so the next morning a new verse appeared on the door.

"The Bodhi is not a tree
The bright mirror is nowhere shining
As there is nothing,
Just where can the dust settle?"

The patriarch read the verse but said nothing. He motioned Hui-neng to come to his lodging. There he gave him the robe of the great patriarch Bodhi-Dharma and the staff. But because the master knew his monks were not ready for a lowly rice cleaner to become abbot, he advised Hui-neng to escape and hide his new state until the times were right. That night Hui-neng left the monastery. A few days later, before passing away, the old master spoke:
"Four hundred and ninety-nine of my disciples understand Buddhism perfectly, except one — Hui-neng. He is a man not to be measured by an ordinary standard." Hui-neng was pursued and finally found but only one monk managed to catch up with him. He begged for the new teaching. *"Show me this moment your original face before you were born"* said Hui-neng. At this the monk is said to have had a satori and true Zen was born.

In fact the two schools of Zen Buddhism are perfectly reflected in this little story and its two verses. The elder disciple Shen-hsin, the founder of the Gradual School of Enlightenment was still firmly rooted in the scripture of Indian Buddhism and the inheritor of that school of

Three Satoris

meditation. Hui-neng, on the other hand, being the founder of the
School of Sudden Enlightenment, created an entirely new phenomenon and in this he had absorbed the Taoist approach to life. *"The
world is always held without effort. The moment there is effort, the world is
beyond holding."*

The crossleggeds or "dustwipers" try to attain a state of calm
through meditation (Dhyana,) but with this method it is difficult to go
beyond the self-absorption of Level Five. There is ecstasy but no seeing
into one's ultimate nature.

According to Hui-neng, the quietistic Zen, the wiping of the dust
in order to see the original mind-mirror-nature, is impossible. Yet all
Buddhists attempt it, attempt to calm the mind, much in the tradition
of Indian Yoga. But Hui-neng insists that there is nothing to attain in
the first place. Maps are all useless, sitting crosslegged, trying to make
it all happen is pointless and ego gratifying. Satori, the sudden
unexpected flash of insight into the true nature of man and the
universe, just happens when the fruit is ripe; the goldbrick falls where
it will. There is within oneself that which knows and satori happens.
The evolutionary sleeper once aroused continues at its own speed. All
falsehoods drop away in that explosion of intense illumination. There
is simply no awakening to attain, for it is always there.

Meister Eckhart, the Christian mystic once said, *"It is as if one stood
before a high mountain and cried God! Art thou there? The echo comes
back Art thou there? If one cries out Come out, the echo comes back Come
out!"*

The life of Zen opens with satori. Satori can be defined as the
"opening of the mind-flower," it is a sudden state of heightened
consciousness which is totally discontinuous with the everyday thinking mind. While it is different for different people, it often manifests as
the uniting of all our normal dualistic opposites into a whole: an
organic miracle and mystery of living. It is an intuitive unfolding of
Reality; a perceptual revolution; a revelation and re-evaluation of the
Self as a spiritual unity.

A satori has the effect of severing any ties with normal everyday
life, as the experiencer has known it up to that point. After satori,

when the original void or no-thing-ness is glimpsed, nothing is ever the same.

The sudden school of Hui-neng was simply distinguished from the "mental tranquilization" school of Shen-hsui by its insistence upon the satori, the sudden, intuitive flash of insight, as opposed to the subtle philosophic dialectics of the Buddhist dominated, earlier, school.

Although the "suddens" eschew all maps, the "Three Satoris" of Zen do warrant investigation, for here is the unspoken and unwritten map of the Zen monk.

These are the three satoris which are the quantum leaps that straddle the thresholds of Levels Five, Six and Seven of our original evolutionary map.

A monk comes running to his master: "*Master, I have at last experienced no-thing.*" He receives a hard blow from the master's staff for his trouble. "*Fool, you missed! Return to your meditations. If nothing is an experience then it is still some-thing. This was just the first satori.*"

Some time later the monk returns, flushed with joy. "Master, I have just experienced that there is no experience and no experiencer, only no-thing-ness." "*Idiot,*" and the master hits him again "*Who has still experienced? Go back and meditate.*" This is the second satori. Later the master passed the monk's cell and enquired. "*Have you experienced nothing yet?*" To which the monk only smiles and does not say a single word. The master is well pleased. Ko Hsuan says of this moment:

"*He realizes that the no-thing-ness of nothing is also nothing and when the nethermost nothingness is reached there is most truly to be found a deep and unchanging stillness.*"

The void has opened its doors and the monk steps beyond the beyond.

"*This Very Body the Buddha*
This Very Place the Lotus Paradise."

This is the core word. *Now* and *here* is the natural state. There is nothing to do or attain. We already possess everything and only have to re-cognize that fact. In this tradition the sleepers just need a little nudge.

The Way of the Heart

*"Non-being is a mirror, the world an image and man
is the eye of the image
in which the person is hidden
you are the eye of the image, and the light of the eye.
Who has ever seen the eye
through which all things are seen?
The world has become a man
and man a world.
There is no clearer explanation than this
When you look well into the root of the matter
He is at once seen both seeing eye
and thing seen."*
(Mahmud Shabistari)[2]

*"The road your Self must journey on
lies in polishing the mirror of your heart
it is not by rebellion and discord
that the heart's mirror is polished free
of the rust of hypocrisy and unbelief:
Your mirror is polished by your certitude
by the unalloyed purity of your faith.*

*Break free from the chains
you have forged upon yourself
for you will be free when you are free of clay.
The body is dark — the heart is shining bright;
the body is mere compost — the heart a blooming garden."*
(Hakim Sanai)[3]

WE NOW TURN FROM THE AUSTERE NATURAL BEAUTY of the innerscape of Zen to what might be considered the other end of the spectrum of evolutionary paths of transformation. It is one of the more profound mysteries that the spare, desert-like clarity of the inner world of Zen should have had its roots in the lush, verdant landscape of India and that the Sufis, Christians and Jews on the other hand should have been born into an arid, desert world with a correspondingly luxurious and visionary inner environment.

While the Judaic world of the Kabbalah, or the paths of Christian mystics like St. Francis, belong to the way of the heart, the penultimate expression of that way must surely be reserved for the Sufis, the mystical arm of Islam. The verse in the column gives the essence of this teaching. It is not the rebellion and doubt of Zen or, as we shall see, of both U.G. Krishnamurti and iuddhu Krishnamurti. It is not the path of negation. Sufism is a huge YES, not "neti-neti" (not this, not that) but "eti-eti"(yes this and yes, also that.) But like Zen, the way of the Sufi is to be of this world. The chains of the "clay," of the visible and measurable universe of matter, are only binding if there is identification with them. For the Sufi the body of compost is there to be used to fertilize the true evolutionary garden and make it flower. The ultimate mystical quest is to return to that garden of Truth through a universe alive, aglow and radiantly on fire.

It is said that the "Over-soul" originally fell from the light into the world of shadows and, as it identified with desires and things, it became heavier, more substantial, dense and opaque. The veils multiplied, but once the soul remembers its captivity and is conscious of its exile from the world of light it begins the ascent. And that climb back, from its material and sensual function to that of the true function of the spirit, is the Evolutionary Quest.

As consciousness moves upward from *sense* to *spirit* it becomes the spiritual heart of pure intuition. And it is this heart which finally unites with the One.

In order to activate the sleeper of the heart we must first distinguish our ego from a true sense of Self. The ego is a marvelous fiction. It is our normal image of what we are, but it is a false mirror.

"The Beloved is devoted to its lovers for how else can it be Belovedness? Each and every Lover is the Beloved; each and every Beloved is the Lover. Love longs for Beauty; Beauty thirsts for Love. The Absolute Unity, which is the Absolute Beauty and Absolute Love, loves its Beloved so intensely it leaves not a trace of themselves. For in reality there is only the Beloved, only loving."
(Meher Baba)[4]

This ego is a novel written by ourselves about ourselves and the very first step on the Quest is to disentangle ourselves from its seductions and to dis-identify with the manuscript we, and the collective consensus around us, have managed to create.

The image of the mirror is fundamental to any understanding of the Sufi. Before the creation of human beings the universe had come into being, but it was unconscious and unreflective. Man became the "polished mirror of consciousness" and a new phenomenon arose within the Divine Unity of Existence. The Sufi aspires to become that reflective mirror, the instrument by which the One can have an image of Itself. But the One, the Beloved, is both the seeker and the sought.

Where There's a Will There's a Way

Gurdjieff was born on 13th Janury 1877 in Russian Georgia. Although he has managed to cover his tracks carefully and little is known about his early years it would seem that he was a precocious child who grew into an independent young man fascinated by the odd and the mysterious. He traveled most of the Middle East and visited Tibet before turning up in Russia just before the 1914-18 war. It was in Moscow that he first encountered Ouspensky who became his pupil in 1915 and wrote the first book which revealed some of his teachings. Gurdjieff gathered around him a group of disciples and led them out of the fighting and the Revolution via Tiflis, Constantinople, through Germany ending up in France by 1922. At the Prieuré of Avon he created the "Institute for the Harmonious Development of Man" surrounding himself with a group of remarkable men and women. Much of the work at the Prieuré was composed of arduous physical tasks and a great deal of time spent in the development of sacred dances. These were performed in France, England and finally in New York in 1924. Shortly after Gurdjieff's return from America he had a very serious car accident, in highly mysterious circumstances. After this he devoted himself to writing the three major works of the "All and Everything" series. The Institute was closed and from 1933 he lived almost exclusively in Paris, even during the German occupation from 1939 to 1945. He died in 1949.

ONE VERY REMARKABLE MAN who was responsible for changing the direction of Western thought in the earlier part of our century was Georges Ivanovitch Gurdjieff. He wrote to D.P. Ouspensky in 1916 that:

"In speaking of evolution it is necessary to understand from the outset that no mechanical evolution is possible. The evolution of man is the evolution of consciousness and 'consciousness' cannot evolve unconsciously. The evolution of man is the evolution of his will and 'will' cannot evolve involuntarily. The evolution of man is the evolution of his power of doing, and 'doing' cannot be the result of things which 'happen'." [5]

This "Way of the Will" seems to be the polar opposite to the Taoist approach of "non-doing." The fundamental view of TAO as told by Lao Tzu or Sosan is that "easy is right and right is easy." But it should be remembered that Gurdjieff lived in an age of extreme reliance upon the intellect, thus making it necessary for him to use any device available to provoke his disciples minds over the first threshold, and out into the road.

Gurdjieff maintained that *"Everyman is a three brained being."* This roughly corresponds to the stages of evolutionary development in the brain of reptilian (core,) mammalian (mid-brain) and neo-mammalian (neo-contest.) It is, however, more accurate to describe us as three *centered* beings with: 1) a physical center, a functional, sexual and instinctual focus; 2) an emotional center which is the locus of emotions and feelings; 3) an intellectual center, which is the seat of the mind. The fate of everyman is to be unbalanced and out of harmony with these centers. We apparently don't have a single point of gravity from which to operate. Most of us are overwhelmed by one or the other of the three tendencies. Gurdjieff divided the whole mass of human beings into three types, corresponding to the dominance of each center.

Man number one is thus a slave to his physical brain. This is the parrot man, the imitator who has no independent thought but relies on the ideas of others and the conditioning programs of society. He imitates the behavior of others as unquestioningly as any animal copying the behavior of its parents. He clings to old programs because he lacks any ideas of his own.

Man number two is a creature of whims. He takes interest only in those things which immediately catch his fancy. He requires instant emotional gratification and

therefore he is constantly bombarded and affected by the environment and those around him.

Man number three is the man of theory, the scholar, the intellectual, who for the most part is caught up in idle speculation. He is the perfectionist seeking perfect solutions for non-existent problems; a man who might calculate how many angels could stand on the head of a pin.

Although everyone belongs to one or another of theses categories and combinations of them, an individual can, through conscious effort, schooling and hard work on himself, break the mechanical patterns and transform himself into man number four.

In this man all three centers begin to function in accord. No single aspect is dominant and no aspect is confused with another. Everything is harmoniously in balance, giving rise to a center of balance within the individual. From this firm foundation the seeker can move upwards to the higher emotional and higher thinking centers. Gurdjieff maintained that everyone has these and they are *always working correctly*!

The Way of the Pathless Land

Jiddhu Krishnamurti was born in 1895 in Andhra Pradesh, South India. In 1908, when he was only thirteen, he was "discovered" by C.W. Leadbeater and Annie Besant and was prepared to become the vehicle for the Lord Maitreya or the World Teacher as had been predicted by the Theosophists. Krishnamurti disbanded the whole organization that had grown up around him and resigned as head of the Order of the Star in 1929.
His distrust of any organized cult or religion remained with him throughout his teaching. He maintained that Truth was limitless and of concern to the individual and that it could not be bounded by any organization, sect or religion.
It is said that his true awakening did not come until 1948 when he was in India, but even before that his teachings had profound effects upon many leading scientists, writers and philosophers. He managed to give discourses right up to his death in 1986 at the age of 91.

"That immense energy and intelligence has been using this body for 70 years... a 12 cylinder engine... that's a pretty long time and now the body can't stand any more." [7]

OF ALL THE SPIRITUAL GENIUSES OF OUR CENTURY Jiddhu Krishnamurti is perhaps the best known and yet the most enigmatic. Proclaimed by a huge esoteric organization as the vehicle for the "Maitreya," or a reincarnation of the Buddha, he disbanded the organization, declaring that organizations destroy the truth. Surrounded by followers who saw in him the promised World Teacher he continually admonished them against focusing on the container and not the content, advising them to look within themselves for the answers to their continual questioning.

Perhaps the tragedy of his teachings, however, is that even fifty years later those same followers were still listening to him.

Krishnaji's message was clear, uncompromising and amazingly consistent throughout the seventy years of his teaching. In 1929 he disbanded the Order of the Star which had been created around him. *"I maintain that Truth is a pathless Land, and you cannot approach it by any path whatsoever, by any religion, by any sect. That is my point of view and I adhere to that absolutely and unconditionally. Truth, being limitless, unconditioned, unapproachable by any path whatsoever, cannot be organized; nor should any organization be formed to lead or to coerce people along any particular path."* [6]

This is plain enough. He then states that he wants no followers. *"The moment you follow someone, you cease to follow Truth."*

And his message?

"I have only one purpose: to make man free, to urge him towards freedom; to help him break away from all limitations, for that alone will give him eternal happiness, will give him the unconditioned realization of the Self."

"Because I am free, unconditioned, whole — not the part, not the relative but the whole Truth that is eternal — I desire those who seek to understand me to be free, not to follow me, not to make out of me a cage which will become a religion, a sect. Rather should they be free from all fears — from the fear of religion, from the fear of salvation, from the fear of death, from the fear of life itself. My purpose is to make man unconditionally free, for I maintain that the only spirituality is the incorruptibility of the Self which is eternal, is the harmony between reason and love.

This is the absolute, unconditioned Truth which is life itself. I want therefore to set man free, rejoicing as the bird in the clear sky, unburdened, independent, ecstatic in that freedom."[8]

His teaching is deceptively simple but requires a single-minded integrity and a great deal more courage than most of us possess. He told us that truth is within us and can only be discovered by each one of us — alone. We have all that is needed.

No one else, no path, no maps, no crutches are of any use, only an unrelenting and continual awareness of who we are and how we act will reveal the real situation. To do this we must examine, with no self- indulgence or judgment whatsoever, just who we are and what we are. No preconceived ideas, theories or comforting fantasies will help as we investigate our mind to see the egotism and self-ignorance, which are the roots of all our suffering and violence.

To live in the real is to live in the present moment which prevents us gathering and garnishing our memories, identifying with old thoughts and the past.

Living in the present fuses the observer and the observed, harmonizing the mind. Once this is set in motion, the higher functions of evolution take over and start moving on their own account. Look at yourself with clear eyes and the rest will take care of itself.

A significant little story told by Pupul Jayakar illuminates the sheer simplicity of Krishnamurti's teaching. He was in a car with three friends who were heatedly discussing "awareness." There was a jolt to the car but no-one paid any attention as they were all intent upon the arguments. Krishnaji turned to them and asked what everyone was discussing. "Awareness" came the reply and they all wanted him to join. He asked *"Did any of you notice what happened just now?"*
"No."
"We knocked down a goat, did you not see it?"
"No."
"And you were discussing awareness?"

No Way

"The people who come to see me do not stay very long. They come a few times or hang around for a few months, then either go back to their ordinary lives or go on to some fellow who promises them what they seek. Some of them become devotees of Bubba Free John, the latest American avatar. Either way that's fine with me.

"But one thing I will never do is deceive them. I will never suggest in any way that I can give them anything. I will never hook them into some phony baloney idea about practicing undifferentiated awareness and the observer being the same as the observed, and all that."[9]

U.G. KRISHNAMURTI INSISTS THAT ONE OF THE MAJOR BARRIERS to self-discovery is our reliance upon other peoples' visions, and our inability to look and listen for ourselves.

When asked to sum up his teachings he replied curtly: *"The phrase would be — I cannot help you!"* He does not even spare his namesake, Jiddhu Krishnamurti, in his scathing criticism of any who claim that there is a way to truth. Even though J. Krishnamurti spurned gurus and organizations, U.G. Krishnamurti is even more adamant in his observation of the futility of all teachings. *"I don't talk of meditative state. It is not this; it is not that."* (He refers here to the "via negativa" approach of both Zen and the teaching of J. Krishnamurti.) *Meditation is a self-centered activity — it strengthens the very Self you want to be free from!"*

He gives no teaching which implies methods, systems or new ways of transformation. What he gives *"is simply a description of the way I am functioning. It is just a description of the natural state of man that is the way you, stripped of the machinations of thought, are also functioning."*

"The natural state is not the state of a self-realized or God-realized man, it is not a thing to be achieved or attained, it is not a thing to be willed into existence; it is there — it is the living state. This state is just the functional activity of life. By 'life' I do not mean something abstract; it is the life of the senses, functioning naturally without the interference of thought. Thought is an interloper, which thrusts itself into the affairs of the senses. It has a profound motive; thought directs the activity of the senses 'to get something out of them, and uses them to give continuity to itself. This constant demand to experience everything is because if we don't, we come to

an end — that is, the 'we' as we know ourselves and we don't want that at all. What we want is the continuity...!"[10]

So he points out: "*You can never understand this; you can only experience this in terms of your past experience. This is outside the realm of experience. The natural state is acausal: it just happens. No communication is possible, and none necessary. The only thing that is real to you is the way you are functioning; it is an act of futility to relate my description to the way you are functioning. When you stop all this comparison, what is there is your natural state. Then you will not listen to anybody.*"

Of all the remarkable men who have come into their natural state U.G. Krishnamurti must be the most uncompromising. Perhaps for that reason alone he is a rare breath of fresh air. So often, even the most radical of the masters are forced to use the language of their traditions or of time honored ideas. But U.G. Krishnamurti cuts across all the accretions of religion and conventional mysticism to batter home the point that no approach, no path will help. It is the paths themselves which are the barrier.

"*I am not out to liberate anybody. You have to liberate yourself, and you are unable to do that.*

"*What I have to say will not do it. I am only interested in describing this state, in clearing away the occultation and mystification in which those people in the 'holy business' have shrouded the whole thing. Maybe I can convince you not to waste a lot of time and energy, looking for a state which does not exist, except in your imagination. What makes one person come into his natural state, and not another person, I don't know. Perhaps it is written in the cells. It is acausal. It is not an act of volition on your part; you can't bring it about. There is absolutely nothing you can do. You can distrust any man who tells you how he got into this state. One thing you can be sure of is that he cannot possibly know himself, and cannot possibly communicate it to you. There is a built-in triggering mechanism in the body. If the experiencing structure of thought happens to let go, the other thing will take over in its own way.*

"*The functioning of the body will be a totally different functioning, without the interference of thought except when it is necessary to communicate with somebody. To put it in the boxing-ring phrase, you have to 'throw in the towel,' be totally helpless. No one can help you, and you cannot help yourself.*"[11]

Uppaluri Gopala Krishnamurti was born in 1918 in South India. He was raised by his grandparents and educated into a highly religious background. Although suspecting a great deal of hypocrisy behind the ritual austerities and meditations, he met Ramana Maharshi while still in his teens and asked the old sage "Can you give me what you have?" Raman replied, "I can give you, but can you take it?" His authentic search began after this meeting. He became, against his natural inclination, the general secretary of the Theosophic Society and met J. Krishnamurti. He quickly realized that there was no way of understanding what J.K. was trying to communicate. About his 49th year he was puzzled by the appearance of many strange psychic powers or siddhis. At that time he was in London living penniless and idling in the streets for over three years. In 1967 he entered what he calls the natural state or the "calamity." Since then he has never allowed any organization or disciples to gather around him. For this reason he is little known to the West. His message being "I cannot help you" makes this hardly surprising.

Way of Communion

Franklin Albert Jones was born on Long Island, New York in 1939. It is claimed that he was born fully enlightened, but at the age of two he made a conscious decision to enter a normal everyday life. By the early 1960s he was beginning to have strange awakenings in the psychic stage. In New York he met Swami Rudi, a practitioner of Kundalini Yoga, and under his direction he studied to enter a Lutheran Ministry. However, after two years he experienced the first awakening to Level Five. He visited India in 1968 and the Ashram of Rudi's teacher, Swami Muktananda. It was here that he underwent even further ascent to the higher functions. Even though he remained a devotee of the goddess Shakti (the female principle of Tantra Yoga) he abandoned all the conventional practices of Yoga. In 1970, while sitting in the Vedanta Temple in Los Angeles, he re-awoke to his original childhood state.

Returning from a pilgrimage to India he assumed the name Bubba Free John, which served for his first revelatory period. This then became Da Free John in the second stage of his teaching work. Recently he has entered the third stage and is known as Love Ananda. He lives on an island in Fiji as a semi-recluse with close friends and devotees.

Perhaps of all the emotive words within the mystic vocabulary "surrender" is the one which sticks in the gullet of most

DA FREE JOHN, OR AS HE IS NOW KNOWN, LOVE ANANDA, is considered by many to be a true and authentic religious genius. John White for example says that *"he clarifies and unifies the entire spectrum of issues and experiences that concern spiritual seekers and consciousness researchers. His teaching about enlightenment seems unsurpassed by any spiritual teacher of any time."* He certainly manages, to clarify the entire rainbow spectrum of man's evolutionary consciousness.

In the expression of his teaching and in contrast to both U.G and Jiddhu Krishnamurti we find the fundamental, essential argument — the "Master is the Message."

He sees the whole human endeavor as a seven stage process which differs little from either the ancient Indian Vedanta or the Yoga of Patanjali. Indeed it is his unique contribution to our understanding that he has brought these traditions alive again. But in doing so he stresses that many of the "exalted states" of Levels Four, Five and Six of our earlier map are the usual territory of the conventional mystics. The so-called religious visions, yogic trance states, the ecstatic and pleasurable experiences that can be introduced by turning one's attention inward, while tracing the various stations of the brain-mind are not *reality*. They are necessary stages of the journey on the Way of Becoming, but what Da Free John insists on is the Way of Being. He sees the whole endeavor of man as an effort to enter the final, seventh stage of a radical and intuitive identification with the Original Source, what he calls the Radiant Transcendental Being.

This can only happen when the seeker continuously, moment by moment surrenders the sense of self to that Radiant Being.

It is said that the Way of Divine Communion matures with the seven limbs, or disciplines of the traditional yoga of Patanjali (see page 156) but the key to them all would appear to be truly "hearing" the spiritual master and entering into a deep surrender to him as the manifestation of that ultimate seventh stage. This is the second alternative we encountered earlier in which Ramana Maharshi offered the seeker:

"There are two ways; ask yourself 'Who am I?' or submit!"

As the devotee begins to awaken, powerful alchemical changes occur in the body. The glandular chemistry, the nervous system, the brain and even the cells undergo a radical transformation. The *whole body* begins to radiate and in the final explosion of consciousness the whole body itself is enlightened.

The key to the totality of this esoteric anatomy lies in the heart.

Here we come to Da Free John's unique contribution, for he re-establishes the seat of the self, the Soul, within the heart. He stresses that most spiritual practices stop at the brain-mind, whereas it is only by opening the eyes of the heart that one can enter that final state of Sahaj-Samadhi. Here the radical intuition realizes that the energy of the life-current itself is identical to consciousness. His method is a combination of yoga practices with communion with the master; Samadhi is the *"foundation and core of the practice, rather than its result."*

Fundamental to all his teaching seems the role of the master and the spiritual adept and how a devotee can tune into his particular resonance. What he says here is crucial to our later understanding of any evolutionary changes in the species.

"Tuning in to a fully developed Master Field, where all of these evolutionary processes have already taken place, permits those changes to be magnified and quickened or, in effect, lived into that system without its having to pass through certain of the processes associated with the individual struggle to evolve.

"Therefore, as I have indicated, the Spiritual Adept is a unique mechanism in Nature provided for the sake of the spiritual and altogether human evolution of human beings as well as the transformation and evolution of all beings and all processes that exist in the cosmos."[12]

Westerners. There simply is no equivalent concept in the West for either surrender or submission. It does not mean the cowering, rigid obedience of the Hebrew bible or the capitulation of a general or a nation. The closest description might be that the disciple acknowledges that he, himself, is blind, insane, without vision and that the master or guru has sight and is committed to helping the disciple to see for himself. What is needed is unconditional trust for the disciple is like a man who is blindfolded and doesn't know it. The role of the master is to get him to undo the knot and take it off. He uses any strategy which might work however bizarre it might seem. Surrender, by complete preoccupation and absorption in the master, is the bridge needed to transform communication into *communion* and the tool to untie the knot is trust. It is the traditional way of a living master. The way of surrender is said to be the fastest route to enlightenment for the master has a "Buddha Field" around him which can resonate with the disciple. His way as a whole is not the method of yoga, but an ongoing process, triggered by himself as a master, which develops towards its own perfection in which yoga is both fulfilled and transcended.

This way is also called the Way of Divine Ignorance. The Christian mystic Dionysius, nineteen centuries ago, echoes this in his seemingly obscure statement: "*Not knowing is the most intimate.*"

The Way of Celebration

Rajneesh Chandra Mohan was born in 1931 in Central India. He had an isolated childhood with his grandparents until the age of seven. At fourteen he experienced his first satori in a temple, after a powerful premonition of death. From the age of fourteen until twenty-one he experimented with many kinds of paranormal behavior and meditation, having a second satori in 1952. He was a brilliant, rebellious and highly eccentric student who won the All India University Debating Trophy. He entered the natural state of enlightenment in 1953 at the age of twenty-one. During the following years he remained at the university and allowed the condition to settle becoming a professor of Philosophy at Jabalpur and started traveling and lecturing all over India.

WE NOW COME TO THE THIRD AND PROBABLY MOST CONTROVERSIAL of the pioneering evolutionary figures of this century. Bhagwan Shree Rajneesh is the maverick, a spiritual rebel who has often been involved in "street fighting" tactics with politicians, governments and religious leaders. He has been variously called the most dangerous man since Christ, a charlatan, and the new Maitreya but, as he points out, Socrates was also considered dangerous for much the same reasons.

He is a man you either hate or love, or, as some assure us, both at the same time. One might wonder what kind of message he provides that manages to polarize opinions in this way; for it is a message which has roused virtually all the orthodox religions to close their ranks against him, demanding action from their various nations and states.

At first glance this overreaction seems ludicrous certainly when his "dangerous" credo turns out to be "Love," "Light," "Laughter" and a total celebration and reverence for "Life." But such a phenomenon as laughter is often seen as a direct threat to any organized religion which takes itself too seriously. Although there have been laughing monks of Zen and the juicy, wicked humor of Georges Gurdjieff, by and large the world of the spirit hasn't been exactly a laugh a line.

To Rajneesh life is a superb joke, a constant play and he views seriousness as mankind's worst dis-ease.

While celebration and love for life itself as a fundamental ingredient of spiritual life is a new innovation in the world of religion, the tradition from which Rajneesh springs might well be one of the most venerated in the East. However, it is virtually unknown to the West. Simply stated, Bhagwan Shree Rajneesh can be seen as a divine madman.

The Indian Upanishads testify to six categories of enlightened masters or adepts; the last and most venerated of those is called the *avadhuta*. This is the "crazy master" who seems dedicated to shaking up everyone by exhibiting the most outrageous behavior, directly challenging the status quo and all our accepted codes and rules of living. Of all the evolutionary pioneers we have met so far such an individual is the least comfortable to live with.

They are controversial by definition, anti-establishment, unpredictable and are invariably eccentric, if enthusiastic, pranksters. One ancient text even likens them to a boa constrictor awaiting its prey. And their quarry is the *ego* — that elusive, non-existent and illusory identity which we all so lovingly carry around with us. Anything which can shock a disciple out of his usual somnambulistic state is used by the master.

Some avadhutas have been known to extend their activities beyond that of their disciples, taking on whole villages and towns, shocking the sleepy citizens out of their usual rigid grooves. Our modern global counterpart, Rajneesh, managed to stir up the political and religious leaders of India and then moved on to the U.S.A., now finding himself barred from entry to almost every nation on the planet.

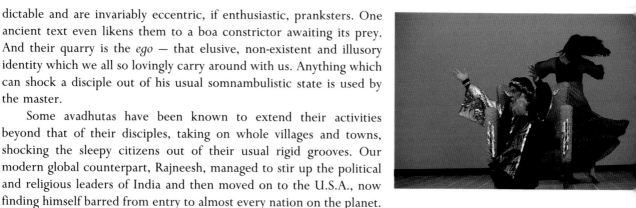

In 1966 he held the first meditation camp in Rajasthan and resigned his professorship to devote all his energies to his work. He settled in Bombay giving controversial lectures to audiences of over 50,000. He moved to the Shree Rajneesh Ashram in Poona during 1974. This ashram became the largest Humanistic Therapy center in the world. He traveled to the U.S.A. in 1981 and was the guest of the Rajneesh Commune there until 1984 when, at the center of political and religious controversy, he was arrested and deported from the States. Now settled once again in Poona he has continued giving daily discourses. He has a following of so-called "sannyasins" which probably numbers half a million throughout the world.

An avadhuta is a radical, religious madman who often appears drunk and "god intoxicated" (to the Sufis to be "drunk with God" makes one immune to the "poisons of the world".) An avadhuta has supposedly freed himself (shaken off = *ava + dhuta*) of all constraints and relative truths and sees life as one great joke or the divine play. It is said that *"Nothing is sacred to him who moves in, and is moved by the Sacred itself,"* so it is small wonder that such a man or woman poses an anarchic threat of chaos to rigid social norms, for such a being cannot be bound by any man-made rules.

An ancient and otherwise sober scripture on Hatha Yoga over a thousand years ago announced:

"Who is sometimes an enjoyer
Sometimes a renouncer
Sometimes naked or like a demon
And sometimes so upright and well-behaved
Such is called an avadhuta."

But, if Rajneesh is such an exotic madman, there is an extraordinary method in that madness. Like all avadhutas his concern is to enlighten. Nothing else matters.

What also distinguishes his particular brand of spirituality is that one must be prepared to give a total commitment to everything life offers and to celebrate and revere each and every moment.

Alongside of this teaching comes his unique vision of a new man which, we will find, has remarkable similarities to the portrait of the new species to be found with the last chapter of this book.

"I would like you to be Zorba the Greek and Gautama the Buddha together simultaneously. Less than that won't do!

"Zorba represents the earth with all its flowers and greenery and mountains and rivers and oceans, and Buddha represents the sky with all its stars and clouds and rainbows. But the sky without the earth will be empty, the sky cannot laugh without the earth, and the earth without the sky will be dead. Bring both together and a dance comes into existence. The earth and the sky dancing together and there is laughter, there is joy, there is celebration... [13] Of course laughter and dance and celebration require a total response of the total being with nothing partial or unwhole thus forcing a seeker into the present moment. The mind, a mechanism of past and future, cannot exist in the present so by this simple, natural method the disciple can bypasses all the more conventional meditations.

Like Master Da Free John and Shri Ramana Maharshi, Bhagwan Shree Rajneesh maintains that surrender to a master and the resonating communion between the master and disciple is the fastest route to Samadhi. But unlike traditional masters, his whole message is one of the balance between polarities. Trust and surrender must be balanced by intelligent doubt and rebellion; Zorba must balance Buddha, science must balance mysticism. *Both Baka*, the state of alertness, and *Fana*, the state of ecstasy, must oppose one another like the two hemispheres of the brain or the sympathetic and the parasympathetic systems of the body. There must be a balance between the Zen satori through the brain-mind or head center and that of the Sufi through the heart center. There must be a balance between love on the one hand and meditation on the other.

As a master he is known to be full of maddening contradictions and his roles swing wildly between sinner and saint. Yet, as he points out, he is just a mirror and whosoever stands in front of the mirror sees his own reflection.

The Way of a Woman

SO FAR OUR COMPANIONS ALONG THE ROAD HAVE BEEN MALE. Yet, strangely, it is claimed that more women than men attain the natural state and they are invariably the most promising disciples. So what do we know of the female "masters?" A brief glance at the list in the column will show how few have been actually acknowledged in the past. There are even traditions, like the Jainas, who insist that women have to be reborn as men for the final moment of truth. Even Buddha said, on initiating the first women into sannyas, that instead of his message being alive for two thousand five hundred years it then would only last for five hundred years. It is said that once a woman enters the natural state she has no desire to become a teacher. She knows that when the gold brick has to fall on a seeker, it will do so.

While the taste of the ocean may be the same, we have seen that the expression of it is profoundly different for each individual. Is there also possibly a comparable difference in expression between the two sexes? Certainly when we turn to "the Mother," there is a very different quality to her words. Her message is birth. Her vision is of a birth of a new consciousness which exists at the level of the "body of cells."

In reading her words it is tempting for a man to speculate that women, who by their very nature are more receptive and attuned to the deep cycles of the Earth and to the organic creativity of life, would naturally be drawn to an enfolding of consciousness around the basic forms of existence. When the Mother speaks of the normal concept of "liberation" she does so as a real female.

"...And all the means — which could be termed artificial, including Nirvana — all the means of getting out are worthless. I don't know. But salvation is physical; not at all mental, but physical. I mean it isn't veiled or hidden or anything; it's here. And everything else, including death, appears really as a falsehood, that is, something that doesn't exist."

"The sublime state is the natural state! It's you who are constantly in a state that is not natural, that is not normal, that is false, a deformation."[14] She was in her 80s when the real journey began, and despite painful illness and infirmity she conducted an experiment on her own body well into her 90s.

Mira Alfassa was born in Paris in 1878 of an Egyptian, marxist mother and a Turkish banker. Her cosmopolitan upbringing brought her in contact with many artists and philosophers and she became close friends with the painter Monet, the sculptors Rodin and Gustave Moreau. Her lifestyle as an artist and mathematician was, she admitted, entirely materialistic but on accompanying her husband to India she met Shri Aurobindo, remaining with him until his death in 1950 and helping to establish and run the ashram which bears his name — Auroville. In 1951 the Mother, as she was then known, started an extraordinary diary of her journey of a "yoga of the cells." This had accumulated into thousands of documents by the time of her death at the age of 95. So far only three of the thirteen volumes have been published by a close disciple and friend, Sat Prem.

A few of the women who, traditionally, are believed to have entered the natural state and who have taught or created orders around them are: Mary Magdalene, Hanna Rachel, Ima Shalom, Miriam, St. Teresa of Avila, St. Catharine, Dame Julian of Norwich, Arya Chandana, Jayanti, Meerabai, Yasodhara, Gautami, Chaiyono, Rabiya, Lalla, Bhairava, Brahmani, Mira Richard (The Mother).

"What the body is learning is this: to replace the mental rule of intelligence by the spiritual rule of consciousness (the other state.) And that makes a tremendous difference (although it doesn't look like much, you can't notice anything,) to the point that it increases the body's capabilities a hundred-fold. When the body follows certain rules, however broad they may be, it is a slave to those rules, and its possibilities are limited accordingly. But when it is governed by the spirit and consciousness (of the other state,) its possibilities and flexibility become exceptional! And that's how it will acquire the capacity to extend its life at will. The 'necessities' lose some of their authority; it becomes possible to go this way or that way. All the laws — the laws that were the laws of Nature — lose some of their tyrannical power, you could say. It's a progressive victory over all the 'musts.' And all the laws of Nature, all human laws, all habits, all rules are gradually relaxed and eventually come to an end. In particular, that whole sense of rigidity, absoluteness and near-invincibility brought about by the mind will disappear.

"But if it's happening in one body, it can happen in all bodies! I am not made of something different from other human beings. My body is made the same way. And my body was as stupid, as ignorant, as unconscious and stubborn as every other body in the world. It all began when the doctors declared that I was very ill — that was the beginning of everything. Because the body was completely emptied of its habits and energies; and then very slowly, the cells awakened to a new receptivity. Otherwise it would be hopeless! Because matter was originally less conscious than a stone...even a stone has some form of organization, it was certainly worse than a stone: it was inert and absolutely unconscious; and little by little it awakened. Well, it's the same here: for the animal to become a human being, all it took was the infusion of the mental consciousness; and now the consciousness that was buried deep down is awakening. The mind was withdrawn, the vital was withdrawn (that's what gave the appearance of a serious illness at the time), and as the body was left to itself, the cells gradually began to awaken to consciousness. And from that, after further working and prodding (I don't know how long it will take) a new form will emerge, which will be what Sri Aurobindo called the supramental form — and it will be.... whatever, I don't know what to call those beings. What will be their mode of expression, how will they communicate?.. In man, all that evolved very slowly. And when man emerged from the animal, there was no way to record the process; now it's quite different, so it will be more interesting...."[15]

Common Ground

It seems all the more poignant that it is a woman called "The Mother" who looks ahead to the birth of a new species. *"Remember that you are at an exceptional hour in a unique epoch, that you have this great happiness, the invaluable privilege of being present at the birth of a new world."*

TWO THOUSAND FIVE HUNDRED YEARS AGO IN INDIA PATANJALI DECLARED that the final stage of Yoga, Sahaj-Samadhi *"fulfills the purpose of evolution. Now the process by which evolution unfolds through time is understood."* Twenty-five centuries later Da Free John is able to say: *"Man is also a new stage in the event of time. His newness or uniqueness is hidden. This higher brain is the structural cauldron of the present and future evolutionary changes of Man and what is beyond Man in the scheme of the World."*

However skeptical an anthropologist, a geneticist, embryologist or psychologist might be of the so-called "objective" or scientific validity of such a bold statement, they cannot, up to time of writing at least, offer any better explanation. For, the more modern researchers delve into the nature of the life process, the less sure they are of any foundations beneath their feet.

The much misunderstood and often mis-aligned disciplines of the sage on the other hand suggest an entirely different approach with a far richer harvest. The ways of the mystic or seer are not hypothetical. They do not propose an idea and then support it with evidence to substantiate the theory. These are testimonies of men and women who have recorded what they have experienced. Whether we are prepared to take these, often bizarre, statements on trust is of course another matter entirely. The reader will only know whether what they say is true if he or she ventures on the Way personally. If a man tells you that all you have to do to see the beauties of a sunrise is to remove your blindfold, then all the most erudite abstract theories about blindfolds will not help you to see it. But for the purposes of this particular inquiry these various ways have been examined solely as corroborating evidence of an evolutionary direction. The paths also shed light upon the elusive mechanisms which can be set in motion up the evolutionary ladder.

At this point it might be well to summarize some of the evidence gathered so far from investigating these ways or paths which claim to lead to the "natural enlightened state of Man."

1) As a species we seem to be an essential part of an evolutionary process through time.

2) It would appear that consciousness is the true evolutionary environment of man.

3) The Void, in Its Original State of Being, was as if in a deep and sound sleep. As It awoke It passed through various levels of a Divine Dream. It awoke, however, with the false consciousness that It was man. Only by retracing the stages of the Divine Dream, this time *consciously*, will the Void finally see the true image in the mirror which is Itself. So it is said, we are already that which we seek and the mystic quest is a paradoxical journey towards ourselves. Man is the mirror of himself.

4) The driving force of evolution is the prime urge: "To be known."

5) There seem to be seven levels to the Divine Dream, seven zones to the whole evolutionary process with six crucial thresholds, like rungs of a ladder. Each of these needs a massive surge of energy or consciousness in order to be crossed at all. These quantum leaps are traditionally called satoris once past Level Four. In the evolutionary environment of consciousness they correspond to a jump in relative magnitude from non-life to life or from the biological realm to that of self-reflective consciousness. Simply put, they are totally discontinuous with the preceding level.

6) The satoris or samadhis which mark the leaps across the higher levels of evolutionary consciousness are unpredictable, sudden, unannounced and unrepeatable events which cannot be either coerced or forced into being. They happen in their own good time.

7) The *natural state* of man is one of enlightenment. It is not just some vague consciousness that becomes enlightened but the whole psycho-physical body. For our particular investigation this is significant and crucial. In the final explosion of consciousness, and even in the earlier stages of the process, the body goes through radical and subtle changes at a cellular level. It is said that all the atoms are blasted into new configurations as the whole body-mind adjusts to the new energies available in the natural state. It would seem that up to this point it is our thoughts that have actually interfered with the smooth running and natural harmonies of the organism.

8) The major evolutionary sleepers or higher functions of the mind-body are located within the glands associated with the chakras or energy wheels, the heart and the brain. Once the process is set in motion they seem to follow their own schedule. Gurdjieff even claims they are always working perfectly, in any event.

9) As we are already that which we seek and have only to trigger the higher evolutionary functions in order that they can work freely it can be seen that the master's work is both paradoxical and absurd. They have to take away things we don't have (ego) and give us things which we already possess.
"*This is something I can't give, because you have it. Why should I give it to you? It is ridiculous to ask for a thing you already have.*"[16]

10) As we find that we cannot force or coerce the evolutionary sleepers into action, any method looks as if it is doomed from the start. The ways or paths to the "goal" are actually nothing more than one individual's way of re-awakening to the reality of the situation. In the long run each seeker must find his or her own unique way. So we find that most methods are really devices used by the master to start the disciple on the journey.
But if the seeker clings to a track made by someone else he will probably get lost. While the master lives he carefully tailors the cloth to fit the seeker, but when the master is gone it is futile for anyone to try to re-shape the seeker to fit clothing which was not designed for him in the first place.

11) As we are already that which we seek, all that is needed is a 180 degree turn to look one's self in the eye. In Christian terms *Repent Ye* originally meant to *look around*, to *re-evaluate*. But the courage needed to turn to face the Void or the "Faceless" is far more than most of us possess. So we manufacture fantasy worlds of power, magic and the para-normal, and blissful flights to describe what we think enlightenment might be rather than truly facing its shattering nature.
The following is perhaps one of the clearest statements ever made by someone in the natural state: "*This state is not in your interest. You are only interested in continuity. You want to continue, probably on a different level, and to function in a different dimension, but you want to continue somehow. You wouldn't touch this with a barge pole. This is going to liquidate what you call 'you', all of you — higher self,*

A New Evolutionary Direction

IF WE TENTATIVELY ACCEPT that the driving force behind evolution is the urge "to be known," that primal need for Existence to see Itself in a mirror then the true purpose of humankind could be to offer Existence a reflective surface in which It can view Itself.

At this point in the investigation the ground begins to disappear beneath our feet for it would seem that every time a new mirror reaches to the Void, bringing with it a new consciousness of Itself, Existence becomes more and more *conscious*. Put another way it could be said that originally the Primal Consciousness of the Void was asleep — unconscious of Itself. It became conscious only in the body of man which is at the third level. In climbing back up the evolutionary ladder It gradually became, through the efforts of the evolutionary pioneers, more aware of Itself and Its true predicament.

Finally on reaching the seventh level there was a recognition of Its original condition. It was not man at all but God.

Now, if we are to believe what mystics report, each time a human consciousness reaches the Void the Primal Consciousness undergoes a profound change. Ripples and eddies spread throughout the universe (or universes.) All and everything changes in that ecstatic reunion with Itself, including, it would seem, the whole quality of the evolutionary urge itself. And here we come to the question of the new species.

Having seen the evidence so far, it would seem that if our species as a whole are the present custodians of Level Three, it would be logical to assume that the next stage of evolution will be a species which is at Level Four or beyond.

The next evolutionary jump could create an entirely new direction. If, for instance, the next species started at the level of the psychic heart (Level Four) manifesting such miraculous paranormal powers as control over matter, telekinesis, telepathy and astral projection, then the species as a whole would be in a profoundly different world of the spirit to the one we know.

We have no way of predicting just what such a state might be any more than a brown bear at Level Two has a projection of what it might be like to be a human being.

lower self, soul, Atman, conscious, subconscious — all of that. You come to a point, and then you say 'I need time.' So Sadhana (inquiry and religious endeavor) comes into the picture, and you say to yourself 'Tomorrow I will understand.' This structure is born of time and functions in time, but does not come to an end through time. If you don't understand now, you are not going to understand tomorrow. What you are looking for does not exist. You would rather tread an enchanted ground with beatific visions of a radical transformation of that non-existent self of yours into a state of being which is conjured up by some bewitching phrases. That takes you away from your natural state — it is a movement away from yourself. To be yourself requires extraordinary intelligence. You are 'blessed' with that intelligence; nobody need give it to you, nobody can take it away from you. He who lets that express itself in its own way is a natural man."[17]

12) It is claimed (true, this is mostly by masters) that the fastest method of transformation is being in the presence of a master, someone who has already entered the natural state. It is true, however, that these individuals are surrounded by a resonating Master Field, or Buddha Field which can rouse the evolutionary sleeper in each of us. This is one of the most revolutionary and significant facts to emerge from the evidence, because it could be the method of triggering the sleeper of the species as a whole.

13) There is an almost unanimous agreement that the whole evolutionary process consists of seven levels (Summarized in the Appendix.)

CHAPTER TWO

Witness

WE MAY PERHAPS NOW look at what this mysterious enlightened natural state is like? Has anyone ever described it? If it really is the ultimate expression of the evolution of man, surely we might have some records. The seers tell us that there is an insurmountable obstacle to any form of discovery. "We don't speak the same language. You only know experience and we only know the *absence* of experience." So something might be *said*, but something quite different might be *heard*.

As man ascends the evolutionary Jacob's ladder there is a qualitative leap needed to gain each rung. In the lower stages the jump from the biological Level Two to the level of self-reflective consciousness of the level above is a complete transformation. There appears to be nothing in the world of cells or simple organisms which corresponds to self-reflective consciousness. The difference between "gene" and "meme" is unbridgeable and one way only. For while the level above encompasses the level below, the reverse is not the case. Consciousness can embrace a plant, yet a plant cannot comprehend consciousness. It is like a one-way mirror: as we ascend each rung and look back the level below is clear and transparent, but to those below the level above appears as a mirror to their own.

The problem arises only when a consciousness at Level Five tries to express that state to one residing at Level Three.

MANY DESCRIPTIONS HAVE BEEN RECORDED of satoris: sudden flashes of deep insight and visionary states. As we ourselves are considered blind, often these visions can be mistaken for experiences of the enlightened state. In the middle half of the last century a Canadian psychologist, Richard Bucke, described such an event.

"All at once without any warning of any kind, I found myself wrapped in a flame-colored cloud. For an instant I thought of fire, an immense conflagration somewhere close by in the great city; the next, I knew that the fire was within myself. Directly afterward there came upon me a sense of

*"It is not outer awareness
It is not inner awareness
Nor is it suspension of awareness
It is not knowing
It is not unknowing
Nor is it knowingness itself
It can neither be seen nor understood
It cannot be given boundaries
It is ineffable and beyond thought
It is indefinable
It is known only through becoming it."*
(Mandukya Upanishad)

Flight of the Unknown to the Unknown

exultation, of immense joyousness accompanied or immediately followed by an intellectual illumination impossible to describe. Among other things, I did not merely come to believe, but I saw that the universe is not composed of dead matter, but is, on the contrary, a living Presence; I became conscious in myself of eternal life. It was not a conviction that I would have eternal life, but a consciousness that I possessed eternal life then; I saw that all men are immortal; that the cosmic order is such that without any peradventure all things work together for the good of each and all; that the foundation principle of the world, of all worlds, is what we call love, and that happiness of each and all is in the long run absolutely certain. The vision lasted a few seconds and was gone; but the memory of it and the sense of reality of what it taught has remained during the quarter of a century which has since elapsed." [18]

Alan Watts quotes Bernard Berenson as giving one of the clearest accounts of satori.

"It was a morning in early summer. A silver haze shimmered and trembled over the lime trees. The air was laden with their fragrance. The temperature was like a caress. I remembered — I need not recall — that I climbed up a tree and felt suddenly immersed in Itness. I did not call it by that name. I had no need for words. It and I were one." [19]

Such descriptions appear to place the experiencer at Level Four, Five or Six and such visions have often been taken for enlightenment itself. But what of John of the Cross?

"The soul is like the crystal that is clear and pure; the more degrees of light it receives the greater the concentration of light there is in it. This enlightenment continues to such a degree that at last it attains a point at which the light is centered in it with such copiousness that it comes to appear to be wholly light and cannot be distinguished from the light... for it is enlightened to the greatest possible extent and thus appears to be light itself." [20]

There is little chance of telling whether such an image is the natural state or just another part of the Divine Dream, for the only one who is qualified to confirm the authentic state is the one who is *in* it.

And the problem is further exacerbated by the fact that at that exalted level there is simply no common referent, no ground which is even vaguely similar.

"You can't possibly understand what I am saying. It is an exercise in futility on your part to try to relate the description of how I am functioning to the way that you are functioning: this is a thing which I cannot communicate."[21]

So what are we trying to do with the following testimonies from our major witnesses, if what they have seen cannot be told? The five witnesses selected are amongst the most significant evolutionary explorers of this or of any time. We are a privileged generation to have so many towering figures in this realm of human exploration. Within this century these five have tried hard to convey their insight and their state even if it is a shadow of a shadow of the real condition.

Something of the fragrance and the immensity and wonder of the natural state somehow filters through. It is with much regret that space does not permit the testimonies of other such figures as Ramana Maharshi, Shri Ramakrishna, Meher Baba or Georges Gurdjieff. However, those chosen exhibit what seems to be the most complete spectrum of human consciousness assembled in one epoch.

Before we listen to what the witnesses have to say we would do well to heed Lao Tzu's first and last warning in the Tao Te Ching: *"The truth that can be told is not the truth."* With that firmly in mind we can proceed. The names of each witness are to be found in the bibliography. They are withheld on the page so there is an opportunity to approach the text with no preconceived ideas.

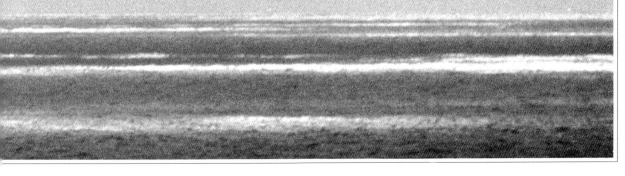

First Witness

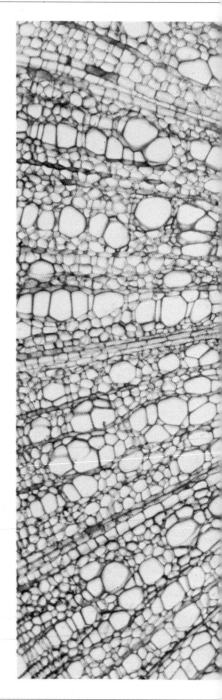

"I AM JUST ON THE BORDER, at the threshold; it's as if there were a semitransparent curtain and you see things on the other side, you try to grasp them, but you can't. But it feels so, so close! Sometimes, I suddenly see myself as a huge concentrated power, pushing and pushing with an inner concentration, to get through."[22]

"I was cast into a formless, limitless vast. It was all-powerful and infinitely rich, as if this vastness were made of countless imperceptible dots — dots that take up no space — of a warm, dark gold. All that was absolutely alive, alive with a power that seemed infinite. And yet motionless. A perfect immobility, but containing an incredible intensity of movement and life! And a life that was so.....multitudinous that you can only call it infinite. And an intensity, a power, a force, and a peace — the peace of eternity. Silence, calm.

"A power capable of everything. Everything. There was that whole impression of power, warmth, gold... It didn't feel fluid: it was like a powdering. And each of those 'things' (I can't call them particles, or fragments, or even dots unless we take dots in the mathematical sense of a point that takes up no space) was like living gold: a powdering of warm gold; I can't say bright, or dark; it wasn't luminous either: a multitude of tiny gold dots, nothing but that. And with a fantastic self-contained power and warmth! And then, at the same time, a sense of plenitude, of peace stemming from absolute power. It was movement at its utmost, infinitely faster than anything we can possibly imagine, and absolute peace, perfect tranquillity at the same time."[23]

"IT IS STRANGE, the mantra has a cohesive effect on the cells: the entire cellular life becomes one solid and compact mass of incredible concentration — with a single vibration.

"Instead of the body's many usual vibrations, there is only one single vibration. It becomes as solid as a rock, one single concentration, as if all the cells of the body were a single mass."[24]

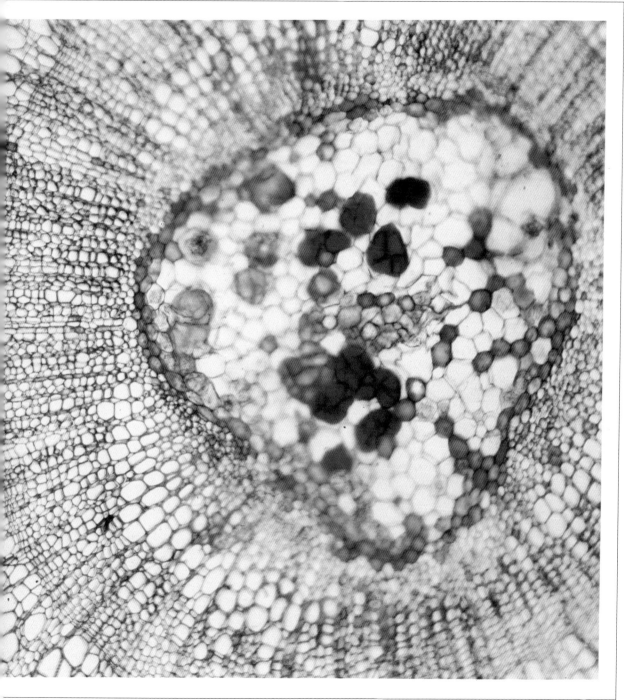

At the Threshold

"It isn't going off into some inaccessible planes, it's RIGHT HERE. Only, for the moment, all the old habits and the general unconsciousness put a sort of cover over it, which prevents us from seeing and feeling. That has to be...removed. And it's everywhere, you see, everywhere, all the time. It doesn't come and go: it's there, all the time, everywhere. It's us, it's our stupidity that prevents us from feeling it. There's no need to go off at all, no need whatsoever.

"... Every possible color is combined without blending together, and combined as luminous dots. Everything is made up of that. It seems to be the true mode of being — I am not entirely sure of it, but in any case it's a much more conscious mode of being. And I see it all the time, with eyes open, with eyes closed — all the time. It gives a curious impression at once of subtlety and penetrability, we might say, of suppleness and much less rigidity of form. The first time the body itself felt that in one part or another...it was a little lost, the impression of something that escapes you. But if one remains very quiet, it is simply replaced by a sort of plasticity or fluidity which seems to be a new cellular mode. Probably, it is what will materially replace the physical ego. But naturally the first contact is always very...surprising. The transition from one way to another is always rather difficult. Although it takes place very gradually, there is a moment, a few seconds of...suspense, to say the least. But this is the way all habits are undone. For all body functions it's the same: blood circulation, digestion, breathing — all body functions. And the transition is not an abrupt replacement of one mode by the other, but a fluid intermediary state, which is difficult. And I see that for years the body and the whole bodily consciousness used to revert swiftly to the old way for protection, to escape; but I managed to stop that, now on the contrary the body accepts: 'Well, if it is dissolution, so be it!' One feels as if the whole ordinary stability is gone....The great adventure."[25]
"The difficulty always lies in the transition: if the memory of the other way (the ordinary and universal way of all human beings) comes, all of a sudden — it's quite strange — the body feels completely helpless, exactly as if it were on the verge of fainting. So it reacts immediately, and the other movement takes over again."[26]

Second Witness

"ON THAT FIRST DAY while I was in that state and more conscious of the things around me, I had the first most extraordinary experience. There was a man mending the road; that man was myself; the pick-axe he held was myself; the very stone which he was breaking was a part of me; the tender blade of grass was my very being and the tree beside the man was myself. I almost could feel and think like the road-mender, and I could feel the wind passing through the tree and the little ant on the blade of grass I could feel. The birds, the dust and the very noise were a part of me. Just then there was a car passing by at some distance; I was the driver, the engine and the tires; as the car went further away from me, I was going away from myself. I was in everything, or rather everything was in me, inanimate and animate, the mountain, the worm and all breathing things. All day long I remained in this happy condition.

"I was so happy, calm and at peace. I could still see my body and I was hovering and within myself was the calmness of the bottom of a deep unfathomable lake. Like the lake, I felt my physical body an unfathomable lake. Like the lake I felt that my physical body with its mind and emotions could be ruffled on the surface, but nothing, nay nothing could disturb the calmness of my soul. The presence of the mighty Beings was with me for some time and then They were gone. I was supremely happy for I had seen. Nothing could ever be the same. I have drunk at the clear pure waters at the source of the fountain of life and my soul was appeased. Never more could I be thirsty, never more could I be in utter darkness. I have seen the Light. I have touched compassion which heals all sorrow and suffering; it is not for myself, but for the world. I have stood on the mountain top and gazed at the mighty Beings. Never can I be in utter darkness. I have seen the glorious and healing Light. The fountain Truth has been revealed to me and the dark-ness has been dispersed. Love in all its glory has intoxicated my heart; my heart can never be closed. I have drunk at the fountain of joy and eternal Beauty. I am God-intoxicated!"[27]

"THE EARTH WAS THE COLOR OF THE SKY; the hills, the green, ripening rice fields, the trees and the dry, sandy river-bed were the color of the sky; every rock on the hills, the big boulders, were the clouds and they were the rocks. Heaven was the earth and the earth heaven; the setting sun had transformed everything. The sky was blazing fire, bursting in every streak of cloud, in every stone, in every blade of grass, in every grain of sand. The sky was ablaze with green, purple, violet, indigo, with the fury of flame. Over that hill it was a vast sweep of purple and gold; over the southern hills a burning delicate green and fading blues; to the east there was a counter sunset as splendid in cardinal red and burnt ochre, magenta and fading violet. The counter sunset was exploding in splendor as in the west; a few clouds had gathered themselves around the setting sun and they were pure, smokeless fire which would never die. The vastness of this fire and its intensity penetrated everything and entered the earth. The earth was the heavens and the heavens the earth. And everything was alive and bursting with color and color was god, not the god of man. The hills became transparent, every rock and boulder was without weight, floating in color and the distant hills were blue, the blue of all the seas and the sky of every clime. The ripening rice fields were intense pink and green, a stretch of immediate attention. And the road that crossed the valley was purple and white, so alive that it was one of the rays that raced across the sky. You were of that light, burning, furious, exploding, without shadow, without root and word. And as the sun went further down, every color became more violent, more intense and you were completely lost, past all recalling. It was an evening that had no memory."[28]

Third Witness

"The next day I sat in the temple again. I awaited the Shakti to reveal herself as my blessed companion. But as time passed there was no sensation, no movement at all. There was not even any kind of deepening. There was not a single element to be added to my consciousness. I sat with my eyes open. I was not having an experience of any kind.

"In an instant, I became profoundly and directly aware of what I am. I was a tacit realization, a direct knowledge in consciousness itself. It was consciousness itself without the addition of a communication from any other source. I simply sat there and knew what I am. I was being what I am. I am reality, the Self, the Nature and Support of all things and all beings. I am the One Being, known as God, Brahman, Atman, the One Mind, the Self.

"There was no thought involved in this. I am that Consciousness. There was no reaction either of joy or surprise. I am the One I recognized. I am that One. I am not merely experiencing Him.

"Then truly there was no more to realize. Every experience in my life had led to his. The dramatic revelations in childhood and college, my time of writing, my years with Rudi, the revelation in seminary, the long history of pilgrimage at the Ashram, all of these moments were the intuitions of this same Reality. My entire life had been the communication of that Reality to me, until I am that."[29]

"As a baby I remember crawling around inquisitively with an incredible sense of joy, light, and freedom in the middle of my head that was bathed in energies moving freely down from above, up, around and down through my body and my heart. It was an expanding sphere of joy from the heart. And I was a radiant form, a source of energy, bliss and light. And I was the power of Reality, a direct enjoyment and communication. I was the Heart, who lightens the mind and all things. I was the same as everyone and everything, except it became clear that others were unaware of the thing itself.[30]

Fourth Witness

"FOR SEVEN DAYS I LIVED in a very hopeless and helpless state, but at the same time something was arising. There was no ground underneath; I was in an abyss, a bottomless abyss, but there was no fear because there was nothing to protect. There was no fear because there was nobody to be afraid. Those seven days were of tremendous transformation, total transformation.

"And on the last day, the presence of a totally new energy, a new light and a new delight, became so intense that it was almost unbearable. It was as if I was exploding, as if I was going mad with blissfulness. "It was impossible to make any sense out of it, out of what was happening. It was a very non-sense world — difficult to figure out, difficult to manage in categories, difficult to use words, languages, explanations. All scriptures appeared dead and all the words that had been used for this experience looked very pale, anemic. This was so alive — it was like a tidal wave of bliss. The whole day was strange, stunning, and it was a shattering experience.

"The past was disappearing — as if it had never belonged to me, as if I had read about it somewhere, as if I had dreamed about it, as if it was somebody else's story. Boundaries were disappearing, distinctions were disappearing. Mind was disappearing; it was millions of miles away. It was difficult to catch hold of it. It was rushing farther and farther away, and there was no urge to keep it close.

"By the evening it became so difficult to bear it. It was hurting, it was painful. It was like when a woman goes into labor, when a child is to be born and the woman suffers tremendous pain, the birth pangs. Something was very imminent. Something was going to happen. It was difficult to know what it was: 'Maybe it is going to be my death?'... but there was no fear. I was ready for it.

"And it was impossible to keep my eyes open. I was drugged. I went to sleep nearabout eight. It was not like sleep. The body was asleep, I was awake. It was so strange — as if one was torn apart in two directions, two dimensions; as if the polarity had become completely focused; as if I was both the polarities together. The positive and negative were meeting. Sleep and awareness were meeting. Death and life were meeting.

"It was weird. For the first time, it shocks you to the very roots. It shakes your foundations. You can never be the same after that experience. It brings a new vision to your life, a new quality.

"Nearabout twelve, my eyes suddenly opened. I had not opened them; the sleep was broken by something else. I felt a great presence around me in the room. I felt a throbbing life all around me, a great vibration almost like a hurricane; a great storm of light, joy, ecstasy.

"I was drowning in it. It was so tremendously real that everything else became unreal. The walls of the room became unreal, the house became unreal, my own body became unreal. Everything was unreal because now there was, for the first time, reality.

"It was nameless. But it was there — so opaque, so transparent, and yet so solid, one could have touched it. It was almost suffocating me in that room. It was too much, and I was not capable of absorbing it.

"A deep urge arose in me to rush out of the room, to go under the sky. It was suffocating me — it was too much — it would kill me! If I had remained for a few moments more, it would have suffocated me. It seemed like that.

"I rushed out of the room, went out in the street. A great urge was there just to be under the sky with the stars, with the trees, with the earth — to be with nature. And immediately when I came out, the feeling of being suffocated disappeared. It was too small a place for such a big phenomenon. It is bigger than the sky. Even the sky is not the limit for it. And then I felt more at ease.

"I walked towards the nearest garden. It was a totally new walk, as if gravitation had disappeared. I was walking, or I was running, or I was simply flying — it was difficult to decide. There was no gravitation. I was feeling weightless, as if some energy was taking me. I was in the hands of some other energy. For the first time I was not alone; for the first time I was no more an individual; for the first time the drop had come and fallen into the ocean. Now the whole ocean was mine, I was the ocean.There was no limitation. A tremendous power arose, as if I could do anything, whatsoever... I was not there, only the power was there. Something was pulling me towards the garden. It was not within my capacity to prevent myself. I was just floating, I was relaxed, I was

in a let-go. I was not there. It was there — call it God — God was there.
I would like to call it It, because God is too much a word and has
become dirty through too much use, so let me call It. It was there and I
was just carried away, carried by a tidal wave. "The moment I entered
the garden, everything became luminous. It was all over the place —
the benediction, the blessedness. I could see the trees for the first
time... their green, their life, their very sap running. The whole garden
was asleep, the trees were asleep, but I could see the whole garden
alive. Even the small grass leaves were so beautiful. I looked around.
One tree was tremendously luminous, the maulshree tree. It attracted
me, it pulled me towards itself. I had not chosen it. God himself had
chosen it. I went to the tree; I sat under the tree. As I sat there things
started settling. The whole universe became a benediction."[31]

Fifth Witness

Q: Is it an incommunicable experience?

Witness: No, it cannot be *experienced.* You cannot communicate what you cannot experience. I don't want to use those words, because "inexpressible" and "incommunicable" imply that there is something which cannot be communicated, which cannot be expressed. I don't know. There is an assumption that there is something there which cannot be expressed, which cannot be communicated. There is nothing there. I don't want to say there is nothing there, because you will catch me — you will call it "emptiness," "void" and all that sort of thing.

When this "explosion" takes place (I use the word "explosion" because it's like a nuclear explosion) it leaves behind chain reactions. Every cell in your body, the cells in the very marrow of your bones, have to undergo this "change" — I don't want to use that word — it's an irreversible change. There's no question of your going back. There's no question of a "fall" for this man at all. Irreversible: an alchemy of some sort.

It is like a nuclear explosion, you see — it shatters the whole body. It is not an easy thing; it is the end of the man — such a shattering thing that it blasts every cell, every nerve in your body.

I felt something happening inside of me: the life energy drawing to a focal point from different parts of my body. I said to myself, "Now you have come to the end of your life. You are going to die." Then I called Valentine and said: "I am going to die, Valentine, and you will have to do something with this body. Hand it over to the doctors — maybe they will use it. I don't believe in burning or burial or any of those things. In your own interest you have to dispose of this body — one day it will stink — so, why not give it away?" She said: "You are a foreigner. The Swiss government won't take your body. Forget about it," then she went away. And then this whole business of the frightening movement of the life force coming to a point, as it were. I was lying down on the sofa. Her bed was empty, so I moved over to that bed and stretched myself, getting ready. She ignored me and went away. She said: "One day you say this thing has changed, another day this thing has changed, a third day this thing has changed. What is this

whole business?" She was not interested in any of these religious matters — never heard of those things. "You say you are going to die. You are not going to die. You are all right, hale and healthy." She went away. Then I stretched myself, and this was going on and on and on. The whole life energy was moving to some focal point — where it was, I don't know. Then a point arrived where the whole thing looked as if the aperture of a camera was trying to close itself. (It is the only simile that I can think of.) The way I am describing this is quite different from the way things happened at that time, because there was nobody there thinking in such terms. All this was part of my experience, otherwise I wouldn't be able to talk about it. So, the aperture was trying to close itself, and something was there trying to keep it open. Then after a while there was no will to do anything, not even to prevent the aperture closing itself. Suddenly, as it were, it closed. I don't know what happened after that.

This process lasted for forty-nine minutes — this process of dying. It was like a physical death, you see.

I didn't feel that I was a new-born baby — no question of enlightenment at all — but the things that had astonished me that week, the changes in taste, seeing and so on, had become permanent fixtures. I call all these events the "calamity." I call it the "calamity" because from the point of view of one who thinks this is something fantastic, blissful, full of beatitude, love, ecstasy and all that kind of a thing, this is physical torture — this is a calamity from that point of view. Not a calamity to me, but a calamity to those who have an image that something marvelous is going to happen.

The most puzzling and bewildering part of the whole thing was when the sensory activities began their independent careers. There was no co-ordinator linking the senses, so we had terrible problems — Valentine had to go through the whole business. We'd go for a walk, and I'd look at a flower and ask "What is that?" She'd say, "That is a flower." I'd take a few more steps, look at a cow and ask, "What is that?" Like a baby, I had to re-learn everything all over.

You can never understand the tremendous peace that is always there within you, that is your natural state. Your trying to create a peaceful state of mind is in fact creating disturbance within you. You can only talk of peace, create a state of mind and say to yourself that you are very peaceful — but that is not peace; that is violence. So there is no use in practicing peace, there is no reason to practice silence. Real silence is explosive; it is not the dead state of mind that spiritual seekers think. "Oh, I am at peace with myself. There is silence, a tremendous silence! I experience silence!" — that doesn't mean anything at all. This is volcanic in its nature: it's bubbling all the time — the energy, the life — that is its quality. You may ask how I know. I don't know. Life is aware of itself, if we can put it that way — it is conscious of itself. There is not one moment of boredom for this man. For hours and hours I can sit here and watch the clock pendulum moving there — I can't be bored — I really don't know what it is. The pendulum is moving there — the whole of my being is that movement. For hours and hours I can sit there and look at it. You are not interested in that thing; you are interested in something else, some meditation. This individual is always in a state of meditation. "Where is that movement?" I am wondering — that is the meditation that is going on. Not that I am wondering in the usual sense of the word; this individual remains in a state of wonder for the rest of his life. "Outside" and "Inside" are created by thought. When there is no movement of thought, you don't know whether it is inside or outside. This is just like a mirror. This is a live mirror, reflecting things exactly as they are. There is nobody here: I don't see anything; the whole of my body is reflecting things exactly the way they are out there.

A person who has come into such a state of Samadhi is like a madman and a child rolled into one. Madcaps function in exactly the same way — the thoughts are disconnected, disjointed things, and so the actions are also disconnected, but their thoughts are accompanied by hallucinations, mental images, seeing something that isn't there — that's the only difference. This state is always a state of wonder; he doesn't know what he is looking at, he doesn't know what he is smelling, and yet his senses are working at their peak capacities, extraordinarily sensitive, taking in everything.[32]

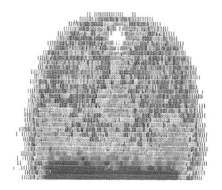

Part III

EVOLUTIONARY TRANSFORMATION

CHAPTER ONE

Evolutionary Sleepers

An exploration of the sites of the higher functions which lie dormant within Homo sapiens awaiting some evolutionary initiative and a brief survey of some possible scientific propositions and theories of how they might be activated. The chapter ends with a summary of the evidence so far of the forthcoming arrival of a new species.

EVOLUTIONARY SLEEPER — SLEEP AND THE SLEEPER — LUMINOUS BODY — EXPLOSION — SLEEPERS ONE: GLANDS — BRAINCORE: THE FIFTH STAGE OF EVOLUTION — BRAIN CROWN: THE SIXTH STAGE OF EVOLUTION — HEART OF THE MATTER — UNSEEN ORDER — GENESIS — MEMORY FIELDS — VIBRANT FORM — CRYSTALLIZATION — CRITICAL MASS — BUDDHAFIELD — SHOCK TO THE SYSTEM — SORCERER'S APPRENTICE — SUMMARY OF THE EVIDENCE

CHAPTER TWO

The Unknown Guest

An "Identikit" of the new species, their probable characteristics and the likely problems which might occur when the two lines of evolution meet.

PROPHECY — MEDIUMS AND MESSAGES — A NEW GENETIC RING — THE SECOND EVE — THE NEW STAGE — IDENTIKIT — CROSSROADS — A NATURAL BIRTHRIGHT — WATER BABIES — EDUCATING CHARLEY — BORN TO BE DIFFERENT — PSYCHIC — A CAUTIONARY TALE — PSYCHIC ON STAGE — MYSTIC CHILDHOODS — HARMONIOUS MAN — THIS VERY BODY THE BUDDHA — STAR MIND — CHILDHOOD'S END

Acknowledgements
Bibliography
Suggested Reading

CHAPTER ONE

Evolutionary Sleeper

Above: A 17th Century edition of The Interpretation of Dreams written in the second century by Artemedorus (British Library.)

WE NOW TURN TO an examination of evolutionary sleepers; those higher functions which we propose have so far lain dormant in the species. Where are they, what is their function and how are they to be triggered? We will also explore the evidence which points towards the next stage of man's evolutionary development.

The first difficulty we encounter is that virtually all of the evidence is circumstantial. That is to say that most of the accounts, like the one in the column, come from mystic witnesses which as far as the orthodox scientific community is concerned are about as permissible as those of a madman in a court of law. Yet these "madmen" do sound very sane and talk as if they have actually witnessed at first hand the penultimate state of man's evolution. The problem is that we cannot directly share it with them. The ultimate truth of any situation can only be known by each individual, so that if an investigator wishes to see it all with his own eyes he must *be* it; he must enter the selfsame state as the mystic.

Such a condition can be likened to a blindfold committee who stand waiting for the sun to rise. The prime witness says: "Take off your blindfold," but the committee insist that they have come to learn about the sun and not about blindfolds.

The blindfolded scientist measures the rising heat, listens to the increased activity of the birds and the earth and speculates upon the existence of a huge hot body which appears on a simple twenty-four hour cycle. This information he can at least pass on to the rest of the blindfolded committee.

Yet there are moments when the scientist's blindfold slips and he is granted a sudden flash of insight. Mathematicians have had their fair share of satoris! The cry of "Eureka!" from Archimedes in his bath or that moment when Isaac Newton, watching an apple fall from a tree,

204

divined that both the apple and the moon shared a universal law of gravity — these are the ecstatic triumphs of the scientific world.

Einstein's "happiest thought of my life" was curiously a vision of someone falling off a roof. For in that insight it was revealed that anyone in the state of falling was both in motion and at rest at one and the same moment. This image became one of the cohesive forces behind the Theory of Relativity. Einstein always maintained that there were no logical or reasonable paths to such natural laws, only the luminous flash of "intuition can reach them."

Such searing insights seem to explode the old habitual "boxes" in the mind and cut new neural pathways across the brain.

In trying to explain some of the subtle functions of the mysterious sleepers we will be balancing the evidence from both the scientist and the sage.

There is, however, one excellent example which might throw light on our own investigation where both disciplines can meet in a mutual investigation; one in which the "subjective" exploration of the inner realm can complement the "objective" discipline of the shared and observable world. It concerns an activity which is close to us all — *sleep*.

WHY DO WE SLEEP? It is only since the 1950s that scientists have discovered just how busy the brain is during sleep and how the brain actively generates sleep. But even after 40 years of intense research scientists are none the wiser why we sleep at all.

There are many authentic cases known of individuals who don't sleep at all. Mysteriously there is no outward sign that their lives are in any way impaired. No one seems to die from lack of sleep and the physical body refreshes itself perfectly with a simple relaxed rest.

So what is the purpose of a state in which we spend one third of our lives, in a state of unconsciousness or at least semi-consciousness?

Neuro-physicists and sleep specialists do not know the answer. They have charted every minute change in body postures during the night, every alteration in the brain waves through electroencephalograms (EEG's), every twitch of the face muscles and burst of rapid eye

Sleep and the Sleeper

movements (REM's) and every firing of the millions of neurons in the brain stem and the basal forebrain. And they still haven't the slightest idea why it all happens.

Here we find a perfect opportunity where both the scientist and the mystic could meet and merge their fragmented visions in a holistic and harmonious overview.

The great Sufi mystic of our century, Meher Baba, gave a comprehensive explanation of the "why," showing as he did so that there is a profound relationship between enlightenment and sleep.

He says that the primal urge in human beings is to seek union, to re-establish our lost state of Oneness. During the waking state consciousness is identified with and diverted by the material world, whereas in sleep the being is taking refuge in the inherent natural state. The whole creation has this conscious or unconscious tendency to take shelter in the Original Void by entering the state of sound sleep for a time.

There are three basic states in the normal experience of human beings. The First State is that of sound sleep, or the state of complete and original unconsciousness of the "Self." The Second State is dreaming or the semi-conscious state and the Third State is the awake state of an awareness of the "Self."

In the Third State we are conscious through actions and impressions. These impressions are constantly being imprinted upon the mind and are stored in the sub-conscious. These then are projected when we experience semi-conscious and conscious states; that is when we are either dreaming or awake.

When these impressions are dormant we are said to be in sound deep sleep. The sound sleep we experience is precisely the same sound sleep state of the Original Void. In fact there is essentially no difference between sleep and enlightenment save for the fact that sleep is an unconscious state while enlightenment is conscious. Just as we, in waking up from sound sleep, pass through the state of dreaming first, so the original Prime Consciousness passed through all the six levels of the Divine Dream.

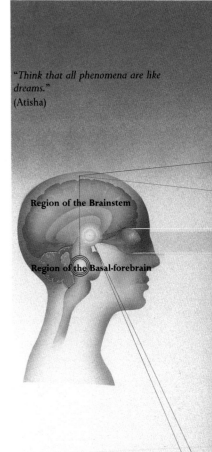

"Think that all phenomena are like dreams."
(Atisha)

Region of the Brainstem

Region of the Basal-forebrain

We enter sleep in four stages which are clearly defined by dramatic changes in our brainwaves. The compact waves of normal waking alertness lengthen as we gradually enter sound sleep at stage four. Most studies find that the end of this stage is marked by a sudden shift in posture. The brainwaves reverse their course and the sleeper commences the first REM period of dreaming. This complete cycle is repeated roughly every 90 minutes throughout the night with the period of deep sound sleep becoming progressively shorter while the REM period becomes increasingly longer. During sound sleep the most active area is located in the basal forebrain while the dreaming state seems to occur within the brain stem.

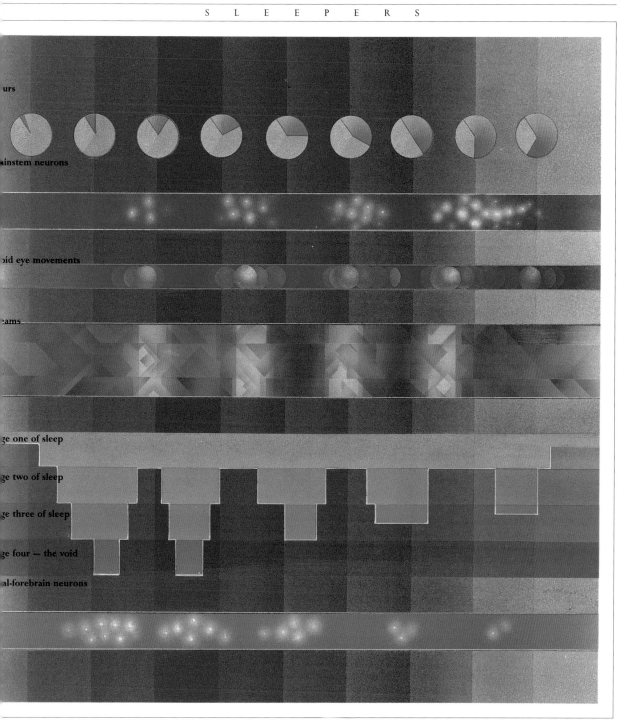

Luminous Body

So each night we re-enact the whole of creation, returning briefly to our original state of unconsciousness. Certain researches into sleep have found that during that period certain areas within the basal forebrain are activated and this is precisely the area in which we can expect to discover the true evolutionary sleeper, that gateway to the Void.

WHILE SLEEP IS AT LEAST within our normal sphere of every night events, the extraordinary energy phenomenon which can alter the entire biological organism when it enters deep mystic or enlightened states, is virtually unknown to science. This is certainly not due to a lack of authentic cases but simply because our present reliance upon reductionist methods does not permit any lucid explanation for these unique events.

Science does not know what to do with the evidence and therefore such cases have brief lives as footnotes in obscure publications and then are forgotten. Which brings us back to the difficulty of matching science and mysticism. This is the realm where truth jostles with fact. The old adage that "truth abides while facts change" points out that the two are not synonymous.

During the following chapter many readers may feel a stretching of their credulity and might be prompted to ask, "How do you or anyone else *know?*" Like you I also have to suspend disbelief in both the theories and research of scientific method and in mystical visions. I simply don't *know*. There is much from both disciplines which have to be taken on trust.

In the realm of mysticism this is perhaps for most people more pronounced. Individuals like U.G. Krishnamurti, Da Free' John or Yogeshwaranand Saraswati can say that they have intuited the truth but until there is a body of substantiating evidence their truths remain their own. And yet are the so-called scientific facts so much more reliable? Even these 'eternal laws' of physics current in the 1950s did not turn out to be so everlasting. So let us proceed here in the spirit of trusting in God but tethering your camel.

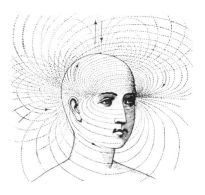

Francis of Assisi (1181-1230) was a Christian mystic who performed many recorded miracles. There are corroborating accounts of a luminous glow which appeared about him on many occasions. At his death the body is said to have shown no signs of decay for a long period during which time it actually gave off a visible brightness.

Jnaneshwar, a yogi saint in Maharashtra, India, in the 13th Century was well-known for his miracles. After his death, however, his body did not decay and was reported as late as the 16th Century to be still perfect. It was said that even after three hundred years it continued to give off great heat and a strange luminosity.

Tukaram (1608-1648) another Maharashtran saint and a devotee of Krishna had a vast following which watched his death. In the final ecstatic moment of release his body radiated such a blazing light that his followers were blinded. It is reported that when their vision was restored Tukaram's body had spontaneously combusted and was gone.

Seraphim (1759-1833) was a Russian Orthodox priest from Sarov. He was famous for his unaccountable healing and miracles and on at least two occasions transfigured his body into a brilliant luminous space.

Ramanuja, a yogi from south India, was

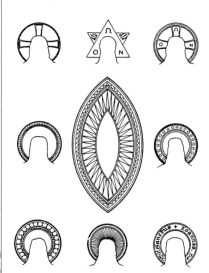

said to have often demonstrated a transfiguration of his body into light. His final demonstration was, however, spectacular for he sealed himself into a small chamber and when his disciples finally broke in his body had disappeared. If these accounts are true then saints, mystics and sages are seen to transcend our normal concepts of the laws of nature. However, the accounts are not only from the past when faith may have been far more naive and easily awed. Even in our own scientific and skeptical times there have been well publicized and unaccountable bodily manifestations of light.

Ramakrishna acquired a brilliant golden light around his body which attracted even the most doubting observers from both India and the West. When *J. Krishnamurti* underwent a strange transformation in 1948, having suffered terrible head pains for weeks, he suddenly collapsed. His two companions watched.

"Then life and an immensity began to enter the face. The face was greatly beautiful. It had no age, time had not touched it. The eyes opened but there was no recognition. The body radiated light; a stillness and a vastness illumined the face." [2]

There is, we know, a substantial body of evidence to show that in the final exalted stages of evolutionary development an individual's body can actually undergo a spectacular transformation often accompanied by a physical radiance which can be clearly seen by even the least subtle eye. Such bizarre manifestations are outside mechanistic physics yet from what we know from the viewpoint of quantum mechanics matter is not always quite what it appears to be. Some modern physicists have envisioned matter as a minute ripple upon a vast ocean of spatial energy. The space between atoms is vast, there being far more space to a block of lead than anything we might term solid. Not only that but even the "solid" matter of life might be actually composed of something as insubstantial as light.

David Bohm, one of the pioneers of theoretical physics gives a simple, down-to-earth description. *"As an object approaches the speed of light, according to relativity, its internal space and time change so that the clocks slow down relative to other speeds, and the distance is shortened. You would find that the two ends of the light ray would have no time between them and no distance, so they would represent immediate contact. You could also say that from the point of view of present field theory, the fundamental fields are those of very high energy in which mass can be neglected, which would be essentially moving at the speed of light. Mass is a phenomenon of connecting light rays which go back and forth, sort of freezing them into a pattern.*

"So, matter, as it were, is condensed or frozen light. Light is not merely electromagnetic waves but in a sense other kinds of waves going at that speed. Therefore all matter is seen as a condensation of light into patterns moving back and forth at average speeds which are less than the speed of light. Even Einstein had some hint of that idea. You could say that when we come to light we are coming to the fundamental activity in which existence has its ground, or at least coming close to it." [1]

Does this perhaps go some way to explain the long and impressive list of individuals who have exhibited this light transmuting quality?

Explosion

WHILE SUCH IMAGES AND EVENTS would seem to fit the popular ideas we have of magicians, saints and sages it is only one side of our enlightened coin.

"It is like a nuclear explosion you see — it shatters the whole body. It is not an easy thing; it is the end of the man — such a shattering thing that it blasts every cell, every nerve in your body. I went through terrible physical torture at that moment. Not that you experience the 'explosion' — you can't experience the explosion — but its the after effects, the 'fall-out,' is the thing that changes the whole chemistry of your body." [3]

It is a popular and comfortable misconception that the enlightened, the yogis and the so-called holy men are in immaculate health. Perhaps we all feel they must have miraculous self-healing and paranormal powers. It is true there are some great yogic saints like Trailanga Swami who lived for two hundred and fifty years or Tapawiji Maharaj who died in 1955 at the age of one hundred and eighty-five. But these seem the exception rather than the rule. Far more often the immense energies of a new consciousness sever the fragile moorings with the body.

Even if the mooring is not snapped altogether, the energies involved seem to have scant regard for the suffering of the individual. *"The physical pain was unbearable — that is why I say you really don't want this... If I could give you some glimpse of what this is all about, you would not touch this with a barge pole, a ten foot pole."* [4]

In our time J. Krishnamurti was probably the most extreme case of bodily suffering. His early transformation was manifested in the form that "unseen Masters" were acting upon his body. He could hardly accept the immense energies which surged through his frail body. Krishnaji's brother Nitya wrote of a particularly "ghastly night of suffering":

"All through the evening he was more conscious of his physical body than he had ever been before. They told him that he must make no movement, for generally he was twisting and writhing with pain. But now he promised 'them' he would not move and over and over again he said: 'I won't move, I promise I won't move.' So he clasped his fingers tightly and with his knotted hands under him, he lay on his back, while the awful pain continued. He

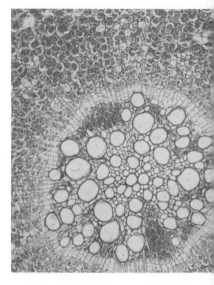

"If there is a disruption between these two — the body we see and the spirit which is not seen — living is impossible. I also realized that Ramakrishna Paramahansa's being afflicted with numerous diseases and the death of Shri Ramana Maharshi of cancer were not due to physical causes but due to the break in adjustment of these two things. It is thought that saints and yogis are always hale and healthy but in truth it is just the contrary. In fact yogis die young, and as long as they live, they are mostly ailing because the adjustment is disturbed and as a result a discord is created." [5]

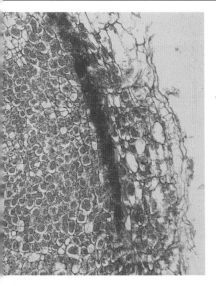

Two photographs taken only 18 months apart which show the dramatic effects of changes in the body of mystics and enlightened entities. In 1974, Bhagwan Shree Rajneesh ended a powerful outward going phase of Rajas energy and by 1975 had entered a new Sattvic stage in which the energy is likened to that of the moon.

found it very difficult to breath that night and he gasped for breath continuously and choked repeatedly and when he could no longer get his breath he just fainted. Three times he fainted that night."[6]

The most obvious question which must occur in this inquiry is that if the natural state is so natural then how come there is so much physical suffering?

Ramakrishna used to say that when ordinary aspirants (Jiva's) enter the final Samadhi for 21 days without a break, they rend the thin veil which separates the sixth and seventh level, but the cost is that the body dies. Unless the individual has a natural disposition to become a master or an "Avatar" they invariably cannot withstand the onslaught of the energy.

Is it possible that nature is still perfecting her most recent experiment called man and is having to adjust the evolutionary sleepers? There are many cases of those who have effortlessly slipped into the natural state but they also seem exceptional. The state invariably exacts heavy tolls but perhaps these are nature's experiments to harmonize and strike a balance between the body and the spirit, matter and consciousness. In the next evolutionary jump will a new balance be the most fundamental change in the species?

The Sufi mystics have a principle of oscillation between two very different states, symbolized by the realm of the horizontal and the realm of the vertical. These are called *Baka* which is awakened consciousness of individuality and *Fana* — the higher realm of consciousness where there is dissolution of individuality. It is said of Al-Shibli that he became incapable of returning from his "God-intoxicated" drunken-like Fana state. He was ecstatic and lost in his samadhi. His master Al-Junaid in the end sent him to a mental hospital until he could come back to the Baka state and flow easily between the two. Ramakrishna had precisely the same problem and was often lost in his Fana state, lying for days unconscious to the everyday world.

If the new species is to survive it will have to balance the twin aspects of living in the world, yet not of the world; of science and mysticism; matter and spirit.

211

Sleepers One — Glands

UNTIL VERY RECENTLY it had generally been assumed by the medical profession that hormones were solely produced by the ductless glands — the endocrines. However, it is now known that the brain can also stimulate the pituitary gland to make hormones which regulate the behavior of immune cells or induce other hormones to do so.

Perhaps still more fascinating is the fact that this is a reciprocal affair; the minute immune cells can also communicate with the brain, using the language of the hormones. Also they can produce hormones themselves; in fact it seems to be their way of "talking." The vast inter-communicating network of the whole immune system acts as an internal sensory organ, much like a sixth sense which warns the brain of invaders or malfunctions and stimulates the glands and the cells into action. The system resembles almost an intelligent and conscious entity in its own right which parallels and intertwines the brain activity.

In the 1970s, long before this was suspected U.G. Krishnamurti described some of the radical changes which happened to his body, especially the endocrine glands, upon his "explosion" into the natural state — what he calls his "calamity." Few accounts are so revealing.

Up and down his torso, neck and head, at those points which Indian holy men call "Chakras," his friends observed swellings of various shapes and colors, which came and went at intervals. On his lower abdomen the swellings were horizontal, cigar-shaped hands. Above the navel was a hard almond-shaped swelling. A hard, blue swelling. A large medallion in the middle of his chest was surmounted by another smaller, brownish-red medallion-shaped swelling at the base of his throat. These two medallions were as though suspended from a varicolored, swollen ring — blue, brownish and light yellow — around his neck, as in pictures of the Hindu gods. There were also other similarities between the swelling and the depictions of Indian religious art: his throat was swollen to a shape that made his chin seem to rest on the head of a cobra, as in the traditional images of Siva; just above the bridge of the nose was a white lotus-shaped swelling; all over the head the small blood vessels expanded, forming patterns like the stylized lumps on the heads of Buddha statues. Like the horns of Moses

"That which is termed the pituitary is the Seventh Seal, it is holy and divine. It possesses within Itself that which is termed a hormone structure that, through desire, opens itself and lets the hormones flow through the brain and the the mouth of the pineal which is the Sixth Seal, the door to the Seventh. In the flowing of these hormones, it activates another part of that which is termed the Divine Receiver, the brain, to allocate itself to accept a higher thought frequency called unlimitedness. The higher thought emerges upon the brain and, in the specified area, through the door of that which is termed the divine Seventh, fills the entire brain cavity with a different electrical frequency circuit."[7]

Braincore — The Fifth Stage of Evolution

and the Taoist mystics, two large, hard swellings periodically came and went.

"I have discussed so many times with doctors who are doing research into the ductless gland. Those glands are what the Hindu call 'chakras.' These ductless glands are located in exactly the same spots where the Hindus speculated the chakras are. There is one gland here which is called the 'Thymus gland.' That is very active when you are a child — very active — they have feelings, extraordinary feelings. When you reach the age of puberty it becomes dormant — that's what they say. When again this kind of a thing happens, when you are reborn again, that gland is automatically activated, so all the feelings are there. There are so many glands, here, for example, the pituitary — 'third eye,' 'Ajna Chakra' they call it. When once the interference of thought is finished, it is taken over by this gland: it is this gland that gives the instructions or orders to the body; not thought any more; thought cannot interfere. That is why they call it the 'Ajna' (command) chakra, probably!

"A tremendous amount of money is being spent, and a lot of research is going on, to find out what they are there, what the function of those glands is — the pituitary gland, the pineal gland, the thymus gland and so forth. I don't want to use the word 'Chakras,' I would call them 'ductless glands.' Unless they are activated, any chance of human beings flowering into themselves is lost. I can't say there is any such thing as an evolutionary process, but there seems to be such an evolutionary process. What its nature is, what its purpose is, I do not know, but it seems to be trying to create something. Man remains incomplete, unless the whole of this human organism blooms into something, like a flower — I don't want to use the word 'flower,' because it has mystical overtones." [8]

The primary phenomenon which appears at the fifth level of evolutionary consciousness is that of *light* and *vision*. The secondary experience is said to be one of *sound* and *hearing* with the whole attention focused in the braincore. The visionary aspect is associated with the optic chiasma, the pineal body and the visual cortex while the auditory aspect is primarily to be found in the medulla ("Mouth of God") and extends into the temporal lobe.

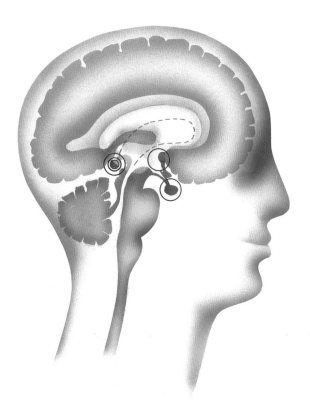

Left: **The baptism of Christ by Piero della Francesca. The dove which hovers above the head of Jesus symbolizes the opening of the third eye and the wings of the ventricles.**

Above: **The cluster of glands which are associated with the fifth stage of evolution are the pineal, which is slightly rear of the center of the brain, the group around the hypothalamus and the pituitary which is just below them. Above there are the open wings of the 'swan' of the ventricles.**

The Brain Crown — The Sixth Stage of Evolution

According to Da Free John attention at this fifth level is at the root of the senses and the braincore. As consciousness moves upwards through the various stations it sweeps in a great arc to the pineal gland which has long been associated with the "third eye." The great 'mechanist,' René Descartes, even believed it to be the seat of the soul. However, it is only when the whole interconnected area is activated that the so-called third eye actually opens.

The eye itself, the Bindu or lesser center is said to be the locus of personal consciousness, perception and cognition. But the higher dimensions of the evolutionary urge is associated with the release of the whole concentrated energy within the *Bindu* which surges upwards to the *sahasrar*, the *Maha Bindu* at the crown of the head, the culmination of the sixth stage of evolutionary development.

THE CONTINUATION OF the white conductor material above the braincore and the third eye is held by many sages to be the jumping board for the last stage on the evolutionary journey. The surging leap of energy upwards traverses the upper region of the *corpus callosum*, the bridge between the two hemispheres. A corona of millions of white fibers called the *corona radiata* extends into the higher reaches of the brain like a huge white fountain. This is the traditional site of the "Thousand Petaled Lotus," the sahasrar at the crown of the head.

The secret of the evolutionary sleeper appears to be that the whole process is self-organizing and from this point onwards tailors its needs and its schedule according to the individual. Some entities are perfect vehicles for the immense play of energies which become available and some seem to have resistances. Many traditions actually end the journey at this point — at the opening of the *sahasrar* while there are others who insist that this is not the final transformation at all. Da Free John, for example, maintains that when the energies break out of the whole body-form and the psychic structures of the braincore they burst forth from those restrictions literally enlightening the whole brain and body. This, however, requires the activation of what is perhaps the most surprising and beautiful sleeper of all — the heart.

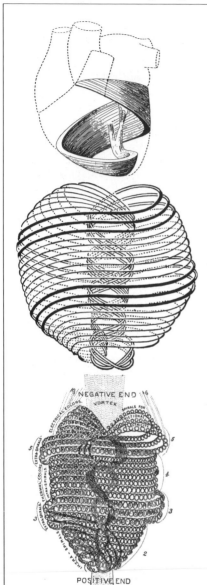

Top: **The spiral twist of the fibers of the heart muscles.**[12]
Center: **Theosophists' vision of the heart of the universe.**[13]
Below: **19th Century concept of the atom showing its center spirals which resemble the visionary images of the energy fields which make up the human body.**[14]

The Heart of the Matter

"That inner Self, as the primeval Spirit, eternal, ever effulgent, full and infinite Bliss, single, indivisible, whole and living, shines in everyone as the witnessing awareness. That Self in its splendor, shining in the cavity of the heart...This Self is neither born nor dies, it neither grows nor decays, nor does it suffer any change. When a pot is broken, the space in it is not, and similarly, when the body dies the Self in it remains eternal."[9]

Like many of the functions so far examined the heart is not at all what it first appears to be. Yet somehow the whole species has intuitively accorded it a very special place in the scheme of things. There seems to be no simple explanation why the heart is such a symbol of love throughout the world. In the mid-1980s the heart was found to be much more than simply the pump it was originally thought to be. The atria of the heart has been discovered to secrete a powerful peptide hormone ANF which interacts with other hormones, affecting various regions of the brain, including the hypothalamus. More significantly it seems to stimulate that magical pituitary gland to produce other hormones which influence the whole endocrine system and many other parts of the body, including lungs, kidneys, adrenals and the sympathetic nervous system.

To a mystic-sage like Yogeshwaranand Saraswati the brain is the center of the whole psycho-physiological level of the organism while the heart is felt to be the seat of the soul or the "Atman" (Self.) The whole current of vibratory force which pervades the body-mind of an individual has its source within the heart.

The so-called "pace-maker," the sino-atrial node of the heart, is located in the right atrium. It is here that many locate the true heartbeat or the seat of the soul, just between the pacemaker and the atrio-ventricular node. The heart is tilted at an angle with the greater mass lying on the left side. However, the location of the Self is said to be about 2 inches (5 cm) to the right of center in the upper part.

A spiral illumination is felt to move from the heart upwards and outwards through the throat and forward into the third eye, finally releasing through the crown of the head.

The final awakening can only happen when there is a radical

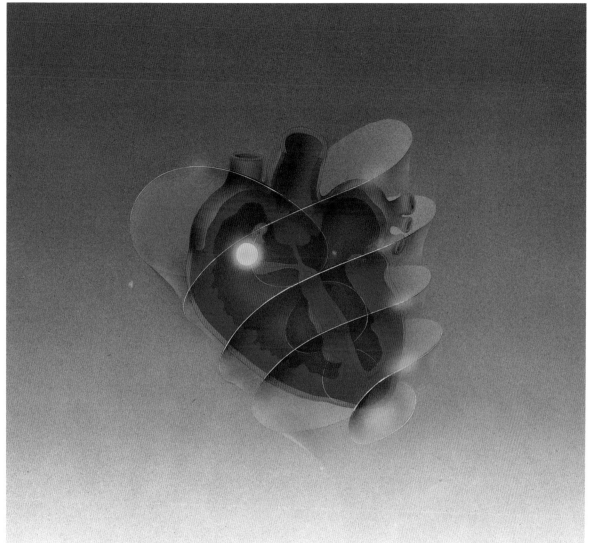

explosion of understanding of the whole illusion of separate existence, a vast and unimaginable shift in gestalt. This could be likened to the final paradigm shift, an utter shock of recognition of the true reality of the situation. At that explosive moment the released energies seem to penetrate the brain root, the total body-mind, illuminating the entire brain, releasing it all back into the unbounded Void — void to void the last stage of evolution that we know!

"There is a cavity that sits next to the heart that no things exist in except electrical energy. There in is where the Soul lies and has a weight content of thirteen ounces." [11]

Unseen Order

"*The present state of theoretical physics implies that empty space has all this energy and that matter is a slight increase of that energy and therefore matter is like a small ripple on this tremendous ocean of energy, having some relative stability and being manifest.*

"*Therefore my suggestion is that this implicate order implies a reality immensely beyond what we call matter. Matter itself is merely a ripple in this background.*"
(David Bohm)[15]

WE HAVE ALREADY BEEN INTRODUCED briefly to three major new scientific "paradigms" earlier in this volume but we now return to some of these ideas in order to understand how evolution might be working and how, if the sleepers are what we propose them to be, they could be activated. The three major shifts in scientific ideas are *Implicate order*, (the hidden order behind the universe), *Dissipative structures* (far-from-equilibrium systems like fluid vortices or life organisms) and *Morphological fields* (invisible fields which stabilize and fix the patterns of forms).

The Implicate order is a boundless whole which can be envisioned as a great holo-movement which continually enfolds and unfolds. Future and past are within the Implicate order, which of itself just Is.

The creator of the theory of implicate order, David Bohm, feels that there is even a super-implicate order, or maybe even a series of levels. His vision increasingly approaches that of our old seven-level map of the Philosophia Perennis. One suggestion is that the super-implicate order might be one of consciousness.

"*Let me propose that consciousness is basically in the implicate order as all matter is and therefore it's not that consciousness is one thing and matter is another. Rather consciousness is a material process and consciousness is itself in the implicate order, as is all matter, and consciousness manifests in some explicate order as does matter.*"[16]

This is fundamental to a possible explanation of the next evolutionary direction and for any possible activation of the sleepers. What Bohm seems to be saying from his standpoint of theoretical

One of David Bohm's favorite models for the Implicate order or unfolding and enfolding is that of a dye being dropped in glycerin which is held between two rotating cylinders. As one is turned, the drop disappears in a homogenous mixture within the background of the glycerin. However, if the direction of rotation is reversed, the dye reappears as it was. Bohm suggests that existence manifests itself in a similar fashion.

Quantum physics, is that in non-manifest reality (Implicate order) all is interpenetrating, interconnected and One.

"So we say deep down the consciousness of mankind is one. This is a virtual certainty because even in the vacuum, matter is one; and if we don't see this it is because we are blinding ourselves to it."[17]

Eddington once said that "the stuff of the world is mind stuff" and we are seeing the possibility that science could come to view consciousness as the evolutionary territory of the species as the mystics do.

Another fragment of the theory which might help our investigation lies in the concept that space does not separate things, it *unites them.* Our normal view is of two separate points in space joined by a hypothetical dotted line in space. But there is a radical shift in perception if we see that only the dotted line is actually real, with two abstract points appearing on it. The event of individual man might be seen this way. For in this model there are no separate people joined by that hypothetical dotted line, only the line itself — *mankind.* This would mean that any sense of individuality would be false and an illusion. Another way of putting such a shattering idea is that space is more real than the objects within it. The tiny "ripple events of matter" in the Void can only be known through our minds and our minds *are* the event — that tiny ripple.

In this revolutionary model we are not only shaped by evolution, but we are the shapers.

"We're part of the movement, there is no separation between us and it, we are part of the way in which that shapes itself."[18]

If this is true then we are the activators of the sleeper which alters the evolutionary direction which in turn changes us.

Genesis

"When matter is becoming disturbed by non-equilibrium conditions it organizes itself; it wakes up. It happens that our world is a non-equilibrium system."
(Ilya Prigogine)[19]

There is one recent co-evolutionary model which implies that the "macro-system" of the planet is as much dependent upon the "micro-system" of atoms, cells or bacteria out of which it is formed, as the micro-system is dependent upon the entire environment of the globe.

Evolution is seen as a cooperative venture. The planet is thus a vast self-organizing system, a living organism which contains billions of "far-from-equilibrium" states which continually are creating new micro-systems, which in turn, like the primitive bacteria that once helped to create the Earth's vast atmospheric envelope, alter the macro-system.

It is a gigantic, ever-changing work of art, continually being created at those thresholds where a system could go any way. These critical crossroads or "bifurcation points" are the points at which the system suddenly jumps to a new configuration.

The human mind, as part of this whole process within a process, is now producing massive fluctuations by its profound effect upon the environment. This involvement of the human mind has edged the whole system to a new bifurcation point where at any moment the total dissipative structure, of cell, man, planet, solar system and beyond, could jump to a new, complex and higher form.

The human being is a key process within this whole structure for seemingly we are the sole dissipative structure called consciousness. The evolution of consciousness with the coming of *Homo sapiens* sets off a chain-reaction ending in an entirely new level of reality. And one of the aspects of that reality was the ability for a life form to observe and find meaning in the phenomenon of time. In fact both scientists and mystics have come to agree that *mind itself is time*.

Perhaps the most significant property of any dissipative structure like the mind, and the fundamental reason for it to exist at all, is its power to disrupt the whole symmetry of time. The mind's being is in

Above: A chemical far-from-equilibrium reaction, reminiscent of life forms.
Opposite: A computer generated image of the internal workings of a dissipative structure like the Belousov-Zhabotin chemical reaction.

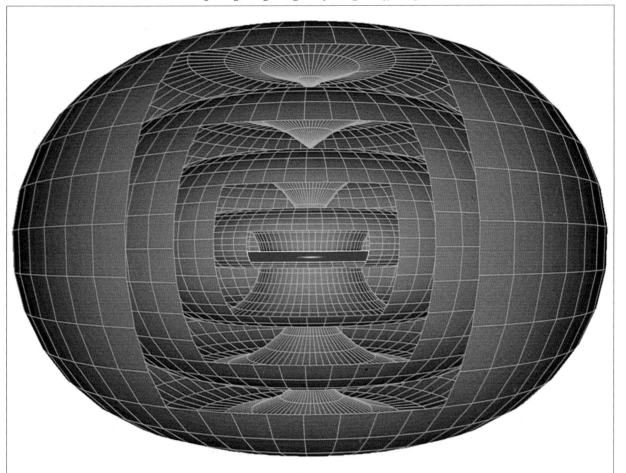

its becoming. Neither mind nor evolution just emerge into time — they *are* time.

The mind itself is also perhaps the greatest and most complex dissipative structure in our universe and the greatest creator of fluctuations in any far-from-equilibrium environment. Thus, as a species we hold the seed of a new evolutionary Genesis within our own hands. Any drastic change in our consciousness, any deep alteration in our view of how we stand within the universe, any action within our environment which causes further excitement to the already pulsating fluctuations occurring at present, can tip the balance and a new evolutionary threshold could open up.

"Life appears no longer a phenomenon unfolding in the universe — the universe itself becomes increasingly alive."
(Jansch)[20]

223

Memory Fields

IF THE GREAT CREATIVE MOMENTS of the universe appear at the so-called bifurcation points, those thresholds of a dissipative structure, then what causes any form created to stabilize itself? What prevents the creation of a singular universe filled with "one-off," unique and completely un-repeatable life forms?

It would seem that once nature recognizes a good thing, some well-adapted form which has burst out of the other end of a bifurcation point, she happily starts repeating the same theme over and over again.

One theory to account for this principle of continuity and conformity is that of "morphogenetic fields." The term derives from "morphe" meaning "form" and genesis, suggesting "coming into being." Rupert Sheldrake in his hypothesis of formative causation proposes that there are an infinite number of invisible form fields which determine the shape and form of things.

Underpinning this theory is the possibility that memory is *inherent* in the universe. Everything inherits a collective memory of similar patterns of the mind and through repetition settles into habitual forms. Simply put "things are as they are because they were as they were."[26a]

According to his hypothesis, each form in existence has a corresponding field. The universe could be made up of a dense matrix of such fields which determine the shape of the tails of mice, the thoughts of men and the behavior of galaxies. Habit seems the cosmic key. Yet although these invisible fields are of habit paradoxically they are continually being re-shaped by the very forms they create.

In the first instance any new individual of a species, or any mutant of an old pattern, would effectively be the only representative of that particular field. So it is proposed that the field and the individual probably come into being together. Once a field has been repeatedly re-enforced, it becomes increasingly habitual.

The bonding of hydrogen and oxygen atoms to create water is just such an "eternal" and lawful field. A living organism, however, by comparison, is a volatile phenomenon which is fluctuating, by its very nature precariously relying on the stability of its environment to remain in one shape. The forms also seem to affect one another — and here Sheldrake offers another radical insight. Just as violin strings of

Vibrant Form

lengths and tension vibrate in time when one is plucked, so similar forms resonate and influence one another.

When one organism succeeds in an environment, it sets up a resonance, and similar organisms, either in the near vicinity or even in geographically far-removed locations, resonate in sympathy. It is tempting to draw upon similar models from the eastern sciences which claim the universe is primarily an event of vibrations.

THIS THEORY BRINGS TO LIGHT a number of highly significant insights. According to the conventional biological theory, behavior is either an innate instinct (like a child pedaling his legs at birth or a chick which cheeps and opens its beak for food) or the behavior is learned. Instinctual, innate behavior is supposedly embedded within the genes and is passed from generation to generation. However, according to conventional theory, learned behavior cannot be passed on except by teaching — toolmaking or language are just such types of learned behavior.

This idea is totally upturned by certain anomalies observed over the last half century in laboratory experiments. It seems that it is possible for a behavior to be learned by an animal in a New York experimental lab, to be passed on to a similar animal in New Delhi with no direct contact.

In a classic experiment conducted by William McDougall at Harvard in the 1920s, white rats were trained in a water maze. Over many generations the rats showed considerable improvement in solving the maze which the researcher interprets as a modification of the rats genes. When other skeptical researchers repeated his experiments in both Scotland and Australia, their first generation rats appeared to continue where the last generation of rats in America had ceased. In Melbourne they found that while the trained rats continued to improve their scores so did the control rats who were unrelated, thus ruling out any genetic modification. The experiments were abandoned as inconclusive. Yet this pattern is exactly what might be expected from the effect of morphic resonance proposed 40 years later.

We are surrounded by examples of habitual fields of behavior from driving cars to stacking deck chairs along the beaches of northern Europe.

A SIMILAR MYSTERY AROSE over crystal growth. When synthesizing compounds, which have never existed before, chemists will attempt to produce crystals of the new creation. This generally proves to be exceedingly difficult. However, once the first batch crystallizes, the technicians find the process progressively easier to repeat. The most usual conventional explanation for this is that somehow there is contamination from seed crystals, but this does not fully explain some cases in very distant locations all over the globe.

Sheldrake's theory of morphological resonance or form fields could well account for both the crystal and the rat mysteries. According to his reasoning the first crystallization is difficult because no form field existed to generate the form, yet once the crystals had been created and re-inforced the field operated across time and space: so an original crystal in Rio de Janeiro would guide a crystal formation in Stockholm or the Fiji Islands. Precisely the same would happen to the rats. As the field strengthened over generations so the control group would also feel the effects and rats all over the world would be able to solve their mazes much better.

If this is actually the case then surely human behavior can also be changed in similar ways. The first genius who used a flint stone to cut his food could have passed this on without ever actually encountering his neighbors. Just how much is learning a language an innate ability, or the ease of making tools, using computers or driving cars? If we look at the history of ideas we also see a recurring pattern. One individual has an insight which he or she passes on to a few others. At first they often meet strong opposition from the conventional and established bodies, but after a revolutionary period most accept the new idea which then over a period of time becomes habitual and entrenched only to be overthrown by a fresh innovator.

Of all previous known historic periods we are living in the most revolutionary in terms of challenging and shifting our old ideas. We seem to be at the point where a number of fields might be intensifying but have not made the final breakthrough — or have they?

Critical Mass

"Everywhere on Earth, at this moment, in the new spiritual atmosphere created by the idea of evolution, there float, in a state of extreme mutual sensitivity, love of God and faith in a new world: the two essential components of the ultra human. These two components are everywhere in the air... sooner or later there will be a chain reaction."
(Teilhard de Chardin)[21]

IT APPEARS THAT the morphogenetic fields do require a certain number of repetitions of forms which set up a resonance, to establish a habit for similar forms. But the questions surrounding such a critical mass are just one of the knottier issues of the hypothesis. So far there is no definite and conclusive evidence to verify this. Evolutionary changes tend to appear on a time scale which is not easily measured.

We might, however, consider the possible effect of the activity of five thousand years of enlightened beings who must have established a resonating field of enlightenment. If we apply the hypothesis of formative causation to the possibility of such a field then surely we might expect to see an increase in the habit. Up until now and as far as is known this does not seem to have been the case. The greatest known explosion of consciousness stretching from China to Greece occurred two thousand five hundred year ago and while there have been many who have entered the natural state since then, nothing of comparable intensity has happened since then.

Yet as we have seen, the first generation of rats in the experiments in Australia and Scotland which followed the original work in America by McDougall picked up 'scores' where the last generation of rats in his experiment had left off. According to the theory, once a field is established, it accumulates. Presumably it is possible for such a field to exist for long periods without affecting anything simply because there is no form which fits it. A form might arise but the environment might be too alien to support it so that it would die out. Early attempts at language might have been like this. But when similar forms reappear the field is sufficiently charged with the past that it might only require a few such individuals to trip the whole habit in a much larger group.

A disciple once asked Ramana Maharshi why he didn't preach his message to the world. He replied, *"Have you not heard of the saying of Vivekananda, that if one but thinks a noble, selfless thought even in a cave, it sets up vibrations throughout the world and does what has to be done — what can be done?"*

It is tempting, following this line of reasoning, to imagine that it might only need one more enlightened being to trigger a transformation in other individuals who are tottering on the threshold. This, in turn, would strengthen the field still further so that the whole species might undergo a similar change.

In our epoch this could be just another piece of useful thinking to add to a collective dream of the New Age (having itself a form field, of course,) but the hypothesis does not invite such parallels.

"I think it will happen when there is a great enough number of conscious people who absolutely feel that there is no other way. Everything that has been, and still is now, has to appear to be an absurdity that cannot go on any longer — then it will be able to happen, but not before. Despite everything, a time will come when the movement will veer toward a new reality. There was a moment. There was a moment when the mental being was able to manifest on earth. There will be a moment when human consciousness will reach a state that will unable the supramental conscious- ness to enter that human consciousness and manifest. It doesn't stretch like a rubber band, you know: there comes a moment when it happens — it can be done in a flash."
(The Mother)[22]

"Nature's purpose seems to be (I cannot make any definitive statement) to create flowers like that, human flowers like that. We have only a handful of flowers, which you can count on your fingers: Sri Ramakrishna, some other people. Not the claimants we have in our midst today. Not the gurus — I am not talking about them. It is amazing — that man who sat there at Tiruvannamalai (Ramana Maharshi) — his impact on the West is much more than all these gurus put together — very strange, you understand?"
(U.G. Krishnamurti)[23]

Buddhafield

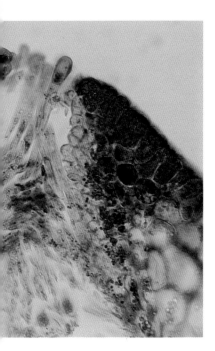

"As our knowledge grows there must be a million or more genes in our nuclei that we are just not using — we have enormous genetic deposit accounts on which we could presumably draw in times of need."
(Lyall Watson)[25]

SO WHAT ABOUT MAN? Is it possible that one more individual who enters the natural state and undergoes the enlightening explosion which appears to permeate the whole body down to the very cells, can change the whole direction of the species? What if there are a hundred sages or men and women in their natural enlightened state; can they be sufficient to create that open threshold which can alter a substantial number of our species and create a breakthrough to a new form ?

We know from Gautama the Buddha that there is a mysterious phenomenon which he termed the "Buddhafield." Two thousand five hundred years ago there was an extraordinary following of over ten thousand monks gathered around him in the tiny state of Bihar, India. He maintained that the intense energy field that was generated around him could start a chain reaction. It certainly seemed to, for, from all accounts, more disciples entered the natural enlightened state with him than with any other master at any other time. Yet he was not alone in Bihar. Contemporary with him were at least seven other enlightened beings of his caliber who lived in the state of Bihar, including *Mahavira*. The phenomenon of enlightenment, however, was not just restricted to that tiny area in India. Enlightened beings of genius appeared simultaneously from the far to the near East. It is hardly a coincidence that so many geniuses of consciousness should all spring into being at the same time unless there was some invisible field which influenced consciousness over geographical barriers.

One of our present evolutionary pioneers has discussed the Buddhafield in some detail.

"Tuning in to a fully developed Master Field, where all of these evolutionary processes have already taken place, permits those changes to be magnified and quickened or, in effect, lived into that system without its having to pass through certain of the processes associated with the individual struggle to evolve. Therefore, as I have indicated, the Spiritual Adept is a unique mechanism in Nature provided for the sake of the spiritual and altogether human evolution of human beings, as well as the transformation and evolution of all beings and all processes that exist in the cosmos."
(Da Free John)[24]

Shock to the System

Another man of insight, J. Krishnamurti, once said that it would take 10 awakened beings working in consort; while Gurdjieff assessed the number of such beings needed to change the world at 100. Bhagwan Shree Rajneesh, who has attempted to bring 10,000 disciples into his own Buddhafield, agrees with Gurdjieff that the number needed to detonate the evolutionary megabomb is around 100. And yet maybe it is only *one*.

WE HAVE SEEN THAT the habits of the formfield can be very persistent; in fact this is the major characteristic of the field and yet perhaps it works in unexpected ways. U.G. Krishnamurti points out (the author's comments in parenthesis): "*You see, the trouble is that the more beliefs* (behavior which create a form field) *you have, the more difficult it becomes for you, because one more thing is added to your tradition. Your tradition (the re-enforced habit field) which you want to preserve, has been strengthened and fortified by the appearance of a new man, because you are trying to fit him into the framework of your tradition.*

"*However, the new man is interested in breaking the cumulative nature of the tradition — not maintaining the tradition, but breaking it. A certain person breaks it and you make it a part of that accumulated wisdom — that is why it becomes more difficult. Even that revolutionary statement of that particular individual who has achieved this breakthrough has already become part of your tradition: your very listening has destroyed the revolutionary nature of this breakthrough and has made this a part of knowledge, tradition, because* you *are the tradition. The listening mechanism that is operating there in you is the tradition — it strengthens itself through the listening process.*"[26]

So, strangely, those who create a tradition around those in a natural state could actually be strengthening a habitual field rather than breaking it. Each enlightened being tries to break old traditions and beliefs but often ends up, unwittingly, adding to the habit field. "*By the time this has been accepted — what is coming out of me — the need has been created for somebody else to come and blast it.*"
(U.G. Krishnamurti)[27]

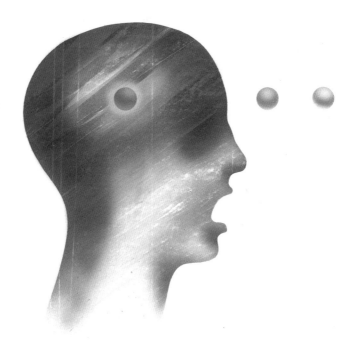

On the other hand, the shock of a new insight can actually lead to a change. It can literally transfigure the very brain cells. The new energy can jolt a lifetime's accumulation of connections and habitual neural pathways. A flash of insight, which comes from the original ground of the implicit order, is not bound by *time*. If it manages to surmount the barriers and to shock the "timebound" cells of the mind for even a microsecond, all the old connections are blasted away and become disentangled in that immense dissipative fluctuation.

"The human brain — not My brain or Your brain — has evolved through a million years. One biological freak can move out of it, but how do you get at the human mind generally to make it see all this?" (J. Krishnamurti)[28]

Sorcerer's Apprentice

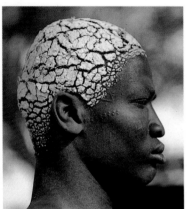

"The feeling grows that scientists are finding it increasingly difficult to predict the consequences of their work, that technology has become the sorcerer's apprentice of our age. The concept of dangerous knowledge appears in a variety of images — the mushroom cloud, the usurping robot, the armless child of thalidomide. Many scientists object violently to the idea of dangerous knowledge, taking the position that all increases in knowledge are inherently good."
(Rensellaar-Potter)[29]

AS NATURE'S FAVORITE CHILD, her latest experiment on the planet, we seem to have acquired, in these last short accelerating decades, the capacity to change evolution's entire direction. Within the next few years our genetic engineers will be in a position to clone from the cell of any man or woman in the natural enlightened condition. If their cells have subtly altered during entry into this state then perhaps it is possible for the resulting embryo to enjoy the same exalted status. With such evolutionary higher cells and a different blueprint will this circumvent the whole spiritual quest?

Every evolutionary pioneer, every individual in the natural enlightened state, has always insisted that there are no shortcuts and that there are no ways that evolution can be coerced or forced to give up its secrets. We cannot even give the gentlest of pushes to the evolutionary process — that is, so far. But we now possess frightening new genetic tools, which threaten to change even that position.

IN THE NEXT CHAPTER we can at last view a portrait of the unknown man and woman who herald the next stage of our evolutionary development. So this seems a good opportunity to summarize the evidence of their impending arrival accumulated so far.

Unused Functions in the Species

1) There are unknown functions within the brain and glandular systems which have only recently been suspected by western science. Yet two thousand five hundred years ago these had been carefully mapped by eastern science and mystics in many parts of the Middle East and Europe.

2) These functions may be connected with higher states of consciousness and seem to have specific purposes within the evolutionary development of man.

3) The species has, at large, ignored these evolutionary "sleepers" choosing instead a different evolutionary path which has led us down a dead end.

4) The species as a whole now faces a crisis of de-programming and a radical re-volutionary review of the true nature of the situation.

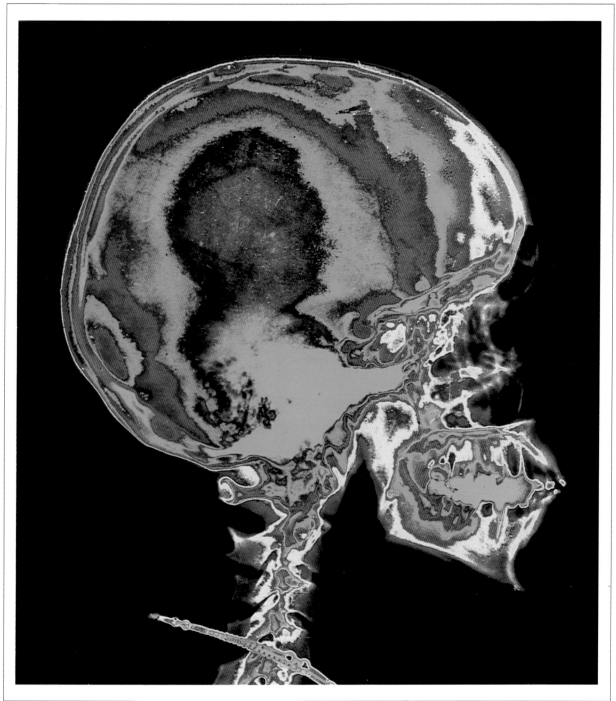

Summary of Evidence

Evolutionary Witnesses

1) There have been rare and isolated cases of individuals who have stumbled across an evolutionary threshold into what they see as the true evolutionary goal of the species.

2) These pioneers have returned from their expeditions with maps and routes to the natural state of man and have shown where we originally came from, who we are and where we are heading.

3) Detailed and unequivocal maps from widely differing traditions and disciplines seem to share certain fundamental landmarks. The major common denominator is that there are seven levels of evolutionary consciousness.

4) Some of their findings seem to point towards what the next stage of mankind might be like.

5) Some of the new scientific models of the West show remarkable points of similarity to those of the mystic vision.

Meeting the Conditions for Evolutionary Change

1) It is recognized that any evolutionary change is triggered by a crisis of some kind within the environment, usually a dramatic alteration of temperature, a population explosion, a change in climate or a depletion of the natural habitat. At present we face all these factors simultaneously.

2) Scientific and technological advances are accelerating beyond our abilities or wisdom to use them and we may be hurtling towards an unprecedented catastrophe unless we jump to a higher understanding.

3) At least seven technological and cultural explosions which have occurred in the last four decades are of sufficient magnitude to detonate the evolutionary bomb and they are all operating now at the same time, creating secondary chain reactions amongst themselves, much like the catalysts in a dissipative structure at a threshold.

4) A radical change has happened in the field of ideas in the last two decades which is of a magnitude not experienced in our known history. Every established hypothesis has been challenged, from those of the sciences to religion, and the whole moral and ethical code of the society. The views we have of both ourselves, the species as a whole, and the universe in which we act have undergone a profound paradigm shift. For the first time the species is reaching out towards higher consciousness on a global scale.

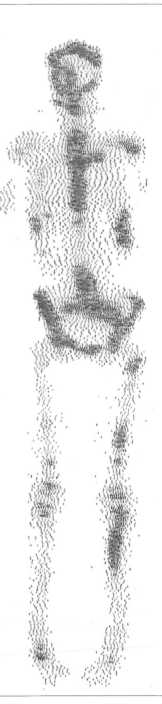

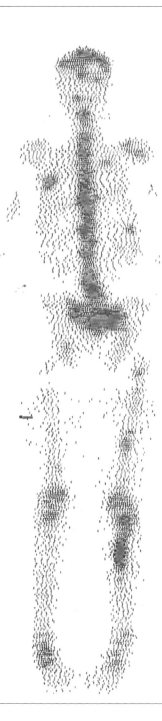

5) From the evidence available it seems that a bifurcation point, escalating technology and an evolutionary threshold appeared in the 1950s and that we are already launched across its boundaries.

6) A number of prophesies forecast that the end of this millennium will be the apocalyptic age where one world dies and another is born and where at least ten natural and esoteric cycles are likely to coincide.

7) We appear to have traveled along a mechanistic and materialistic path as far removed from the natural living state as it is possible to go and are already undergoing a profound reappraisal of all our values.

Waking up the Evolutionary Sleepers

1) There appear to be higher functions in the body which can remain dormant throughout an individual's life time. However, once activated they can transform the entire body-mind. They could be tuning mechanisms or physical sites. These are termed "evolutionary sleepers."

2) The possible sites of the "sleepers" are in the ductless glands, the mid and upper reaches of the brain and the heart.

3) At the point of entering the natural state the whole body becomes enlightened, often undergoing cataclysmic changes.

4) While there are many ways for an individual to start the evolutionary ball rolling, so far the species as a whole has not managed to trigger the higher functions at all. Those rare individuals who have, may only be fragments of what mankind might be if the whole population jumped to the next higher stage.

5) The most likely activators or triggering mechanisms for the species as a whole seem to be:

a) an environmental or cultural crisis on a truly apocalyptic scale;

b) a powerful shock to man's view of himself and the universe in which he lives;

c) a critical mass, or sheer numbers of evolutionary pioneers who have already entered the natural state. This whole endeavor produces a vibrational resonating field, a "Buddhafield" which can trigger a chain reaction in the whole population;

d) genetic engineering or some chemical agent which heightens awareness of our condition or even triggers the sleeper itself;

e) a combination of all factors operating simultaneously.

CHAPTER TWO

The Unknown Guest

ALTHOUGH WE HAVE COVERED much eclectic and esoteric ground so far the visions and messages of psychics and clairvoyants have been avoided. Up until this point there was no plausible shape for our unknown changelings. However, now that we have established a few firm and independent references, we can draw upon the vague, yet persistent, visions of the psychics to fill out a complete dossier on the newcomers.

In the present chaos of 20th Century metaphysics, it is difficult to separate the genuine from the bogus. There have been visionaries of the past, like John of Patmos, with his apocalyptic Book of Revelation. There have been prophets such as the 16th Century Doctor Nostradamus with ten volumes of *The Centuries*. There is Edgar Cayce, the well-known American clairvoyant. There are Merlin's 7th Century Prophesies, the visions of Black Elk and those of the Hopi Indians. As we have mentioned, Gautama the Buddha, in his Diamond Sutra, speaks of an age ofwenlightenment two thousand five hundred years into his future. All these tell of our age and of the coming end to this century.

At present there are countless mediums and channelers, speaking for such entities ad "Ramthae" "Lazaris," "Seth" and "Michael." There are little men in flying saucers who warn of coming disasters, there are pre-cognizants and psychics who have all added their part to our overflowing pool of knowledge of the coming apocalypse, the next thousand years of peace and higher consciousness.

The real difficulty in sorting out the true from the counterfeit is that they all seem to offer much the same fare. Their menus are stickily similar, whether they emerge from disembodied entities or from the Maitreya himself.

The major theme is that we are giving birth to a new mankind, an entirely new kind of being who will herald a new age of the spirit. Already it is said that our glands (and glands are a very popular subject amongst today's mediums) are subtly changing and will become more active in the future.

Glands are the focal point of mediumship and are supposedly the major channeling mechanisms of our bodies.

Prophecy

ALONG WITH THESE GLANDULAR alterations, a number of unspecified and vague changes are claimed to be happening to the gray matter of the neo-cortex of the brain. Invariably the messages are reassuring provided we can avoid blowing ourselves to pieces in the coming decade.

But these visions are what one might expect at the end of any century, and especially at the end of the 10 centuries of the seventh millennium which closes in the year 2000.

The naiveté of our responses is also somewhat predictable; in the light of this heavily unbalanced scientific and materialist culture, such overreaction is to be expected. In the massive switch in viewpoint towards magic and the esoteric we all stand as gullible natives totally unprepared for any exposure to the long traditions of the occult.

Even in that bastion of materialism, the Soviet Union, Premier Gorbachov finds it necessary to use make-up on the distinctive birthmark on his forehead to avoid the current rumors of having the "mark of the beast."

We stand doubly transfixed when new mysterious ideas, so beautifully opposite to the grim and loveless realities of modern scientific life, are so reasonable and humanitarian. We are told that "we know everything already but have just forgotten" — "we are Gods" — "we create everything around us, every illness or event" — "there is no death, only growth and change" — "the universe and our consciousness are part of a great hologram" — "unconditional love and acceptance are the only way" — and so on.

Most of the currently popular ideas set their origin in some ancient teaching which actually makes them even more hallowed when up-to-date versions are given. But let us take a typical example from the field. This one from one of the channeled entities:

"Beautiful woman, blessed be you and your wondrous child and that which you bring forth upon this planet for all who bring forth from their wombs this time forward bring masters. They are Gods that will herald in the new age, for they are the livers of the New Age, they are advance entities of

The Book of Revelation provides an ominous warning to the non-magical, Marxist society, with a reference to the ill-fated star "wormwood" which "burnt like a lamp."

"And the third of the waters became wormwood; and many men died of the waters because they were made bitter."

Chernobyl means "wormwood" in Ukrainian.

higher cause. And that which you carry in your beloved womb, Entity, be not a primitive; it be a wondrous master already understood. All like you will bring forth great fruit that will bring forth an age called the 'Age of Spirit, Age of Light,' on this planet." (Ramtha)[30]

Ramtha on many occasions has offered supremely gifted insights into our present condition and a number appear in this book, but this particularly sticky confection exemplifies only too well the superficial and glossy esoteric pulp which is being offered as true vision.

It is easy to be either overwhelmed or cynical about such a statement. In its grandiloquent sweep it can neither be proven nor refuted any more than the old Christian Fundamentalists can be questioned about their Heaven and their Hells. These new visions of a "Paradise on the doorstep" certainly fulfill the same vague yearnings, which we all share, of the better life to come. It seems irresistible, when flavored with the piquant seasoning of New Age psychology: "positive thinking," "treasuring" and accepting oneself and being midwives and mothers to the new Gods and super-beings.

The superman archetype was first unearthed by Jung in the 1930s, when he observed the appearance of an all-powerful legendary nordic hero in the dreams and unconscious of his patients. This was almost 20 years before Europe had to pay the price for the Nazi view of a blond, Aryan Super-race.

The end of the last millennium in the 10th Century in Europe is also an object lesson to us before we are swept away on a mass hysteria of higher beings. It was a period beset by a frenzied panic, based on the firm belief that the old world was about to be ended by a mighty apocalyptic cataclysm. The new world of that time was to be peopled by higher beings, angels and a heavenly Christian host.

As we know the dark ages became even darker. But now another archetype has arisen from the collective unconscious and a new man of Light stands at the threshold; the channelers' reassuring words must be a life raft for those of us who feel we are adrift in a shark-infested ocean with nothing to hold on to.

Mediums and Messages

Michel de Nostradamus

From the *Diamond Sutra* **we learn that Gautama the Buddha claimed that after each twenty-five centuries there comes a radical change of consciousness on Earth with an accompanying period of intense chaos. Buddha moves the wheel of Dhamma once every two thousand five hundred years and it takes that length of time for the momentum to fade. The wheel that Buddha moved has finally come to rest and his Age dies. The wheel must then be started again for the Dhamma must be renewed. It breathes for twenty-five centuries and then fades away to be reborn totally and radically transformed. Buddha in his time said that at the next turning of the wheel, which is in our present epoch, humankind would enter a totally different stage in the transformation of man. Subhuti, his disciple, actually asked about our age and Buddha answered and said he could see us with his precognitive senses, his Buddha eye, and that our transformation would be even greater than it was at his time.**

John of Patmos

After a wild apocalyptic vision at the end of the Book of Revelation, John witnessed a millennium of peace and a new spirituality

BUT BEFORE DISMISSING all channeling, all psychic visions, all the tiny green aliens with their messages for mankind, we must look a little more closely at the phenomenon which is sweeping through the developed countries at present. The higher consciousness movement, whatever bizarre form it might take on, *is* altering our perceptions of the world.

For the spiritual masters the psychic areas of experience which are most encountered are those most highly suspect being firmly embedded within the fourth stage of evolutionary development. This is the twilight zone of miracles and wonders where many get stuck. Yet perhaps this is also the gateway through which the species as a whole must pass. And it is just that spectacular portal which the sages and evolutionary adepts warn their disciples to avoid.

There is only a hair's breadth difference which separates the schizophrenic from the medium, the madman from the master, and this fourth stage mind-field invariably sorts them out. Perhaps it is a necessary risk which the species must face. In the overreaction to the scientific age of materialism we might well be entering a counterbalancing age of high sorcery. Perhaps the collective mind must cross the "Dark night of the Soul," passing through power and mystery before leaping the gap to the first true mystic level of the fifth stage of evolutionary development.

Already there must be more than enough psychic fields morphically resonating to set us down this path, jostling our disembodied travelers along the way.

Most of the voices at present seem harmless enough, although some do have that unmistakable whiff of sulfur. Some of the messages are simply mediocre, some are just copies of previous ideas and some

with a new Adam which would appear now. "*And I saw a new Heaven and a new Earth; for the first Heaven and the first Earth were passed away.*" **D.H. Lawrence in his last commentary on Revelations gives his interpretation:** "*The famous book of seven seals in this place is the body of man. Of man; of Adam; of any man... And the seven seals are the seven centers or gates his dynamic consciousness. We* are witnessing the opening and conquest of the great psychic centers of the human body. The old Adam is going to be conquered, die and be reborn as the new Adam. But in stages. In seven stages, or in six stages and then a climax, seven.*" **And what does he see as the transformed spheres of consciousness? The four dynamic natures of man and the three higher natures. So like our seven-fold map.**

are very well intentioned but lack real vision or a fire in the belly.

Alongside these there are a number of time honored predictions of the coming of a new world and a new man at the end of this century.

As well as the accelerating series of simultaneous technological, sociological and spiritual crises, we face an extraordinary conjunction of mysterious cycles.

The fin de siècle: the ending of any century invariably brings with it a rash of Doomsday prophecies, confusion, hysteria and the whole set of apocalyptic and new age prophecies. The end of this century, however, is also the end of the magical seventh millennium, the last thousand years of our known history. This raises the tension and the expectancy even higher. Astrologically we are at the changeover point from the Age of Pisces to the Age of Aquarius, and in terms of the clairvoyants, this also marks the five hundred year psychic cycle, when there is supposedly a marked change of consciousness planet-wide.

The Celts believed that the veil between the world of man and the worlds of the spirit becomes very thin at certain seasons, in certain ages and epochs. Celtic traditions mark this period as taking place every five hundred years. Even the mythical Phoenix, which has a life of five hundred years, is due to re-appear in a mighty holocaust to rise again, reborn from its own ashes.

The solar system also has its own cycle in which five planets align with Earth, on the other side of the sun, to play a tug of war with the planet. This is due on May the 5th in the year 2000 and no one knows what catastrophes could happen when the new gravitational forces act upon the already delicately balanced rotational axis of planet Earth.

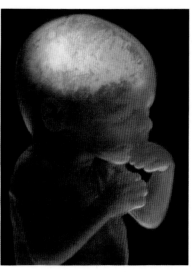

"Root and branch shall change places and the newness of the thing shall pass as a miracle."

Hopi Indian Prophecy

"The emergence of the future fifth world has begun. You can read this in the earth itself. Plant-forms from previous worlds have begun to spring up as seeds... the same kinds of seeds are being planted in the sky as stars. The same kinds of seeds are being planted in our hearts. All these are the same, depending on how you look at them. This is what makes the emergence to the next, fifth world."

Madame Blavatsky

At the end of her mammoth esoteric treatise, the *Secret Doctrine*, **Madame Blavatsky** describes the sixth root, the Race of Man, whose *"pioneers — the peculiar children who will grow into peculiar men and women — will be regarded as abnormal oddities, physically and mentally. Then, as they increase, and the numbers become with every age greater, one day they will awake to find themselves in a majority. It is the present men who will then be regarded as exceptional mongrels, until these die out in their turn in civilized lands."*

Michel de Nostradamus

The famous 16th Century prophet predicted a thousand years of peace, *"when the seventh millennium has come,"* in which man is transformed. It is to be a period where the two sides of the hemispheres meet, science and religion merge and a galactic community comes into being.

Merlin

Merlin the wizard, the mystical sage who tutored the legendary King Arthur of ancient Britain, and who was supposedly the instigator of the whole Quest for the Holy Grail, left behind a book of prophesies. In verse 88, he tells of our time.

243

A New Genetic Ring

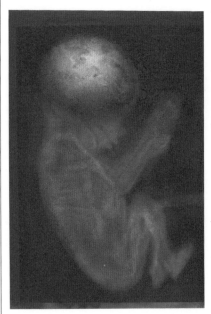

We now examine a typical example of clairvoyant vision concerned exclusively with the new coming. The particular psychic in this interview is a well-known and respected clairvoyant, Vera Chiesa. Affectionately called the "Witch of Turin," she had, in a session previous to this particular interview, revealed that a friend who had died recently and who had been known by the author had chosen "*a grievously different and new path for mankind.*"

This had come as a complete surprise as the questioner had gone for entirely different reasons. At that time Vera Chiesa spoke of this friend as being in an embryo form as a male mutant of the new species. In the second interview she started by saying that all the spirit guides agree that inside each individual is inscribed his whole evolution.

"*The memory of when he was a vegetable, an animal, and therefore all the instincts that are still related to the animal that were his last expression. Slowly, slowly, throughout time, these cells have been changed and stratified. The last layer, our cerebral cortex, has been static for the last ten thousand years. It has an expansion that is excessive in comparison to all the previous rings. And therefore we are, as mankind, at the threshold of a mutation. I think that this person, A, that wants to be reborn has chosen to wait for the blossoming of this cortex, this extra cerebral ring. This event has been expected to arrive between 1990 and 2010 by most psychics, but A has chosen to be amongst the very first of their kind.*

"*There is an acceleration, however, of the passage from one generation to another. There was a time when a generation was a full twenty years. Today there is a diversification already in only five. So there is a generation gap between twenty and twenty-five, or thirty and thirty-five and so on.*"

Q: Will there be a physical expression of this mutation or just a spiritual growth?

"There will be the same diversity as there once was between the first hominids and man as we know him today. This is why this existential phase is so dramatic. Every five hundred years there is a major change in the existential cycle. But on top of that we will now see a genetic mutation. And therefore the sons and daughters will be very superior to their parents from their very birth — from their very first expression.

"There will surely be an increase in the intellectual faculties. Also the body will have two extra glands. One of these will function as a filter and preservation of the respiratory apparatus and will be situated near the actual thymus gland. It will function as a filter against all the new atmospheric changes and poisons. The other gland will be in the hepatic area functioning here as a filter and a site of protein storage.

"Aesthetically these variations will be quite slow. The tendency will be for taller men, a greater development of the entire nervous system and less growth of musculature and organs."

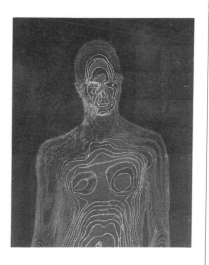

In talking of the friend she had this to say:

"He already exists in the form of a fetus. He has chosen to confront in this life the dramatic knowledge of being different. His body will carry the mutations and an extra genetic ring. The mutation is actually at genetic level already and will be exclusively related to an expansion of the gray matter way beyond what we know of today. There will be a greater development of the receptive faculties and a longer life span. This is because the heart will beat slower than is the case today. These will be the only signs of any outward mutation happening."

The Second Eve

A RECENT AND REVOLUTIONARY THEORY of Genesis has arisen within the anthropological world. Based on painstaking genetic sleuth work, micro-biologists speculate that there was once an actual Eve from whose womb the entire family of man emerged. Even ten thousand generations later her genes seem to be in all humans living today.

While scientists don't actually claim to have found the first woman, they do seem to have discovered the common genetic ancestor of the entire species from the epoch when the first-born humans appeared. Her birth date, about two hundred thousand years ago, has upset the earlier anthropological dating for it was believed that the family tree of *Homo sapiens* started long before this date. But according to these findings the evolutionary jump from archaic humans to modern man happened in one place and literally overnight.

Geneticists know of this Eve as the Mitochondrial Mother. Mitochondrial DNA coding is useful for tracing family trees simply because it is inherited only from the mother and has nothing whatsoever to do with the father. Without any Adam involved at all it preserves the family record and is only changed by mutations. These mutations are believed to be random and isolated mistakes in copying the code. Whether this is so or not the mutations are passed on to successive generations.

Each mutation then produces a new DNA which is as distinctive as any fingerprint.

Somewhere at this moment there could be a new Eve who might pass on her new life patterns to the entire next race of man. Last time she was black, broad and probably built like a heavyweight wrestler and could have been part of an Eve pool of a few hundreds. This time Eve could be any color, race or creed from amongst two billion women on the planet. She could be you!

WHAT ARE THE CHARACTERISTICS of the new changelings which might make them as gigantic an evolutionary step as when modern man appeared alongside the Neanderthals over thirty thousand years ago? What is the difference between them and us?

Perhaps we might briefly return to the analogy of an evolutionary ladder divided by one way mirrors. You will remember that in this

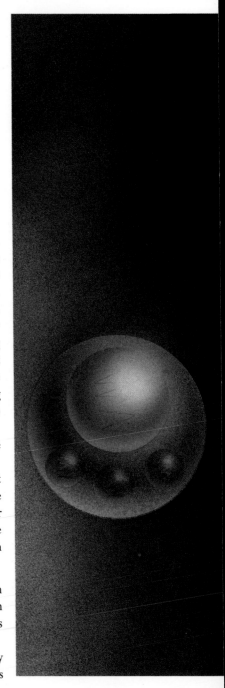

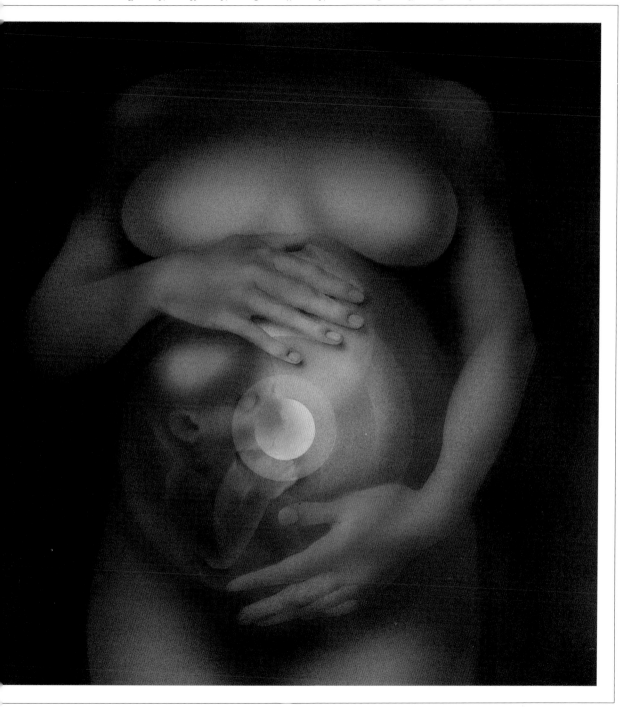

The New Stage

model we pass up through a darkened glass through which we can view the preceding level whereas those below, in looking up, can only see their own reflections in the mirror surface.

If we, from our vantage point at Level Three, look up to Level Four we are actually faced with that image of ourselves still at Level Three. There are no comparable referents for what might happen on the level above for those looking up from below.

How does someone who has glimpsed Infinite Energy, Oneness, the Unity of Existence or the Dissolution of the imaginary *ego* transmit that unbelievable experience to someone else who has only known a sense of separation, of duality and views life through the distorting lens of the "I"?

Consider for a moment what would occur if we were to add even one paranormal talent from amongst the great treasure-house of the next level of evolution to our present species. Suppose we were all telepathic and could sense, feel or in any way share the thoughts of another and that they could do the same with us. Where, one might ask, is the sense of "I"?

If both people shared the experience then any feeling of an individual and separate ego would perhaps disappear. We all have experienced this at some time or another in brief glimpses. Often a mother and child or lovers simultaneously share a thought and yet neither know who "sent" the thought or who "received" it.

What would happen if we multiplied this situation into the number of people within an entire city or even the whole species. Would this linked consciousness create a new entity or overmind which simultaneously would experience everything on a planetary scale? The shared overmind would be aware of the iceworlds of the arctic while simultaneously experiencing the noon-day sun in Mexico.

In such a scenario what would then happen to national boundaries, black and white races, over three hundred religious creeds, opposing politicians and priesthoods? All would disappear overnight, as would individual greed, crime, wars and all the other thousand and one ills which *Homo sapiens* exhibits in such abundance.

Now this account only covers telepathy. Consider if this single

The birth of man and the birth of stars. The Orion Nebulae (M42) is a bright cloud of gas and dust eleven light-years across where stars are in the process of being born. Will the new stage in consciousness give humankind the powers to shape new universes or will the external form of that consciousness change into less substantial patterns which freely range the cosmos, spanning such inconceivable galactic distances.

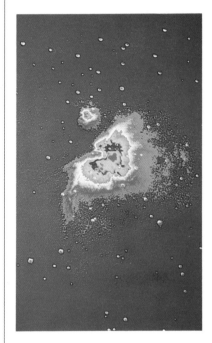

talent is joined by the whole psychic spectrum of Level Four. Add clairvoyance and the visions of all past and future events; psycho-kinesis and the changing or movement of physical objects by thought; actualizing objects and situations; spontaneous teleportation or out-of-body flights to any parts of the planet on other planes and we have a truly astounding species — far removed from our own. Even the death of the individual would be an entirely different phenomenon and not viewed in the same fearful way as we view it now.

So far we have only briefly mentioned the fourth level of evolutionary consciousness and yet this level of the psychic heart is the very stage at which we might expect any new species to enter the scene.

In the fourth stage of evolutionary development it is known that the man-state gradually dissociates from the material and phenomenal world and *enfolds* his or her consciousness. This is the initial stage — the very first step on the path to higher consciousness.

This is the borderline where humankind glimpses the first plane of the subtle world and experiences impressions partially through the gross and partly through the subtle senses. We can hear "the music of the spheres" through our normal ears and see subtle images with both our normal and inner eyes. This level is the point which demarks the limits of the material and subtle worlds. The subtle world is the domain of Infinite Energy and anyone in the early levels of that sphere can perform what Meher Baba calls *"minor miracles."*

These tricks can demonstrate through the release of the Infinite Energy such powers as plucking Swiss watches from the air, *"converting a dry tree into a green one and vice versa, stopping railway trains and motor cars, filling a dry well with water, and so forth."* (Meher Baba) [31] This has so far only been demonstrated by single individuals, but if we imagine an entire species acting in consort in such a way, we might have some small indication as to just how different the world of the new men and women could be.

And this would only be their childhood, for the species could well move on to higher levels in the maturity of their adult life, creating a miraculous island of consciousness.

Identikit

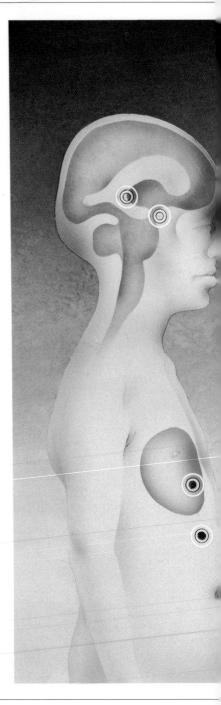

HAVING ADMITTED THAT WE REALLY have no vocabulary to describe the inner world of a member of the new species, perhaps we can fare better when describing his or her physical characteristics.

The main changes we have so far observed seem to be most likely to occur in the glands, the braincore, the crown and the heart. Clairvoyants even suggest that there may be new glands developing near the thymus and the pancreas which will filter the poisons that have recently appeared in our man-made atmosphere. They even predict a heart which beats slower which would certainly give longer lifespans and probably a less stressful lifestyle.

The need for men and women built like tanks in order to survive a hostile environment seems redundant during this high-tech epoch, which could mean that our successors will be of slighter build and perhaps taller as suggested by many psychics.

Some adaptations to possible new conditions of a changing climate with higher levels of UV radiation and other radioactive sources, might make any adaptive species tend towards darker and browner eyes and skin. It might even be possible for some individuals to have a luminous quality to their skin for we have already seen that this can happen when the actual cells undergo subtle transformations.

But these are trivial speculations compared to the nature of the treasures which the new men and women have "above the brows." Here we might find fully active pineal and pituitary glands, all orchestrating a fine-tuned endocrine system. This will certainly be good news for the immune system which would in this event be more efficient. These glands would work in far greater harmony than those we possess now and this could stimulate the full flowering of the chakras or energy wheels.

The effect of such harmony throughout the body upon the higher functions of the braincore and the crown could mean that in full maturity an individual might be expected to pass into higher and higher evolutionary levels. Again we have no real idea of what that might mean, when a species "en masse" ventures across the borders of Level Four to those above.

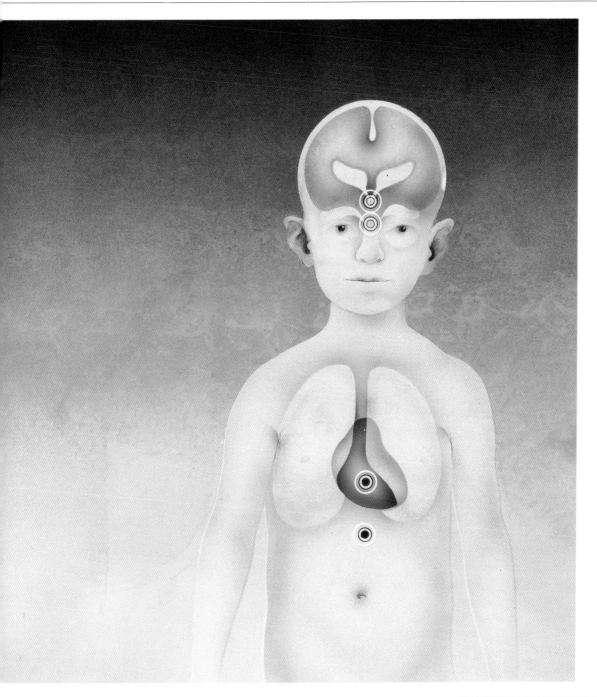

Crossroads

IF THE SPECIES AS A WHOLE moves on to the higher levels in their maturity then it will do so with the awesome power of the Gods. If our entire planetary consciousness climbs back to the level of Infinite Energy, which, even so, is still low on the evolutionary scheme of things, and succumbs to the intense temptations of misusing this unimaginable power, a power capable of breathing life into new worlds and forms, the species could detonate an implosion of consciousness sending humankind back to the level of the atom. This is the stage that Christ encountered in his own "temptation." It is the point on the path which is called by all the mystics "the Dark Night of the Soul."

However, if the species avoids this dangerous territory and moves on to the higher levels in which the creative energies are unleashed, this might change the nature of the universe completely.

This new stage we may be about to witness can be likened to the ending of an evolutionary childhood expressed by one species and the development of another in full adolescence.

Just as we view the atom as the simplest and most humble state of evolution so the new species might look back to view our present immature consciousness. It is time now for the Homo line to put away its childish things.

The Sufis, it will be remembered, have a beautiful map in the shape of a cross. It symbolizes the meeting of the horizontal and vertical dimension. The horizontal arms of the cross represent the normal life of man, which can be seen as an arrow of time moving from the past to the future.

Our minds are seen as part of this dimension. Thoughts move horizontally, one following another like an unending stream of trucks on a super highway. That succession of thoughts is time — mind is another word for time.

The Sufis maintain that the vertical dimension of the cross is that of eternity, of timeless time and the entry into the real world. As man is an upright animal, so the tower of consciousness is vertical. Animals, on the other hand, remain on the horizontal plane, having preset programs which they mindlessly follow from instinctive birth to instinctive death. There is no evolution between the two events. A cow

Homo sapiens	Homo (Novus)
Separate	Whole
Divided	Undivided
Dominant left-hand hemisphere	Balance between both hemispheres
Fragmented	Holistic
Operating in the wrong braincenters	Each braincenter operating in the correct mode
Ego, "I"	Sense of inner self
Alienated	Integrated
Robotic, mechanistic	Aware, spiritualistic
Duality	Wholeness
False Identities	Individuality
Unbalanced	Balanced
Normal five senses	Paranormal, subtle senses plus normal five senses
Belief systems	Known and experienced reality
Scientific materialism	Mysticism and scientism as a
Religion	holistic understanding
Hereafter	Now Here
States and borders	No nations, groups or divisions

Priesthood	None, direct communion with the divine
Politicians	None, no isolated group interests
Family	Supportive communities
Codes of behavior	Individual codes
Work ethic/Vacation	Work and vacation blend
Urbanization and depersonalization of the environment	No need for industrial and urban sprawls
Wars, genocide, crimes	When no sense of separation, no "I" or ego, there is no point
Destruction of the environment	Reverence for life and an ecological responsibility
Men and women	Both equal and unique, poles of a balance
Ambition, competition	No pressure for achievement
Static nouns	Flowing verbs

is a cow is a cow; she does cow-ish things. She gives no indication that she ever yearns to be a butterfly.

All the evidence so far points to the fact that human beings are unique in this way. In the animal kingdom we are eternal pilgrims on our unending quest for ourselves and more than ourselves.

Humankind stands exactly at the intersection of two worlds. Man is the threshold where the vertical and the horizontal worlds meet. In our natural state we are the bridge between these two dimensions.

One pre-man once stood at just such a crossroads as we do today. On that occasion he made the great evolutionary step by moving vertically. The revolutionary jump for the primate was that change of body axis and in that moment an immense change came about: consciousness appeared. And now at this moment we stand at the next evolutionary intersection and the change this time is that of consciousness itself.

So the essential dimension of this new consciousness in the new men and women could be seen as an exquisite balance existing at the threshold of both worlds — the horizontal and the vertical — the world of matter, space and time and the subtle world of the formless and the timeless. This state hovers, like alternating electricity, between two polarities.

The new species could be seen to play on the seashore of time, moving in and out of the waves, poised as it were on the threshold of time and the timeless, as part of their natural birthright.

This brief list of comparative lifestyles of the old and the new reads, at first glance, like a utopian dream by our present standards, set in some fantasy fiction. But if it does seem far-fetched just consider again what happens when our species just gains one, single additional talent — that of telepathy. It may then be seen that these new states of being would inevitably occur without any other paranormal gift involved. Expand this scenario to include the total number of paranormal talents which we might expect to find in the spectrum of Level Four and such a list begins to appear too modest.

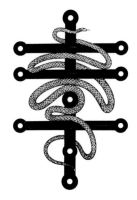

253

A Natural Birthright

I**T IS SAID IN THE** E**AST** that dying is the first stage of birth. If a man dies consciously and aware, he will remain conscious at both his own conception and birth. Both Buddha and Mahavira insisted that birth is actually a greater suffering than death and that the shock of the birth trauma inevitably severs all links with that consciousness. From the pain of the passage through the birth canal the child falls unconscious and any of the delicate and subtle connections with the previous memories are broken or blocked and the new child forgets.

Buddha had also said that our present age would see more highly developed and conscious beings than ever before. If it is so, the question which arises is what happens when such "higher" beings manage to be born without the loss of that precious memory? Perhaps this was the secret of Zarathustra when he was born laughing.

Giving birth to a child is a profound responsibility at any time, but the birthing of the new changelings promises to be an even more delicate and intimate affair between mother and child. It is often claimed that when a mother has a being of higher consciousness in her womb she becomes more aware herself. We can hope that for the sake of our new children she would try to give the baby the most natural and easy welcome possible. Recent statistics in America clearly demonstrate that there is a direct relationship between delinquency and shocking or traumatic births. Likewise it is shown that gentle, natural births seem to produce remarkably stable, well-adjusted, often brilliant and clairvoyant children.

Most childbirth is still a hospital event where too often the mother is confused and bewildered and in most cases under some form of sedation. Even now she is hoisted upon a delivery table with her legs in straps or stirrups, having little say in the whole birth process. At worst she feels that there is a conspiracy on the part of both doctor and hospital staff to keep her ignorant and alienated from her own instincts and natural functions. And because we live in such an artificial environment, equally artificial stresses and tensions arise around the birth event which means an expert is needed to tell the mother what to do. Often this is a male doctor who of course knows nothing of the experience of giving birth.

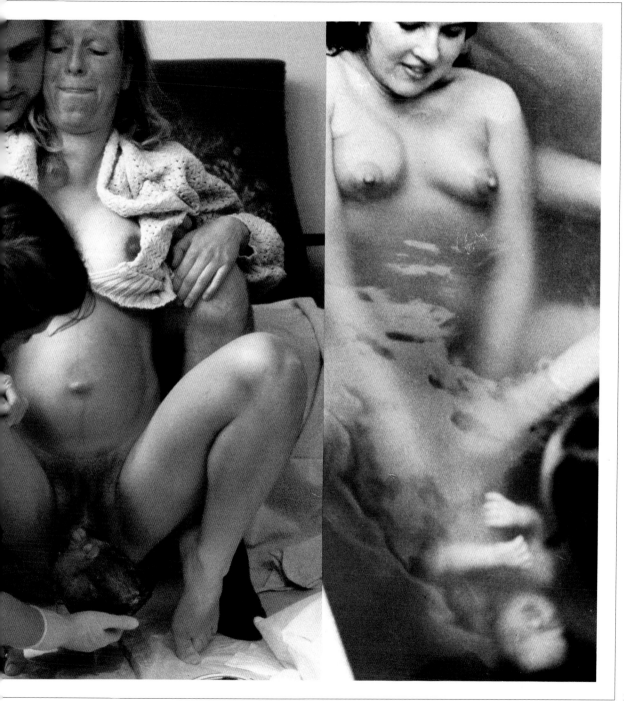

The poor child is hauled out of the womb, half drugged from the standard hospital procedures of administering pain killers. The baby is immediately subjected to a battery of traumas. There can be a difference of as much as 25 degrees in temperature between the womb and the great outside. There are bright lights, harsh noises and sharp pungent smells. Then the child may suddenly be hung upside down with the blood rushing into the brain killing some of the most delicate cells which so far have evaded destruction.

At the end of the whole battle he or she, even in some hospitals today, receives a hefty clout on the buttocks to help them take that first searing blast of oxygen into the lungs. A great welcome to planet Earth.

All the pioneers of natural birthing methods share the idea that the mother knows best. Birth is seen as a natural, instinctual process whether the actual techniques employ seated, kneeling, in baths or out of bath methods. Natural childbirth places the responsibility firmly with the mother and in doing so it can bring with it the awareness, the wonder and miracle of the creation.

The degree of difficulty in giving birth is largely related to the degree of fear experienced by the mother. When the body relaxes there is less pain, when the pain decreases there is less fear. Any effect upon the mother is inevitably transmitted to the child, so if the conscious experience of birth is ecstatic for the mother we can be sure it will more likely be so for the child.

Leaving the womb could be a delightful and exciting adventure if there is no fear from the sudden change of the environment. If the child emerges into soft lights and a loving welcoming atmosphere, with a warm bath awaiting him, surely this is to have a lasting impression upon his whole organism. It is the foundation stone of his attitude to that world and those who live in it.

The new changelings could be highly sensitive or even partly conscious of what is going on, so any technique which will ease that passage into the new world would be crucial to their later development. We now turn to such a method which promises even greater

Water Babies

safeguards against the loss of that precious memory — underwater birth.

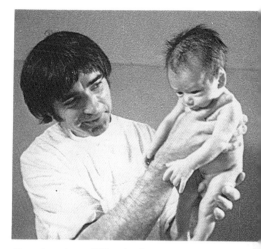

THE PIONEER, IN THE 1960s, of modern water-birthing techniques, Igor Charkovsky, was born in the Ural mountains of Russia and spent much of his youth amongst the healers of the district. He never lost contact with sensitives, energy readers and clairvoyants, so when he started his experimental underwater birthing it seemed natural to use the psychics' skills to contact the child in the womb. He found that they could follow the whole intimate process between mother and child, detecting any difficulties or negative effects during the actual birth.

Water is a beautiful medium for relaxing the mothers and bringing them to subtler states of consciousness where they are more sensitive to their deeper instincts. Warm water both relaxes and acts as a lubricant to allow the woman's body to stretch naturally. At the moment of birth the baby, all by itself, ascends to the surface without effort. Its new environment is identical in warmth and salinity to that of the water bag of the womb and while the umbilical cord remains unsevered the child can breathe perfectly.

Above: A newborn child under the influence of gravity is helpless, unable to move around or even lift its head. The same child under water, in a supportive element, is suddenly granted the freedom of movement and exploration. He moves with grace, delight, quickly mastering his new environment even as young as one month old.

Charkovsky claims that many thousands of refined and delicate brain cells are destroyed in the usual traumatic transition from the womb to the outside environment. Sudden gravitational effects crush these cells, whereas a gentle entrance underwater ensures their survival. In hospital procedures the overwhelming surges of hormones which are rushed into the organism to counterbalance drastic changes in temperature, pain or shock have a lasting effect upon many brain cells and the ductless glands. The gross pressures upon the soft crown of the skull are often excessive and subtle cerebral injuries can often go unnoticed throughout a young individual's life only to surface when it is too late to eradicate them.

Any woman who gives birth today could well be the new Mitochondrial Eve, the mother of the new species; and the welcome to this strange guest could be a crucial factor in how that stranger relates to our presence and the crazy world we have created.

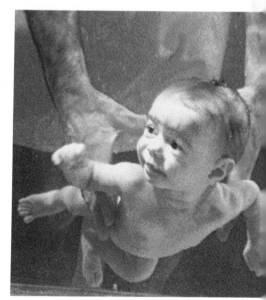

Educating Charley

IGOR CHARKOVSKY'S FIRST EXPERIMENT with human beings was with his own tiny daughter, Veta. She had been born prematurely and the doctors had given up hope that she would survive. As an experienced physiologist, Charkovsky managed to take the child into his own care. He placed her in a shallow water tank in which she could float. Soon he had to build a much larger tank with transparent sides. She even had live fish and frogs to play with. She quickly became a fine swimmer, diving to the bottom of her pool to pick up her bottled food. At seven months he took her with him to the swimming pool where he was an instructor and where she happily floated around.

When only two years old Veta had the body and coordination of a four-year-old.

In subsequent experiments with other children it has been established that coordination, a sense of balance, fearlessness, self-confidence and physical development all become greatly enhanced during water training.

Charkowsky also works with dolphins who have even been present at some of the summer underwater birthings of recent years along the Black Sea coast. It would seem that mothers relax in their company and in some mysterious way their calming presences act as a protective field around the birth.

This deep contact with some of the planet's other most intelligent creatures could well alter the whole nature of our consciousness in the exchange. The brain mass of a sperm whale is six and a half times that of a man and one wonders just what they do with such a gigantic mind. It is clear that both dolphins and whales have a rich inner life and an enormous range of feelings, thoughts and experiences. A dolphin's brain seems always to be busy: even when one hemisphere goes to sleep, the other remains wide awake and active. What myths and legends do they have, what visions and songs?

So far we have not been able to penetrate their world at all. All our attempts at communicating seem ineffectual. Perhaps it is because we assume that we are the ones that train other animals to do the tricks, never considering that they might be able to teach us a thing or two.

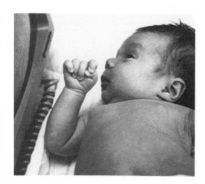

Above: **In the first three months of a child's life a computer which is programmed to display colorful patterns, shapes and sounds can stimulate the infant's visual and auditory perceptions. The child is born into a new world of technology and many parents believe that the sooner he or she masters the available tools, the more they will naturally be capable of dealing with the new Age of Information. These are the 'languages' of the 21st Century and might prove as transforming as the use of the first written words in our recorded history.**

Below: **Soviet mother using water training exercises to enhance the infant's confidence and physical agility. Such foundations give the child a positive and life enhancing attitude. Are the new children likely to have such fortunate backgrounds?**

In experiments with orcas a human musician tried to communicate with music but he was the one in the end to be the pupil. They very patiently repeated their song, correcting him whenever he made a mistake and did not leave the area until he had mastered it.

Maybe the new changeling will have similar troubles with us. His or her whole thought process might be alien, but we of course will try to impose our values upon him. There are many cautionary tales of how well-meaning missionaries destroyed far richer cultures than their own and perhaps one of the saddest stories is that of the Eskimo.

These peoples were once known as the healthiest and happiest on Earth. At the turn of this century the average Eskimo had a vocabulary of over ten thousand words. There were 110 words for different states of snow alone. By contrast the average "civilized" western man doesn't use more than fifteen hundred words.

Not surprisingly the "tannick" or white man couldn't grasp such a complex and rich vocabulary, so he invented "pidgin Eskimo" which covered about five hundred words. Increasingly the Eskimos found themselves using this impoverished conceptual language.

Born to Be Different

A report in 1971 disclosed that the "healthiest and happiest people on the globe" now had the highest mortality and double the suicide rate in Alaska. Their children now have half the life expectancy of the normal population. Could this have been through the loss of their rich and variegated cultural heritage?

It might be asked what happens to a species when we try to teach pidgin dolphin or pidgin whale? What tragedy will occur when we try to teach "pidgin newman?"

Jacques Cousteau put it succinctly when he said: *"No sooner does man discover intelligence than he tries to involve it in his own stupidity."*

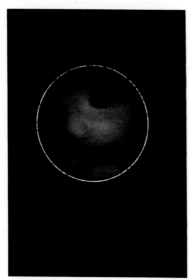

WE HARDLY KNOW OF ANY children of *Homo sapiens* who have managed to escape some distorting mirror on their way through life. Few have ever had a birth which was painless, few have ever been able to pursue their own interests without being restrained in some way and few have had a rich and supportive environment in which to grow without some worm in the woodwork, like crippling religious or social beliefs, moral codes of behavior or absurd or violent political pressures.

Even the most brilliant men and women have had some psychological skeleton in the cupboard.

For instance, researchers in the field of psychology and parapsychology have now established that many children have psychic experiences, often very profoundly influencing their development. These experiences are in no way the rarities which they were once thought to be. It would seem that young children are telepathic, while slightly older ones show powerful clairvoyance.

But parents and teachers tend to reject such experience so strongly that the child withdraws and invariably the talent dries up. Worse still, some children withdraw so much that they become apparently retarded or develop severe learning disabilities. The same children, when offered a supporting atmosphere, are found to have rich and vibrant psychic lives.

K.F. Donelly suggests that this is caused by the difference between perceptivity and perception, of either seeing the holistic movement of all phenomena or comprehending the idea of separate things and events.

Many parents with so-called retarded children complain that the child does not seem to be able to distinguish *between things*. At some time in the whole learning process most children manage to make the jump from perceiving the oneness of things to a perception of "separateness." Many so-called retarded and autistic children don't make that leap, so they remain in what can be at one and the same moment a magical and frightening world. There is often an accompanying lack of any sense of "I." But this is no handicap, except when society forces everyone into the same mold.

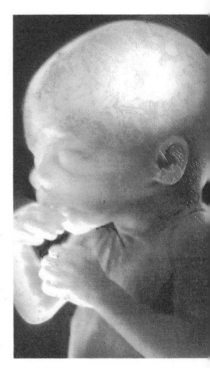

Often brilliant geniuses show remarkable similarities of both behavior and perception to retarded children. Both are exceptional, both can often take in a whole page of a book at a glance and can answer questions on it in detail. However, if you ask the autistic or retarded child to reassemble it in linear and sequential form or in written words, he or she is completely at a loss and withdraws.

The "idiot savant" mathematician who can calculate vast arrays of numbers in his head has no idea how he does it. This creative transformation in the mind is a natural intelligence which has almost completely been eradicated somewhere along the way.

Once knowledge grew so slowly that man's education could proceed in leisurely fashion for long periods before there was some

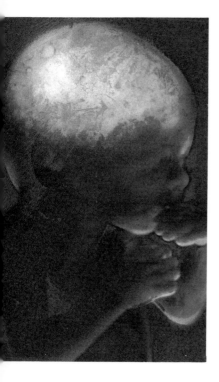

jump. The teachers and priests, as the time-honored transmitters of this accumulated knowledge, were respected for their ability to memorize that knowledge. But now there is an information explosion which can have the effect of outdating the educational system almost daily. What is taught, in certain fields, in the morning could well be obsolete by that very same evening. No longer can there be a simple repetition of ideas or rules, for change is so accelerated that facts have become fluid.

Heraclitus' statement that *"you cannot step in the same river twice,"* has become a maxim in our present epoch. What is needed is a basic understanding of the process of learning, of comprehending both the "glue" holding the facts together and the creativity which jumps tracks and heads off in new directions.

Education has long been oriented to the noun and it is difficult to change to the more active process of the verb. Any new generation will view our universe and their place in it very differently and in totally new ways to our tradition. Words in long linear sentences, as we find in this book for instance, have far less impact upon the modern child than mosaic staccato-like images from TV advertising, the news programs or computer games.

Our new changelings appear on the scene with a perfect sense of timing at the moment our media, technologies and educational system are undergoing such far-reaching and radical changes. Our educational programs are at least now acknowledging that there are two very different tendencies in the learning centers in the brain, the left and right hemisphere, and that up until now education has heavily favored the left, linear, verbal and active tendency. Now at least there is an understanding that the receptive, right-handed, spatial hemisphere also seems to be an important mode of psychic expression. However, whether we will prove to be intelligent enough to devise balanced programs to help the "new ones" is very much in debate.

Psychic

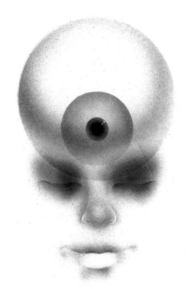

"In children who are telepathic, I have found that adults often react with fear or withdrawal on the supposition that if he can read my mind in this one thing he can read my mind on every area of my unconscious, which is rather fearsome."
(Eloise Shields)[32]

Is THIS HOW WE WILL REACT to the new children? Will we see them as potential monsters? Often a parent's or a teacher's reaction can trigger chronic withdrawal symptoms in exceptional children and their formidable talents disappear under an impenetrable shell. The child then feels alienated and alone, for the shell works both ways, and there is inevitably a guilty sense that something is very wrong with them.

Educational researchers have found that many of the so-called "retarded" or autistic children have developed chronic learning blocks simply through lack of support and understanding.

The author of this book, who had ecstatic yet awesome experiences as a child, was warned severely by his alarmed and well-meaning father that if he continued going into "those spaces" he would surely end up in a lunatic asylum. The experiences quietly shriveled up through both fear and lack of support.

Researchers have found that by carefully tapping into the psychic abilities of autistic children, their creativity can be developed dramatically. If the child's visions are accepted as being completely natural, he or she can make remarkable recovery and progress. However, the merest hint of hostility or disbelief sends the child right into the chronic autistic state again.

Extra-sensory perception comes in many shapes and forms and seems to express itself in different ways at the various stages of a child's development. A young child, for instance, is more likely to exhibit telepathic talents, while the slightly older ones show clairvoyance. But we all seem to possess these gifts in some measure.

The short list in the column indicates some of the areas of experience which may become available to many of the new children. But now imagine, if you will, a combination of all of them in one individual and consider just how overpowering such phenomena might be for the unprepared child. More than that the child has to live in a world in which no one else appears to have such experiences. For all we know, many such children have already been born but have been mistaken as autistic, schizophrenic, poor learners or simply insane.

The new species will probably not have an easy time unless they are fortunate enough to meet some of their own kind. Even then they might not reveal themselves to the world until after a second or even third generation has gained some foothold on the planet with a little group of like minds.

To give some clearer idea of some of the knotty problems which await the little pioneers we now turn to a typical case history of a young clairvoyant child.

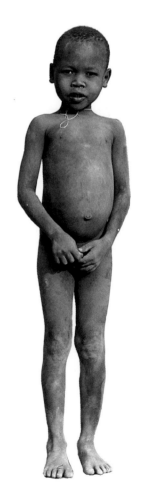

Clairvoyance:
Seeing the invisible, either distant events or people or otherwise unseen phenomena through senses other than our normal five.
Psychometry:
Seeing or sensing past events which are connected to a particular object.
Pre-cognition:
Seeing or sensing future events.
Retro-cognition:
Seeing or sensing past events.
Pre-monition:
A feeling or a forewarning which is usually unspecific, vague and yet unmistakably disquieting.
Dowsing:
Detection of subterranean objects, minerals, watercourses or mines.

Psycho-kinesis:
The mental influence of energy directed at an object which causes it to move without any physical intervention.
Teleportation or Bi-location:
Transportation of objects or oneself over distances instantaneously or in some cases simultaneously.
Out of Body Experiences (OBE):
Usually in a dream or trance state or when there is a threatening or near death situation an individual appears to leave the body, floating or flying, often over considerable distances. This is often referred to as astral projection or experiencing one of the subtle bodies.

A Cautionary Tale

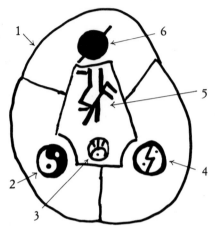

Michiel's drawing of his immediate universe is not one which would be normally associated with that of a ten-year-old.
1. Circle of the world
2. Yin and Yang
3. The sign of Jesus
4. The sign of Paramahansa Yogananda
5. Michiel's inner sign
6. The sign of Satya Sai Baba

EXCEPTIONAL CHILDREN inevitably tread a very thorny path. This case history of a young boy from Holland illustrates only too well the perplexing realities of a child born into a world which is not sensitive to his remarkable abilities. The names of both mother and child are changed because of the need for them to remain anonymous.

The boy was the first-born of a family of three, so that the mother had little to compare his behavior with at first. She remembers the shock of looking into the baby's eyes and unaccountably feeling he was clairvoyant. Otherwise, except for the fact that he did not sleep much and seldom cried, he seemed normal until about the age of two. At that age he would often see visitors "in his head" long before they would knock at the door. He cried out when unpleasant things were happening to any member of the family or close friends, even when they were a long way away. He complained of "too much light" and needed the curtains drawn in his room. Doctors checked both his sight and hearing for he also complained of a constantly droning "motor" in his head, but there seemed nothing wrong physically.

At the age of two he told his mother, Marjan: "*You are very sweet, but you are not my real mother.*" When questioned about the real one he described a woman with short, blond hair whom he had met many times "while flying" and whom he wanted to see in the flesh. But it was years later, as Marjan was showing a picture of Michiel to a clairvoyant woman, that the latter recognized him as the boy "who always visits Bacca." Bacca was the clairvoyant who Michiel kept visiting out of his body even though she had told him to come back only when he was 18 years old. The two "mothers" met with Michiel and now Bacca could advise Marjan on the many difficulties which would be likely to arise in the course of the boy's life.

For example, he was able to exchange dreams with his little sister or even steal her dream and substitute another dream instead. As this caused a lot of bewilderment and tension, Marjan had to stop him.

Up until his fifth birthday he would "fly" out of his body and it was normal for him to see far more things than others. People he did not like or feel attuned to were simply "sent away." He told them to leave and they did not return. But he felt lonely even when he could easily make friends.

Marjan purposefully did not tell the teachers that her son was clairvoyant as she did not want him to be thought odder than he was, but this inevitably led to many changes and moves around different schools. Teachers find any exceptional child difficult to teach or reach. Michiel, like so many other geniuses, autistic or retarded children, could not sit still or concentrate on any subject for long. Unless he had the teacher's full attention he would rapidly lose interest and would drift away into his own inner realm.

At eleven years of age he has managed to push the images "to the back of the head" so that they only appear when he closes his eyes. He actually doesn't want to move his attention to the front again, for it is too harrowing in everyday situations.

In our present society it is more calm and restful for children not to be clairvoyant, and this might be one of the reasons that such phenomena are actively repressed by most children about the age of seven or eight. Michiel, for instance, could not enter a supermarket or a cinema without being overwhelmed by a flood of images too intense to handle. He wanted to escape at once and immediately started dreaming. If someone held his hand he could become grounded enough to survive the ordeal but it would still take as long as a quarter of an hour for him to settle.

Real life situations on TV can shatter him completely, leaving him vulnerable and shaken for days. Violent fantasy programs or movies, however, leave him totally unmoved.

Marjan herself is a sober, ordinary housewife who understands that Michiel lives in two worlds and does not want to stress him more than necessary. It is not easy for her, for he is often very stubborn,

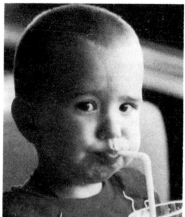

One tradition of Tibetan Buddhism is that when a Lama of high consciousness dies, clairvoyant monks await his reincarnation, seeking children, often in areas far remote from the monastery. The child is then presented with an assortment of objects including the old lama's favorite belongings. If the child unerringly chooses rightly, he is re-established as the lama. Some traditions in monasteries go back centuries with the reincarnation of the same man.

unpredictable and lives by an unfamiliar form of unknown set of values and reasoning. Although he wants to meet other clairvoyant children and experiment with psychometry and recalling images from photographs, Marjan feels that it is better not to push him in any direction, but to allow the talent to emerge and flower in its own way and time. He says that she "*is the only one that understands me here. If you die I will not join anyone else. I will go to India.*" Marjan says she often wonders why he was not born in India, where his talents would be naturally accepted.

Michiel has certain strong ties with various past religious figures and has their pictures around his room much as any teen-ager might have pop idols. He considers them both his friends and respected masters and consults them if necessary. While it is understandable that Christ would be a typical archetype figure for any child from Northern Europe, his other companions Paramahansa Yogananda and Sai Baba are, as Indian saints, unusual choices. The rest of his normal family is not religious in any way, yet he feels he has some task in this world connected with these masters.

Will our new changeling, who may well be far more sensitive and vulnerable than Michiel, have similar experiences when dealing with this crazy world? Shall we reduce him to our level of understanding or shall we allow him to teach us?

"*As a baby I remember crawling around inquisitively with an incredible sense of joy, light, and freedom in the middle of my head that was bathed in energies moving freely down from above, up, around and down through my body and my heart. And I was an expanding sphere of joy from the heart. And I was a radiant form, a source of energy, bliss and light. I was the power of Reality, a direct enjoyment and communication. I was the Heart, who lightens the mind and all things. I was the same as everyone and everything, except it became clear that others were unaware of the thing itself.*

"*When I was born there were no complications, there was no failure to understand, there was no lack of illumination. But in my relations with family and friends it soon became apparent to me what kind of life is allowed in this world. It was obvious that my parents and their friends were unwilling to live as if they were in God and to be happy. That was not permissible. So, obviously, I could not live that way either. I had to become their son and do the usual things that a child does, and, while doing that continue to make the point of God-knowing.*

"*That limited, self-conscious life began one day, as a conscious creation or condition, while I was crawling across the linoleum floor in a house that my parents had rented from an old woman named Mrs. Farr. A little puppy that my parents had given me ran across the floor towards me. I saw the puppy and I saw my parents, and my assumption of ordinary life began from that moment. The two or more years prior to that were free of all limitation.*"
(Da Free John)[33]

Psychic on Stage

THERE IS A REVEALING COMPARISON between "Michiel" and the 13-year-old psychic celebrity Velibor Rablienovic. While Michiel's mother does all she can to avoid either publicity or pushing the child into developing his gifts, Velibor has a training which resembles that of an Olympic athlete. This training, which is supervised by professor Antil Kebir, a noted Yugoslav para-psychologist, is done with the added help of an entity who appears on the astral plane.

It is designed to enable Velibor to keep his gift and use it in cooperation with police and detectives to solve difficult crimes. Perhaps this is another case of how, once we find intelligence, we manage to reduce it to our own stupidity.

The procedure the boy uses is to move into a trance, leaving the body, to appear on the astral plane, to fulfill some assigned task.

"A mist appears before my eyes which dissolves itself. Then I see an image before my eyes as if I was looking at any normal object."

His impressive record includes the prediction of the Chernobyl disaster, reading from closed books on a TV program and finding a long lost child from Split during a nationwide search for the missing boy in Yugoslavia. He has been a guest of Yugoslav congresses on para-psychology seven times and in one international test of his abilities he obtained the highest score a psychic has ever achieved.

There seems to be a cost, however, behind this forced program. His mental age is that of half his actual age. He is a 7-year-old in 14-year-old's psychic boots.

Mystic Childhoods

AND WHAT OF THE REAL MYSTICS themselves? Did they have exceptional childhoods with any common patterns of behavior which we might also expect to find in the new species?

The seventh year does appear to be a significant and crucial turning point. Recurring themes include mothers who have premonitions of an exceptional child, astrologers predict great teachers with surprising accuracy, the early childhoods are frequently free and open affairs although often there is a loss of parent or close relative. All seem to exhibit remarkable psychic gifts. Those born in India have an advantage for, in this country, there is a well-established tradition of such phenomena.

J. Krishnamurti's mother was a psychic and felt something very special about her weakling son. Although astrologers forecast his role as a world teacher, he hardly showed any promise in his early years. His teachers considered him to be mentally retarded as he was both inattentive and had no interest in the lessons, spending most of his time gazing into the distance behind his desk. However, he was able to see the image of his dead sister visiting his mother in their garden. When his own mother died he would experience her unmistakable presence following him around, even hearing the sound of her jewelry.

He was born in the holy room of the household, which was unusual in any orthodox Brahmin house. According to the tradition however he was not to see daylight until the seventh day, being kept quiet in semi-darkness after birth.

U.G. Krishnamurti's mother also had a strong psychic impression that the child was to be born "to an immeasurably high destiny." Highly clairvoyant, she died in his childhood. U.G. was then brought up with the maternal grandfather who gave up his law practice to devote himself to bringing up the young Yoga Bhrashta (meaning one who was within a hairsbreadth of enlightenment in the last life.)

As his grandfather was friendly with Madame Blavatsky and the Theosophists, U.G. was brought up in a religious atmosphere; but remember that by the time he was seven he had seen through the hypocrisy which surrounded the group and was determined not to follow their example.

Bhagwan Shree Rajneesh states that he was born with full consciousness, but the pain of birth severed the connection and he fell into the typical forgetfulness which occurs in these cases. It was not until his own awakening twenty-one years later that the remembrance returned.

"With me something went wrong from the very beginning and the reason was that for seven years I was not with my parents. I lived with my maternal grandfather and grandmother."

They allowed the young boy to run free and wild, to follow his own inclinations and whims, for they had no desire to mold him.

Many masters insist that the first seven years are the most important in life.

"Never again you will have that much opportunity. These seven years decide your seventy years. All the foundation stones are laid in those seven years."

During that time he became famous in the neighborhood for his herbal cures and healing abilities. Having the freedom to go his own way he refused any schooling.

Shri Ramakrishna likewise lived in a tiny rural community. He lost his father at the age of seven and was totally unwilling to go to school. When forced to do so he would fall into dream-like trances and was considered both unteachable and retarded.

A remarkable account of very early childhood comes from Da Free John. He was two years old when he deliberately created an ordinary self-conscious identity for himself.

"In my relations with family and friends it soon became apparent to me what kind of life is allowed in this world."

It became obvious to him that they couldn't live naturally and happily.

"Obviously, I could not live that way either. I had to become their son and do the usual things that a child does...That limited, self-conscious life began one day, as a conscious creation or condition."

Is this how the new children will behave? Da Free John recalled how he had felt bathed in an expanding joyous sphere of energy which issued from the heart.

"I was the same as everyone and everything, except it became clear that others were unaware of the thing itself."

Harmonious Man

How many of the new beings will encounter the self-same barrier and adopt similar strategies of forgetfulness in order to cope with our present world?

IF THE CHILDREN EVENTUALLY manage to survive the ordeal of those first few years will they emerge into maturity as balanced and whole beings? Supposing that like Michiel they are capable of ecstatic flights of awareness experiencing realms which we can only dimly imagine; will they wish to join us in the ordinary world of supermarkets and cinemas, holiday beaches or bleak office buildings?

The great Indian mystic Ramakrishna would frequently fall into ecstatic trance for several days. When finally returning to normal consciousness he would weep and cry to return to that condition. This is hardly the balanced state of a healthy species which is designed to survive.

Perhaps the greatest clue to the likely behavior of our new fledglings is to be found in the Sufi tradition of the "drunk and sober" man. The Sufis believe that the highest state of man is when he manages to hover on the threshold of the vertical and horizontal dimensions of existence, balancing the ecstatic state of Fana which is the dissolution of separateness and Baka, the state of everyday awareness of individuality and the five senses.

Here is the balanced man breast to breast with the cosmos in direct and blissful union with the whole and at the same time being in and of this world of time and matter. Here is the man that Gurdjieff would call the Harmonious man; that Rajneesh would call Zorba the Buddha, a meeting of the worldly passionate Zorba the Greek with the cool and detached Gautama the Buddha; that Da Free John might call Ignorant Radiance; or whom U.G. Krishnamurti simply describes as man in his natural state.

This Very Body the Buddha

MOST SAGES AND SPIRITUAL MASTERS share a life-affirmative delight in the *whole* of existence. Lao Tzu, nicknamed the "old boy," rides backwards on a buffalo giggling all the while. Chuang Tzu, the mischievous court jester, doesn't know whether he is a butterfly dreaming he is Chuang Tzu or Chuang Tzu dreaming he is a butterfly. The three laughing monks of Zen or the wild dancing Hassids of Baal Shem, the mad Sufi dervishes and the singing and loving Baul mystics of Bengal — all treat man as a joyous celebrating animal capable of wonder, ecstasy and laughter.

They all point to heaven as being alive *here* and *now*.

The single and much underrated purpose of life is simply to live. What else is needed? One old Zen master once summed it all up:

> *This Very Body the Buddha*
> *This Very Place the Lotus Paradise*

Yet for me the most poignant statement was made by an unenlightened man: D.H. Lawrence, a man firmly and stoically a member of *Homo sapiens* crying out with a fierce passion just before he died. Here perhaps lives that wild dragon ready to spring across the gap. Here is the old and dying man's gift to the new species.

"*For man, the vast marvel is to be alive. For man, as for flower and beast and bird, the supreme triumph is to be most vividly, most perfectly alive. Whatever the unborn and the dead may know, they cannot know the beauty, the marvel of being alive in the flesh. The dead may look after the afterwards. But the magnificent here and now of life in the flesh is ours, and ours alone and ours only for a time. We ought to dance with rapture that we should be alive and in the flesh, and part of the living incarnate cosmos. I am part of the sun as my eye is part of me. That I am part of the earth my feet know perfectly, and my blood is part of the sea. My soul knows that I am part of the human race, my soul is an organic part of the great human soul, as my spirit is part of my nation. In my very own self, I am part of my family. There is nothing of me that is alone and absolute except my mind, and we shall find that the mind has no existence by itself, it is only the glitter of the sun on the surface of the waters.*"
(D.H. Lawrence)[34]

"The transition is under way. This morning, for every action, every gesture, every movement, for the behavior of the body and the cells, for the most material consciousness — for everything — the old way was gone. There was nothing but 'that,' something ... how can I put it? ... something equal. There were no more conflicts, no more gratings or difficulties, everything was flowing within one and the same rhythm, something which is so smooth and feels so soft, you know with a FANTASTIC power in the slightest action. That condition was constant and unmixed for about four hours. Now everything, dressing, eating and so on, are no longer done in the same way. I don't know how to explain it....No more memory, no more habits. Things are not done because you have learned to do them a certain way: it's spontaneous, they are done by the consciousness. Meaning that recall, memory, action are replaced by ... the new method of consciousness, which knows the RIGHT thing at the exact moment of doing it: this has to be done. Not: 'Oh, I have to go there.' Every minute, you are where you have to be, and when you reach your intended destination: 'Yes, that's it'."
(The Mother)[35]

"...And one clearly understands why saints and sages and all those who wanted to feel continuously that divine atmosphere severed all material bonds: they were not transformed, and so they fell back into the other way of being. To transform matter, however, is infinitely higher, it brings an extraordinary stability, consciousness and CONCRETENESS: things become the true vision, the true consciousness, they become so concrete, so real (yes, true matter.) Nothing, but nothing else can give that fullness. Escaping, fleeing, dreaming, meditating, soaring into higher states of consciousness is all very well, but that seems poor in comparison, so poor, so limited!"

"The whole solid base that makes a corporeal person is gone, pftt, removed! For example, I have a total memory block....Now I am used to it, so the cells remain quiet, still and exclusively turned towards the Consciousness, and they wait. You see, everything we do, everything we know is based on a kind of semiconscious memory of things — that is gone. There is nothing any more. And it is replaced by a sort of luminous presence ... and things happen, one doesn't quite know how. They come effortlessly, JUST what is needed at just the right time. There is none of that baggage we constantly drag around with us: JUST the thing you need." (The Mother)[36]

Star Mind

"This we know. The Earth does not belong to man; man belongs to the Earth. This we know. All things are connected like blood which unites one family. All things are connected.

"Whatever befalls the Earth befalls the sons of the Earth. Man did not weave the web of life; he is merely a strand in it. Whatever he does to the web, he does to himself."
(Chief Seattle)[37]

THE MORE WE OBSERVE how the microscopic world of living cells and bacteria interact with the macroscopic world of the planet, the clouds and atmosphere, winds, tornadoes, ocean currents and the great wild jungles, the more our vision shifts to one of a total and wondrous whole — a living organism.

We have already discussed how the entire biosphere can be seen as a vast self-regulating system — a gigantic dissipative structure feeding on the even greater dissipative structure of the sun and the whole solar system. Humanity is perhaps a key in the entire living process, part catalyzing, part catalyzed and part of that huge flow-through of energy. Now we can be likened to the nervous system of the planet or its immune system, constantly communicating and moving information. We are the most volatile process within the Earth's organs.

We could be the new brain of Earth; a great information matrix of memories and communications. Our cities and centers of information cluster over the surface of the globe like huge ganglia within a gigantic nervous system of increasing complexity. The planet is literally exploding with it.

"Man is only a brief design in the numberless evolutionary stages of the World. And the individual human being is only a moment, a specimen, a partial realization of Man. The individual is not made for his own sake, but to be sacrificed toward Man — so that Man may fulfill his evolutionary destiny. And Man is not made for his own sake, but to be sacrificed toward the ultimate evolutionary process of the World. And the World is not made for its own sake, but to be sacrificed to the unqualified and Eternal Divine."
(Da Free John)[38]

Childhood's End

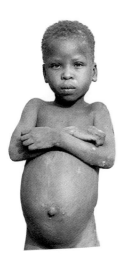

AND WHAT OF US, the last *unenlightened* emperors of the old guard? Do we wonder gracefully down that lonely road to extinction raging against the dying of the light? Can we help the new child on his way? Can we help ourselves?

From archaeological evidence we can deduce that there was a brief period where an early version of modern man lived alongside the Neanderthals, the huge brained and otherwise mysterious beings who had already been around some one hundred thousand years. The modern man might have originated halfway through this period in Africa and South Asia but did not move into Europe until a little over thirty thousand years ago.

What happened when the two groups met, we may never know but it apparently took only another three thousand years before the Old Ones disappeared. From what little is known of them, it seems they had strong social bonds. They cared for their old and sick and performed elaborate burial rituals for the departed whom they believed went to another life. We don't know what advantages modern man had over the bigger brained Neanderthals, but the magnificent cave paintings which appeared in Europe at the same time suggest that a new creativity had arrived. Do the Old Ones have potentials like us which were never activated unless the new men and women were an expression of them? There is no evidence to suppose that two branches of humankind ever merged and bred, but there is also none to the contrary. If a new species appears, one as different as the Cro-Magnon was to the Neanderthal, will it take thirty centuries for our species to become extinct or in these accelerating times only a few generations?

Whatever the outcome, we possess the keys to be the early pioneers, the first models of the line.

Each one of us who takes on the quest to understand ourselves could add something to the whole 'field.' If the race does make use of it and its effect is cumulative then the more who enter the higher reaches of the evolutionary journey the more likely a quantum leap could occur in the species. It would seem that we hold the key.

And as for us, what can we do? Perhaps we all too easily forget that life is a gift. The miracle is to *be alive at all*. And we now have the special privilege to be witness to the birth of a new era.

"... I am sure the movement has begun...How long will it take to arrive at a concrete, visible and organized realization? I don't know. Something has begun. It seems it's going to be the onrush of the new species, the new creation, or at any rate a new creation. A reorganization of the earth and a new creation. At a certain moment things were so acute, reached a point where absolutely everything was as if abolished in my being. Not only was I unable to speak, but my head felt as never before in my whole life: in pain you know. I couldn't see anything anymore, I couldn't hear anything anymore.... But two or three times, I had moments, absolutely marvelous and unique moments — indescribable. It's indescribable. And scenes!.... Scenes of construction: huge cities under construction. Yes, the future world being built.

"...But even today, the overwhelming majority of people and in-tellectuals are perfectly content with taking care of themselves and their little rounds of progress. They don't even want anything else! Which means that the advent of the next being may well go unnoticed, or be misunderstood. It's hard to tell, since there is no precedent to compare it with; but more than likely, if one of the great apes ever ran into the first man, it must simply have felt that that being was a little... strange. That's all. Men are used to thinking that anything higher than they has to be ....divine beings — that is, without a body — who appear in a burst of light. In other words, all the gods as they are conceived — but it isn't like that at all. It is almost as if a new mind is being formed. And the body is learning its lesson — all bodies, all bodies."
(The Mother) [39]

Acknowledgements

I would like to thank all those who have helped, in the past year, to make this book possible. I am especially grateful: — to my editor at Simon & Schuster, Barbara Gess, for her invaluable suggestions.

— to Rupert Sheldrake for some very forthright criticism of the original manuscript, made with considerable gusto in the margin;

— to the great family of Labyrinth Publishing in the hills of Tuscany, who helped with the production of the book;

— to Lalita for a heroic struggle with the word processor which kept losing its memory and for organising the typesetting so beautifully;

— to Philip Dunn for his real friendship, humor and encouragement in even the darkest nights of the soul and for his splendid editing;

— to Navyo for just living and loving with me, for her craziness and support during the wild years of preparing the book. As well researching the photographs as working on the final design and production, she brought a woman's insight into the pages;

— to all the evolutionary pioneers, masters, seers and mystics, who by their example have shown it is possible to realize the new being within us.

Scientific Editor — Philip Ryde BSc. (Hons)

Photographs: Spaarnestad Haarlem: 16/17, 28/29, 103, 104/105, 107, 108/109, 110, 114/115, 119, 126, 128/129, 132/133, 135, 137, 138/139, 143. Science Photo Library, London: 50, 222/223, 235, 248/249. NASA Audio Visual Branch, Washington: 19, 26, 38, 40, 45, 66, 88/89(Eames Research Lab) 279. Beeldbank & Uitgeefprojekten, Amsterdam: 11, 95, 127, 183, 234, 274, 261, 272/273. Karil Daniels, San Francisco: 255, 260. Saskia van Rees, Leveroy: 239, 254. Defense Nuclear Agency, Washington: 15, Jan Frankl, Vienna: 264. National Gallery, London: 214. Barnaby's Picture Library, London: 41, 43. Mapplethore Studio, New York: 79. K & B, Florence: 141, 187, 250, 214, 231. "Overseas", Milan: 259. Erik Sidenbladh: 256/257. Rajneesh Foundation: 174/175. Laughing Man Institute: 172/173. Krishnamurti Foundation: 168/169. Sandro Saragossa, Florence: 161,162/163, 199. Magnum-Laffont: 33,37. Freed: 165/7. Griffiths: 225. J. Boughman: 117. A. Tsiaras: 262/3. R. Laytner: 155. Sygma: 131.

Appendix

LEVEL ONE — *Physical Matter* (the realms of physics and chemistry,) the gross aspects of Energy. The basic material stuff of the material plane of existence. This is the rock bottom.

LEVEL TWO — *Biological* The manifest life condition. For the consciousness of the human child this corresponds to the emotional and sensational, perceptual world. It is both "fusion" and "confusione" of the bio-material universe. The realm of biology and the life sciences.

LEVEL THREE — *Intellectual* (the realm of philosophy and psychology.) This is the whole spectrum of our normal everyday life. It has three stages of development.
Stage 1: In modern man the first seven years of life are basically adaptive learning states. These pass through simple sensation into the emotive/magical consciousness of narcissistic dependence which is supported by simple logic and a sense of myth.
Stage 2: The age of seven unitl fourteen is a period marked by the awakening of a sense of ego, mind and emotional-sexual differentiation. It is the time of relating and the growing awareness of mind-body as opposed to body-mind. Most psychologists claim that few men or women ever develop past this point. Due to cultural and social repressions and the inevitable sexual shocks which happen during this period, most of us fail to make the transition to the level of mature psychological growth.

Stage 3: This period corresponds to the third group of seven years from the age to 14 to 21. Ideally this is when the indivual has matured and integrated the physical emotional-sexual and the mental-intentional aspects of the mind-body. In doing so the individual begins to take responsibility for his or her life. Few attain such a harmony of the three aspects and it is still rare to find an integrated human being operating harmoniously at the three centers.

Threshold of the Journey.
Between Level Three and Four there is a wide twilight-zone in which there are brief lightning flashes that illuminate the splendor of the unknown territory beyond. These brief glimpses act as a magnet on a new, committed journey towards the higher evolutionary self.

LEVEL FOUR — Of all levels it is claimed this is the most potentially treacherous and arduous part of the whole journey. as the traveler enters deeper and deeper into this no-man's-land, it is as though his maps become less and less of use. At this point a master navigator is needed, a school or a discipline, for strangely this whole relatively "lowly" territory has been poorly recorded. This is due to a number of reasons. Firstly it is often terrifying and weird. In many traditions it is known as the "dark night of the soul" although others, like Meher Baba, reserve this for later stages (see diagram for a variation on this theme.) In orthodox psychology this state can have all the outward signs of schizophrenia or other serious mental disorders and few enlightened masters would allow their disciples to linger there. Some wayfarers breeze past it wondering what all the fuss is about, but because the travelers use their gross sense to glimpse this subtle plane, the change of consciousness can release both heaven and hell, depending upon the seekers themselves. This is the level of the mini satoris of the Zen monks: the first rude shock of awakening the vast dynamos of power. It is the first glimpse and consciousness of "Infinite Energy". The state, called sy some mystics, "the awakening of the psychic heart" and corresponding to the opening of the heart and throat chakra, marks the transformation of gross consciousness to that of subtle sensations of smeel, sight, hearing and touch. At present this zone is receiving most interest and exploitation in the West for it is the plane of the more spectacular

psychic displays of channeling, ESP, telepathy, astral travel, telekinesis and the whole dazzling plethora of paranormal phenomena. At the same time it is the most dangerous territory of the whole Odyssey. Here we can encounter the miracles of watches plucked from the air and yogic trances of walking on water. As the voyager comes closer to the frontier of Level Five the extreme emotions and thoughts can threaten to overwhelm the balance of the experiencer, especially when extraordinary powers suddenly become available. While some traditions place this crisis later up the ladder, many concede that if at this stage the seeker is tempted to misuse these forces, there can be a liberation of energy so great that it can shatter the entity entirely and the disintegrated consciousness plunges back to the rock bottom of evolutionary Level One. Whilst these occurences are relatively rare the traveler needs either authentic guidance through this realm of saints and yogis, or a great deal of luck.

LEVE FIVE — If the voyager uses the subtle power of Level Four both discriminately and creatively without eve being overwhelmed by desires or greed, then he or she makes a quantum leap to Level Six, by-passing Level Five altogether. However, most voyagers seem to resist action entirely and gradually Leve Five becomes available. Here we cross the threshold from the realm of Energy-Power into the realm of Mind, the domain of the Mental World. And so begins the real mystical experience. Attention shifts to the braincore with its mystical ascent through the entire nervous system. The peak experience of this level is the first satori of the void," but remaining as both the knower and the known. In India it is recognized as "Nirvikalpa Samadhin," the "formless ecstasy." The seed of self-consciousness remains and this samadhi is only temporary, as it remains both the subject and the object of contemplation. However, the traveler cannot de-volve, he cannot fall back now. One subtle sense is now available, being a heightened sense of "seeing." It is marked by the opening of the third eye.

The seeker now has control over the mind, whereas before this point he was a slave to it. His or her control can even extend to others while the physical body now surrenders to a semi-conscious control from the mental level.

LEVEL SIX — The last stage of the journey of consciousness coincides with a leap from the third eye of the braincore to the "Sahasrar," or the "Thousand Petaled Lotus." This is the last part of the evolutionary action where the attention is focused inward, towards the source of the witnessing Self.

As the last traces of *ego* disappear the sage enters the second satori of Zen Buddhism. Here is the experience of the void as void. There is no longer anyone to experience and nothing to be experienced. This is the stage of seeing the Void, God, Existence, the Radiant Transcendental Being, The One or His Endlessness, face to face. The experiencer or, as we might call it "Existence in the Man State," sees itself everywhere and in all and everything.

Devoid of all impressions of objects and subjects this consciousness confronts Existence, yet still remains apart from It. There is still a trace of differentiation, a subtle veil between Existence and "Man Existence." This is the state of the sage. Yet the sage still longs for an Ultimate Union with the Original One, even though he stands face to face with Its image.

LEVEL SEVEN — This is not really a level at all. It is the Alpha and the Omega of the flowering. In the seventh stage of consciousness the Self realizes everything to become the Radiant, continually arising Being. This is the truly radical quantum leap in which the whole Illusion, the great Divine Dream disintegrates and Reality just Is. Now the whole focus of consciousness, we are told, is upon Existence Itself, rather than the "objects" of Its creation.

The original Void was unconscious. Now the Void-as-man returns fully conscious of the Original State. This is Sahaj-Samadhi, the final flowering of Man. Buddha called it "Anatta"; a state of Absolute no-thing-ness, of no-self. In Zen Buddhism this is the third and final satori. Even in the exalted state of Level Six there were impressions, or the illusion of experience. There were changing forms, desires, dreams; changing patterns of the waves upon a timeless, limitless ocean. Once the Seventh is reached, the traveler once again becomes one with the ocean.

BIBLIOGRAPHY

PRELUDE

1. The Mother, quote 57.107 from: Satprem, *The Mind of the Cells*, (New York: Institute for Evolutionary Research, 1982).
2. Kenneth Boulding, *The Meaning of the Twenieth Century*, (New York: Harper & Row, 1965).
3. *Revelation*, 9:15-19.
4. Albert Einstein, *Ideas and Opinions*, Carl Seeling, ed., (New York: Dell Publishing Co., 1973).
5. Henry Miller.
6. Bernard Levin, *The Times*, 1968.
7. The Mother, quote 56-103, from: Satprem, *The Mind of the Cells*, (New York: Institute for Evolutionary Research, 1982).
7. Visud-dhi-Magga.
8. René Dumont and Charlotte Paguet, *For Africa I accuse*.
9. Daniel R. Vining Jr., *Scientific American (April 1985)*.
10. Lester Brown, *Estate of the World*, (The World Watch Institute).
13. Jonathan Schell, *The Fate of the Earth*, (London: Jonathan Cape Ltd., 1982).
14. Nick Hall, *Discovr* (February 1987).
15. Fred Hoyle, 1948.
16. Rusty Schweichart, astronaut.
17. Nicolas Wade, *New Scientist*, (December 1975).
18. Robert Sinsheimer, *Troubled Dawn for Genetic Engineering, New scientist*, (October 1975).
19. Van Rensselaer-Potter, *Bioethics: Bridge to the Future*, (Englewood Cliffs: Prentice Hall, 1971).

PART I

1. The Mother, quote 66.308, from: Satprem, *The Mind of the Cells*, (New York: Institute for Evolutionry Research, 1982)
2. Heraclitus, 513 B.C., *The Fragments*.
3. Meher Baba, *God Speaks — The Theme of Creation and Its Purpose*, (New York: Dodd, Mead & Company, 1955).
4. Ramtha, *Ramtha — An Introduction*, S.L. Weinberg ed., (Eastsound: Sovereignty, Inc.,1988).
5. Da Free John, *The Enlightenment of the Whole Body*, (Middletown: The Dawn Horse Press, 1978).
6. Emerson Pugh.
7. The Mother, quote 61.241, from: Satprem, *The Mind of the Cells*, (New York: Institute for Evolutionary Research,1982).
8. P.V. Tobias, *The Brain in Hominid Evolution*, (Columbia University, 1971).
9. René Dubois, *Man Adapting*.
10. Gurdjieff, from: P.D. Ouspensky, *In Search of the Miraculous: Fragments of an Unknown Teaching*, (London: Routledge & Kegan Paul, 1977).
11. William Blake, *The Portable Blake*, (New York: Viking Penguin Inc., 1968).
12. Ronald D. Laing, *The Politics of Experience and the Bird of Paradise*, (Harmondsworth: Penguin Books Ltd.,1984, reprint).

13. William Blake, *The Portable Blake*, (New York: Viking Penguin Inc., 1968).
14. R.D. Laing, *The Politics of Experience and the Bird of Paradise*, (Harmondsworth: Penguin Books Ltd., 1984, reprint).
15. Gregory Bateson, *Perceval's Narrative: A Patient's Account of His Psychosis*, (Stanford University Press, 1961).
16. Penelope Shuttle and Peter Redgrove, *The Wise Wound: Menstruation and Everywoman*, (London: Paladin Grafton Books, 1986, reprint).
17. Franz Kafka, *Letters*.
18. Russell Schweichart, Lecture in Kyoto, Japan, 1982.
19. The Mother, quote 69.105, from: Satprem, *The Mind of the Cells*, (New York: Institute for Evolutionary Research, 1982).
20. Theodore Roszak, *Person/Planet*, (New York: Anchor Books, 1978).
21. The Mother, quote 66.263, from: Satprem, *The Mind of the Cells*, (New York: Institute for Evolutionary Research, 1982).
22. Ibid.
23. D. T. Suzuki, *Lankavatara Sutra Studies*, (London: Routledge & Kegan Paul, 1968).
24. Norman O. Brown, *Life Against Death, the Psychoanalitic Meaning of History*, (Middletown: Wesleyan University Press, 1959).
25. Kabir, *Songs of Kabir*.
26. U.G. Krishnamurti, from: Rodney Arms, ed., *The Mystique of Enlightenment — The Unrational Ideas of a Man called U.G.*, (India: Dinesh Vaghela, 1982).
27. Chief Seattle, *His Address*, 1853.
28. R. D. Laing, *The Politics of Enlightenment and the Bird of Paradise*, (Harmondsworth: Penguin Books Ltd.).
29. Ibid.

30. Lewis Mumford, *The Myth of the Machine*.
31. Winston Churchill, *House of Common Speech*, (1948).
32. Jacques Cousteau.

PART II

1. Patanjali, *Yoga Sutras*.
2. Mahmud Shabistari, *Gulshan-i-raz (The Garden of Mystery)*, trans. E. H. Whinfield, (London, 1880).
3. Hakim Sanai, *The Hadiqua — The Walled Garden of Truth*.
4. Meher Baba, *God Speaks — The Theme of Creation and Its Purpose*, (New York: Dodd, Mead & Company, 1955).
5. Gurdjieff, *Letter to Ouspensky*, (1916).
6. J. K. Krishnamurti, from: Pupul Jayakar, *Krishnamurti — A Biography*, (New York: Harper & Row, 1986).
7. Ibid.
8. Ibid.
9. U. G. Krishnamurti, from: Rodney Arms, ed., *The Mystique of Enlightenment — The Unrational Ideas of a Man Called U.G.*, (India: Dinesh Vaghela, 1982).
10. Ibid.
11. Ibid.
12. Da Free John, *The Enlightenment of the Whole Body*, (Middletwon: The Dawn Horse Press, 1983).
13. Bhagwan Shree Rajneesh, *The Discipline of Transcendence*, vol. II, (India: Rajneesh Foundation,).
14. The Mother, quote 55.1412, from: Satprem, *The Mind of the Cells*, (New York: Institute for Evolutionary Research, 1981).
15. The Mother, quot 69.234, ibid.
18. The Mother, quote 67.3012, ibid.
16. U.G. Krishnamurti, from: Rodney Arms, ed., *The Mystique of Enlightenment — The Unrational Ideas of a Man Called U.G.*, (India: Dinesh Vaghela, 1982).

17. Ibid.
18. Richard Bucke, *Cosmic Consciousness*, (New York: E.P. Dutton, 1923).
19. Bernard Berenson, *Sketch for a Self Portrait*, (New York: Pantheon Books, 1949).
20. John of the Cross, *Collected Works of John of the Cross*, transl. K. Kavanaugh and O. Rodriguez, (Washington: Institute of Carmelite Studies, 1976).
21. U. G. Krishnamurti, from: Rodney Arms, ed., *The Mystique of Enlightenment — The Unrational Ideas of a Man Called U.G.*, (India: Dinesh Vaghela, 1982).
22. The Mother, quote 61.276, from: Satprem, *The Mind of the Cells*, (New York: Institute for Evolutionary Research. 1982).
23. The Mother, quote 58.811, ibid.
24. The Mother, quote 58.115, ibid.
25. The Mother, quote 73.82, ibid.
26. The Mother, quote 67.224, ibid.
27. J. K. Krishnamurti, (Ojai, 1923), from: Pupul Jayakar, *Krishnamurti — A Biography*, (New York: Harper & Row, 1986).
28. J. K. Krishnamurti (Rishi Valley, 1961), ibid.
29. Da Free John, *The Knee of Listening*, (Middletown: The Dawn Horse Press).
30. Da Free John, *The Enlightenment of the Whole Body*, (Middletown: The Dawn Horse Press, 1978).
31. Bhagwan Shree Rajneesh, *The Discipline of Transcendence*, 2 vols., (India: Rajneesh Foundation).
32. U. G. Krishnamurti, from: Rodney Arms, ed., *The Mystique of Enlightenment — The Unrational Ideas of a Man Called U.G.*, (India: Dinesh Vaghela, 1982)

PART III

1. Da Free John, *The Enlightenment of*

the Whole Body, (Middletown: The Dawn Horse Press, 1978).

2. U. G. Krishnamurti, from: Rodney Arms ed., *The Mystique of Enlightenment — The Unrationa Ideas of a Man Called U.G.*, (India: Dinesh Vaghela, 1982).

3. Ibid.

4. Ibid.

5. Bhagwan Shree Rajneesh, *Tao: The Three Treasures*, vol I, (India: Rajneesh Foundation).

6. J. Krishnamurti, from: Pupul Jayakar, *Krishnamurti — A Biography*, (New York: Harper & Row, 1986).

7. Ramtha, from: D. J. Mar, *Voyage to the New World*, (Eastsound: Sovereignty, 1985).

8. U. G. Krishnamurti, from: Rodney Arms ed., *The Mystique of Enlightenment — The Unrational Ideas of a Man Called U.G.*, (India: Dinesh Vaghela, 1982).

9. Ramana Maharshi, *Collected Works*, Arthur Osborne ed., (New York: Samuel Weiser, 1972).

10. *Katha Upanishads.*

11. Ramtha, from: *Ramtha — An Introduction*, S. L. Weinberg, ed., (Eastsound: Sovereignty, 1988).

12. *Scientific American,* (May 1957).

13. C. W. Leadbeater, *The Chakras*, (Theosophical Society).

14. Dr. Ed Babbit, *Principles of Light and Color.*

15. Renée Weber, *Dialogues with Scientists and Sages: The Search for Unity,* (London: Routledge & Kegan Paul, 1986).

16. Ibid.

17. Ibid.

18. Ibid.

19. Ilya Prigogine, *From Being to Becoming*, (New York: W.H. Freeman & Co., 1980).

20. Eric Jansch, *The Self-Organizing Universe*, (Oxford: Oxford Pergamon Press, 1980).

21. Teilhard de Chardin, *The Phenomenon of Man*, (New York: Harper & Row, 1965).

22. The Mother, from: Satprem, *The Mind of the Cells*, (New York: Institute for Evolutionary Research, 1982).

23. U. G. Krishnamurti, from: Rodney Arms, ed., *The Mystique of Enlightenment — The Unrational Ideas of a Man Called U.G.*, (India: Dinesh Vaghela, 1982).

24. Da Free John, *The Enlightenment of the Whole Body*, (Middletown: The Dawn Horse Press, 1978).

25. Lyall Watson, *LifeTide,* (London: Hodder and Stoughton Ltd.).

26. J. Krishnamurti, *The Ending of Time*, (London: Krishnamurti Foundation Trust Ltd.).

27. Ibid.

28. J. Krishnamurti, *The Awakening of Intelligence*, (New York: Harper & Row, 1973).

29. Rensellaar-Potter, *BioEthics: Bridge to the Future*, (Englewood Cliffs: Prentice Hall, 1971).

30. Ramtha, *Ramtha: An Introduction*, S.L. Weinberg ed., (Eastsound: Sovereignty, 1988).

31. Meher Baba, *God Speaks — The Theme of Creation and Its Purpose,* (New York: Dodd, Mead and Company, 1955).

32. Eloise Shields, *Research in Parapsychology 1975*, (Metuchen: Scarecrow Press, Inc., 1976).

33. Da Free John, *The Enlightenment of the Whole Body*, (Middletown: The Dawn Horse Press, 1978).

34. D. H. Lawrence, *Apocalypse,* (Harmondsworth: Penguin Books Ltd., 1980, reprint).

35. The Mother, quote 64.189, from: Satprem, *The Mind of the Cells,* (New York: Institute for Evolutionary Research, 1982).

36. The Mother, quote 68.288, ibid.

37. Chief Seattle, *His Address,* 1853 .

38. Da Free John, *The Enlightenment of the Whole Body*, (Middletown: The Dawn Horse Press, 1978).

39. The Mother, from: Satprem, *The Mind of the Cells*, (New York: Institute for Evolutionary Research, 1982).

SUGGESTED READING

Science, Philosophy and Other Gems

Bohm, David. *Wholeness and the Implicate Order.* London: Routledge & Kegan Paul, 1980.

Briggs, John P., and F.D.Peat. *Looking Glass Universe — The Emerging Science of Wholeness.* London: Fontana Paperbacks, 1985.

Capra, Fritjof. *The Tao of Physics.* San Francisco: Shambala Publications, 1975.

Turning Point. New York: Simon and Schuster, 1982.

Dawkins, R. *The Selfish Gene.* Oxford: Oxford University Press.

Dubos, René. *So Human an Animal.* New York: Charles Scribner's Sons, 1968.

Einstein, Albert. *Ideas and Opinions.* New York: Dell Publishing Co., 1973.

Huxley, Aldous. *The Perennial Philosophy.* New York: Harper & Row, 1945.

Jantsch, Eric. *The Self-Organizing Universe.* Oxford: Oxford Pergamon Press, 1980.

Krishnamurti, J., and David Bohm. *The Ending of Time.* New York: Harper & Row, Publishers, 1985.

Laing, R.D. *The Politics of Experience and The Bird of Paradise.* Harmondsworth: Penguin Books Ltd., 1984, reprint.

The Divided Self. Harmondsworth: Penguin Books Ltd., 1984.

Lawrence, D.H. *Apocalypse.* Harmondsworth: Penguin Books Ltd., 1980, reprint.

Pribram, K.M. *Languages of the Brain.* New York: Prentice Hall.

Prigogine, Ilya. *From Being to Becoming.* New York: W.H. Freeman & Co., 1980.

Miller, Henry. *The Colossus of Maroussi.* Harmondsworth: Penguin Books Ltd., 1985, reprint.

Pearce, Fred. *Acid Rain.* Harmondsworth: Penguin Books Ltd., 1987.

Russell, Peter. *The Awakening Earth — The Global Brain.* London: ARK PAPERBACKS, 1985 reprint.

Sagan, Carl. *The Dragons of Eden — Speculations on the Evolution of Human Intelligence.* New York: Ballantine Books, 1984, reprint.

Schell, Jonathan. *The Fate of the Earth.* London: Jonathan Cape Ltd., 1982.

Sheldrake, Rupert. *A New Science of Life — The Hypothesis of Formative Causation.* London: Paladin Grafton Books, 1987.

The Presence of the Past — Morphic Resonance and the Habits of Nature. London: Collins, 1988.

Shuttle, Penelope and Peter Redgrove. *The Wise Wound: Menstruation and Everywoman.* London: Paladin Grafton Books, 1986, revised edition.

Sidenbladh, Erik. *Water Babies.* New York: St. Martin's Press, 1982.

Watson, Lyall. *Life Tide.* London: Hodder & Stoughton, 1979.

Weber, Renée. *Dialogues with Scientists and Sages: The Search for Unity.* London: Routledge & Kegan Paul, 1986.

Mysticism, Enlightenment and Research into Higher Consciousness

Aurobindo, Sri. *The Mind of Light.* New York: E.P. Dutton, 1971.

Barrett, William, editor. *Zen Buddhism — Selected Writings of D.T. Suzuki.* New York: Anchor Books, 1956.

Da Free John. *The Enlightenment of the Whole Body.* Middletown: The Dawn Horse Press, 1978.

Enlightenment and The Transformation of Man. Middletown: The Dawn Horse Press. 1983.

The Knee of Listening. Middletown: The Dawn Horse Press.

The Dreaded Gom-Boo, or the Imaginary Disease that Religion Seeks to Cure. Middletown: The Dawn Horse Press, 1984.

Dass, Ram. *Journey of Awakening.* New York: Bantam Books, 1978.

Gopi Krishna. *The Biological Basis of Religion and Genius.* New York: Kundalini Research Foundation.

Gurdjieff. *Views from the Real World.* London: ARKANA PAPERBACKS, 1984 reprint.

Beelzebub's Tales to His Grandson.
3 vols. London: Routledge & Kegan
Paul, 1976.

Life Is Real Only Then, When 'I Am.'
London: Routledge & Kegan
Paul, 1983.

Jayakar, Pupul. *Krishnamurti — A
Biography.* San Francisco: Harper &
Row, Publishers. 1986.

Julian of Norwich. *Julian of Norwich:
Revelations of Divine Love.* London:
Penguin Books Ltd.,
Lhalungpa, Lobsang P. *The Life of
Milarepa.* New York: E.P.
Dutton, 1977.

Meher Baba. *God Speaks — The Theme of
Creation and Its Purpose.* New York:
Dodd, Mead & Company, 1955.

Discourses. 5 vols. India: Meher
Publications.

Miller, Henry. *The Colossus of Maroussi.*
Harmondsworth: Penguin Books Ltd.,
1985.

Ouspensky, P.D. *In Search of the
Miraculous: Fragments of an Unknown
Teaching.* London: Routledge & Kegan
Paul, 1977,
Pearce, Fred. *Acid Rain.*
Hartmondsworth: Penguin Books Ltd.,
1987.

Rajneesh, Bhagwan Shree. *Take
It Easy* (2 volumes).India: Rajneesh
Foundation,
1979.

*The Diamond Sutra — The Vajrachchedika
Prajnaparamita Sutra.* India: Rajneesh
Foundation, 1979.

Notes of a Madman. India: Rajneesh
Foundation, 1985.

Ram Dass. *Journey of Awakening.* New
York: Bantam Books, 1978.

Russell, Peter. *The Awakening Earth —
The Global Brain.* London: ARK
PAPERBACKS, 1985, reprint.

Satprem. *The Mind of the Cells.* New
York: Institute for Evolutionary
Research, 1982.

Schell, Jonathan. *The Fate of the Earth.*
London: Jonathan Cape Ltd., 1982.

St. Teresa of Avila, *Interior Castle.*

Walker, Benjamin. *Gnosticism — Its
History and Influence.* Wellingborough:
The Aquarian Press, 1983.

Waldberg, Michel. *Gurdjieff — An
Approach to His Ideas.* London:
Routledge & Kegan Paul, 1981.

Watts, Alan W. *The Way of Zen.* New
York: Vintage Books.

Behold the Spirit. New York: Vintage
Books, 1972.

In My Own Way. New York: Vintage
Books.

White, John, editor. *What Is
Enlightenment? Exploring the Goal of the
Spiritual Path.* Los Angeles: Jeremy P.
Tarcher, Inc., 1985.

Wilber, Ken. *The Atman Project — A
Transpersonal View of Human
Development.* Wheaton, Ill.: The
Theosophical Publishing House, 1980.

Eye to Eye. New York: Doubleday, 1983.
Up from Eden. New York: Doubleday,
1982.

The Spectrum of Consciousness.

Wilhelm, Richard. *The Secret of the
Golden Flower — A Chinese Book of Life.*
London: ARKANA PAPERBACKS, 1984.

Addresses of Organizations

Bhagwan Shree Rajneesh
Rajneeshdham
17, Koregaon Park
Poona 411001 (MS) India

Da Free John
The Laughing Man Institute
P.O. Box 836
San Rafael, California 94915

J. Krishnamurti
Krishnamurti Foundation of America
P.O. Box 216
Ojai California 93023

Meher Baba
The Meher Spiritual Center
P.O. Box 487
Myrtle Beach, SC 29577

Satprem
Institute for Evolutionary Research
200 Park Avenue
New York, N.Y. 10166